Swamp Song

Ron Larson

Swamp Song

A Natural History of Florida's Swamps

University Press of Florida

Gainesville Tallahassee Tampa Boca Raton

Pensacola Orlando Miami Jacksonville

00 99 98 97 96 95   6 5 4 3 2 1

Library of Congress Cataloging-in-Publication Data
Larson, Ron, 1946-
Swamp song: a natural history of Florida's swamps / Ron Larson.
p. cm.
Includes bibliographical references and index.
ISBN 0-8130-1355-0
1. Swamp ecology–Florida. 2. Swamp fauna–Florida. 3. Swamp plants–
Florida. 4. Swamps–Florida. I. Title.
QH105.F6L37 1995
574.5'26325'09759–dc20   95-9806

The University Press of Florida is the scholarly publishing agency for the
State University System of Florida, comprised of Florida A & M University,
Florida Atlantic University, Florida International University, Florida State
University, University of Central Florida, University of Florida, University of
North Florida, University of South Florida, and University of West Florida.

University Press of Florida
15 Northwest 15th Street
Gainesville, FL 32611

Contents

 # Illustrations

Figures

Plates *(following page 110)*

 Preface

Why write a book about swamps? Because swamps, to me, are among the most alluring natural areas in Florida. I will never forget the first time I waded knee-deep in the cool, dark waters of Fakahatchee Strand. The dense green forest flourished with pop-ash trees resplendent with ferns and orchids and armfuls of spiky bromeliads. The sheer beauty of it all drew me deeper into the trackless wetlands. Unfortunately, not enough people realize that such places exist, or even that swamps are worth experiencing.

I had two main goals in writing this book. First, I want to entice people to explore and enjoy swamps. Second, I want Floridians, and everyone interested in the natural world, to understand these environments better so that they can make informed decisions affecting the future of the wetlands around them.

Swamp Song is a primer on Florida's forested wetlands—swamps. It describes various types of swamps, how they are formed, and how they function. The biota is featured through descriptions and personal anecdotes—several hundred species are mentioned. Yet these are but a fraction of the many thousands of species, from bacteria to panthers, that live in Florida's swamps.

Swamps and other wetlands are complex and dynamic systems, with diverse plant and animal life intricately connected by a web of interactions. I have tried to unravel some parts of that rich tapestry. The reference list can lead interested readers to more detailed information.

Swamp Song is based on studies by wetland scientists and naturalists and on my own observations. My wife, Kathy, often has accompanied me on field trips across the state. Our treks sometimes take us to wetlands nearly as wild as those seen by John and William Bartram more than two hundred years ago. *Swamp Song* is the culmination of our journeys. If it inspires your own quest for Florida's fascinating swamps, then this book will have served its purpose.

Swamp Song was written to describe the swamps of Florida. Similar wetlands and many of the same species occur along the coastal plain from the Carolinas to east Texas, so readers from other areas should also find the book of interest. Furthermore, the book is only an introduction to Florida's swamps. In a volume of this size it would be impossible to cover such a broad subject in more than just a cursory manner. What I have covered is biased by my own interests. I encourage readers to make their own discoveries and consult the references listed at the end of the book to further their knowledge of wetlands.

The text is organized into nine chapters. The first five introduce swamps: what they are, how they formed, how they can be explored, what can be seen, and when to see them. The remaining four discuss the biota—the flora and fauna—of Florida swamps. Readers wanting to learn about the various kinds of swamps in Florida should read chapters 1 and 2. Those wanting to find and explore swamps can go to chapter 3. Chapter 4 describes what can be seen in a few of Florida's notable forested wetlands. The dramatic and colorful seasonal changes that occur in swamps are described in chapter 5. Natural-history accounts of some swamp plants and animals are presented in chapters 6 through 9. Scientific names for species mentioned in the text and shown in photos are in the index; common names are used in the text, with such names as Magnolia, Luna, and Vireo capitalized because they are also the scientific names.

Many people generously contributed their time to improve the manuscript for *Swamp Song*. Without their help, publication of the book would not have been possible. My sincere thanks go to Ray Ashton of Water and Air Research; Daniel Austin of Florida Atlantic University; David Benzing of Antioch College; Bob Butler, John Hefner, Dennis Jordan, Dave Martin, and Greg Masson of the U.S. Fish and Wildlife Service; Charles DuToit and Walt Thompson of the Florida Department of Natural Resources; Thomas Emmel, Dana Griffin III, and Larry Harris of the University of Florida; Malcolm

Hodges and Carl Nordman of The Nature Conservancy; Herbert Kale II of the Florida Audubon Society; Randy Kautz, David Maehr, Paul Mohler, and Brian Tolson of the Florida Game and Fresh Water Fish Commission; James Layne of Archbold Biological Station; Phil Lounibos of the Florida Medical Entomology Laboratory; Orson Miller of Virginia Polytechnic Institute; Petra Sierwald of Chicago's Field Museum of Natural History; Peter Stiling of the University of South Florida; David Webb of the Florida Museum of Natural History; and Robert Williams of Sarasota. I also appreciate the help provided by several anonymous reviewers.

Thanks also to my copyeditor, Beth Morrison, and to the staff of the University Press of Florida, especially Walda Metcalf, associate director and editor in chief, for starting it all, Alexandra Leader for her encouragement, Larry Leshan for layout and cover design, and Michael Senecal for overseeing production.

I am most grateful to Jennifer Smith, a medical and natural-history illustrator from St. Simons Island, Georgia, for providing the frontispiece, figures 4, 5, 9, and 12, the spot illustrations scattered throughout the book, and the illustration on the back of the cover. Printing assistance for the color slides was provided by Brian Ainsworth (president), Theresa Redding (lab manager), and the helpful staff at Harmon's Photos Ar' Nice in Gainesville, Florida. Photographs were kindly provided by Charissa Baker, Robert Bennetts, Joan Hesterberg, Kathy Larson, and David Maehr; these greatly enhance the book.

Finally, I am indebted to my wife, Kathy, who has shared my passion for swamps. Despite the torments of mosquitos and yellowflies, she fought the urge to flee and adventured through the swamps with me. Many memorable days of camping, canoeing, and hiking together provided rewarding photographic opportunities, which led Kathy to many more months of darkroom photography work and countless color slides to organize and label. Continual viewing of such beauty on film and in the Florida wilds over many years prompted the progression of this book through numerous manuscript revisions by experts and persistent editing by Kathy; now it has become a reality.

 Introduction

Where land and water intermingle, something magical occurs: a landscape both luxuriant and alluring. Gleaming lily-covered ponds are nearly everywhere, dotted with white egrets silently stalking small fish. Along winding, cypress-lined rivers, stately blue herons wade amid aquatic gardens profuse with scalloped pennyworts and blue-flowered pickerelweeds. In the dark recesses of remote swamps, canary-yellow prothonotary warblers build their nests in the hollows of cypress and tupelo trees whose strangely swollen trunks rise from midnight-black water.

The seasons too impart a special ambience. In spring and early summer, the air is filled with the lemony scent of sweetbay and the roselike fragrance of loblolly bay. After fresh summer rains, moist pine flatwoods revel in pastel-pink orchids and golden wildflowers that sway on thin stems. In autumn, when the sky is blue as a robin's egg, the swamps of north Florida are emblazoned with the fiery reds and yellows of maple leaves. Hungry swallowtail butterflies sift through the warm sunlit swamps, hurriedly sipping the last drops of nectar from fading flowers. In winter, cool winds blow through moss-draped cypresses where multicolored warblers glean insects from the bare branches. There is both beauty and abundant life here.

Florida is richly endowed with wetlands (fig. 1). They cover over 17,000 square miles (one square mile = 640 acres), nearly one-third of

Figure 1. Distribution of major forested wetlands in Florida. Redrawn from Wharton et al. 1976.

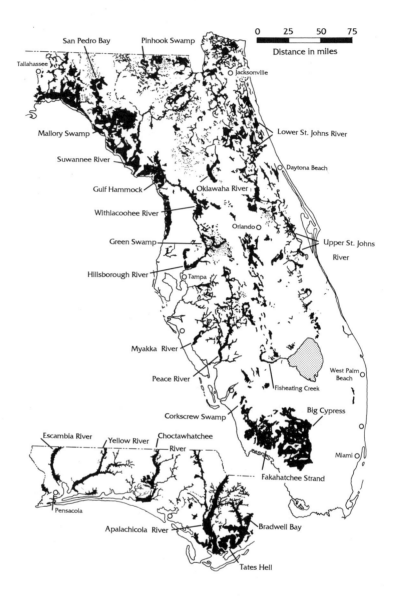

the state. In fact, Florida has more swamps and marshes than any other state except Alaska.

Florida is unimaginable without cypress domes, pitcher plant savannahs, bayheads, wet prairies, mangrove swamps, and sawgrass glades, yet all of these are disappearing! In just twenty years, from 1955 to 1975, more than two thousand square miles of wetlands in Florida were lost—a rate of eight acres each hour (Hefner 1986). Over the next ten years this loss slowed to three acres per hour—four hundred square miles (Frayer and Hefner 1991).

Wetland losses may have slackened, but species dependent on south Florida's wetlands have been severely affected, especially birds. Populations of herons, egrets, storks, and other wetland-dependent birds have drastically declined (Crowder 1974; Kushlan, Ogden, and Higer 1975; Bildstein et al. 1990). Alteration of the Kissimmee River has reduced waterfowl usage by more than 90 percent, and bald eagle nesting has declined by more than 70 percent (Perrin 1986). Gleason (1984) estimated that more than 175 wildlife species in south Florida are imperiled, the primary cause being loss of wetlands and other habitats.

Florida has compiled a tragic record of wetland destruction (Carter 1974; Blake 1980). It began with an era that scientist and conservationist Patrick Gleason (1984) called "The Age of Rapacious Drainage." Nationally this age started in 1849 when the federal government, through the Swamp Lands Acts of 1849, gave millions of acres of virgin wetland to the states. In Florida the damage began in 1882 with Philadelphia industrialist Hamilton Disston's grand scheme to drain the Kissimmee River Basin. In 1945 the era abruptly ended when one of the worst droughts in recorded history hit south Florida. The ill-planned system of canals had lowered water tables, with devastating results. Marjory Stoneman Douglas (1947) poignantly described what happened: "The whole Everglades was burning. What had been a river of grass and sweet water that had given meaning and life and uniqueness to this whole enormous geography through centuries in which man had no place here was made, in one chaotic gesture of greed and ignorance and folly, a river of fire."

Finally, in 1946 two hurricanes dumped more than eight feet of rain, and south Florida became a vast lake. The stage was set for an "Age of Structural Solutions," which began when the U.S. Army Corps of Engineers began building a system of canals to regulate south Florida's water. "From Disney World to Homestead," wrote Gleason (1984), "700 miles of canals and innumerable control structures predetermine the path of every raindrop from cloud to sea." By 1990, such "structural solutions" had expanded to more than a thousand miles of canals, several thousand floodgates, and numerous pumping stations. What may have been a dream to water managers and engineers had become an ecologist's nightmare. Domination of south Florida's water was accomplished at the expense of an irreplaceable natural ecosystem that had been fine-tuned over millennia to cope with the vagaries and extremes of rainfall. The resultant ecological damage now extends from Orlando to Florida Bay, affecting nearly every habitat from pine flatwoods to coral reefs—the price we are paying for having tried to master a natural system that did not meet our immediate needs.

Florida has come a long way since those early days of rampant wetland devastation, but the fight is not over. Every day a wetland is filled, drained, or ecologically altered. Overpumping of aquifers sucks surface water from isolated wetlands, killing cypress and altering the ecosystem. The plight of wetlands and other wild lands must be brought to the forefront. Each of us should know what wetlands are and why they are important and that they can be fascinating and unforgettably beautiful.

1

Swamps and Hammocks

What's in a Name?

Florida has many kinds of wetlands. Knowing more about them makes them more fascinating. Florida's wetlands can be divided into two broad categories: marshes (and glades like Florida's Everglades), where grasses, sedges, reeds, and other herbaceous plants are prevalent, and forested wetlands, where trees are prevalent. Forested wetlands in turn can be divided into two categories: swamps and hydric hammocks. Swamps and hammocks are seasonally flooded forests.

Swamps are divided into two categories: estuarine and freshwater. Estuarine swamps occur near the ocean and are dominated by mangroves—one of the few trees tolerant of salt water. In Florida there are three types of freshwater swamps: depression swamps, river swamps, and strands. Depression swamps occur in low areas that are flooded primarily by rain rather than runoff. Water also percolates from surrounding higher ground, or, in the case of large depression swamps such as the Okefenokee, streams feed into the depression. Six categories of depression swamps are recognized: basin swamps, shrub bogs, bayheads, cypress domes, gum swamps, and Carolina bays. Cypress domes are easily recognizable because normally they are inundated with water and their vegetation is different from the vegetation in adjacent uplands.

River swamps are found along rivers and creeks and are also known as floodplain swamps. They are inundated during periods of high runoff. The large watersheds sometimes associated with them means that flooding can be extensive. There are two types of river swamps in Florida: alluvial and blackwater.

Strands are swamps that in some respects occupy an intermediate position between depression swamps and river swamps. Like depression swamps, strands are fed mostly by rain rather than runoff. But, like river swamps, the water in strands flows, although in a slow, broad sheet, not a relatively narrow channel.

Swamps are usually fairly easy to identify. Hydric hammocks are more difficult. Hydric hammocks are hardwood-dominated wetlands that have a seasonally high water table but that are flooded only immediately after heavy rains. They are not considered "true" swamps because standing water is present only intermittently. They may be covered with water for only a week or two each year, and they support plants found in both wetlands and uplands. Because hammock soils are usually fully saturated, however, they are indeed forested wetlands.

Florida's freshwater swamps and hydric hammocks are the subjects of this book. Together they cover between 7,000 and 8,500 square miles of Florida—12 to 15 percent of the state's area. The remainder of this chapter will tell you more about what makes these valuable wetlands distinctive.

Depression Swamps

Basin Swamps

Basin swamps occur in large, sandy depressions on the coastal plain of north Florida and south Georgia (Wharton et al. 1976; Wharton 1977). Because basin swamps often contain an abundance of Sphagnum moss and can even have floating islands of peat called batteries, they are sometimes called bog swamps. The largest basin swamp in the Southeast is the six-hundred-square-mile Okefenokee Swamp in southeastern Georgia, which extends into northeast Florida where it is known as Pinhook Swamp (fig. 2). Bradwell Bay in Florida's Apalachicola National Forest is another basin swamp, occupying about thirty square miles.

Perhaps the largest basin swamp system in Florida is the Mallory Swamp–San Pedro Bay–California Swamp system in Dixie, Lafayette, and Taylor Counties. This complex of forested wetlands covers more than five hundred square miles of the Big Bend region north of the mouth of the Suwannee River and forms the headwaters of the Econfina, Fenholloway, and Steinhatchee Rivers.

Basin swamps trap much water because they are large, they have restricted outflow, and they contain deep layers of water-retaining peat. These deposits, which can be more than fifteen feet thick, are, in fact, the basis for the Indian name *Okefenokee*, which means "shaking earth." Peat in basin swamps accumulates at a rate of only about one inch per fifty years. This peat may eventually become coal, since similar peat-forming conditions probably existed in ancient swamps that have been transformed into coal.

The Okefenokee Basin was probably formed during the Pleistocene epoch, more than 250,000 years ago, when the Atlantic Ocean was about 150 feet higher (Schlesinger 1978). Wind and wave action formed a 130-mile-long sand sill, the Trail Ridge, which extends from Florida into Georgia (fig. 2). As the ocean retreated, an extensive silty depression was left behind. The depression may have deepened further as underlying carbonate layers dissolved. Freshwater marshes formed behind the ridge. Only about seven thousand years ago did peat formation start, because of higher water levels. On a smaller scale, similar marshes occur behind more recent beach ridges like those at the Savannas State Preserve south of Fort Pierce.

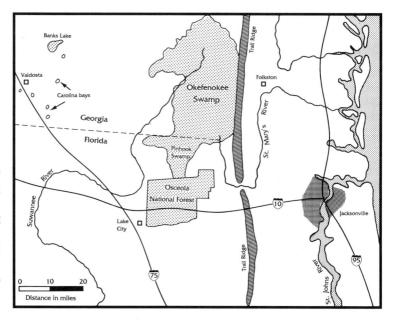

Figure 2. Map of northeast Florida and southeast Georgia showing Okefenokee Swamp, Pinhook Swamp, Banks Lake, Trail Ridge, and smaller Carolina bays.

Although the Okefenokee is referred to as a swamp, it is actually a highly complex jigsaw puzzle of ponds, marshes, bayheads, scrub bogs, cypress and gum swamps, and pine-dominated uplands. On peat islands called "houses" there are shrub thickets (similar to shrub bogs, described below) composed of shrubs and small trees like titi, dahoon holly, loblolly bay, and pond cypress. Shrubs are the dominant woody vegetation in Okefenokee's wetlands and are also the most diverse, comprising about thirty species. Trees account for less than half this number. Tough, sprawling vines called greenbriers are also abundant in the swamp.

In the Okefenokee, there is a relationship between the underlying topography and the overlying plant communities. Marshes called "prairies" occur where the peat is deepest. Pond cypress, swamp tupelo, and swampbay dominate in areas that have shallower peat deposits. Giant pond cypress that were more than three feet in diameter and nine hundred years old once grew in the swamp; now few trees exceed five hundred years of age (Duever and Riopelle 1984).

The Okefenokee has had an interesting recent history. Between 1909 and 1927, an industrious logging company—the Hebard Lumber Company—employed three hundred loggers to cut timber in the swamp, from which they eventually wrestled enough cypress, pine, and hardwood to build a city. A railway built on piers and fallen trees moved the logs to nearby mills. Logging removed 90 percent of the valuable timber and has changed the face of the swamp, perhaps for centuries. Because conditions no longer favor cypress, there is little recruitment. Consequently, the cypress in the swamp may not recover for hundreds of years (Hamilton 1984). Before the logging, there was a futile attempt in the 1890s to drain the Okefenokee. After ditching only thirteen miles, at a rate of three miles per year, the Suwannee Canal Company finally went bankrupt.

From about 2000 B.C. the swamp was home to Native Americans, who lived in the area until European settlers arrived in the mid-nineteenth century. These British immigrants, known as Okefenokee Crackers, or Swampers, were culturally related to the Appalachian hillbillies and, like them, retained an identity that was mostly lost elsewhere. The Swampers survived by harvesting the rich natural resources of the area. The last of them left in the 1940s, after most of the swamp was purchased by the federal government and became the Okefenokee National Wildlife Refuge.

Although the ecology of the Okefenokee is largely determined by water depth and duration of flooding (hydroperiod), fires also play a crucial role (Schlesinger 1978; Hamilton 1984). Small fires are frequent; one in June 1993, dubbed the Gnatcatcher, burned six thousand acres. Major conflagrations are rare, occurring on average only three to four times per century, yet their effect has been great. Although these fires burn much of the swamp, they are very spotty. Large fires start during rare drought years when the peat dries sufficiently for lightning-started blazes to spread. Peat fires travel slowly outward and down. Loss of peat effectively raises the water table, so ponds and marshes replace "houses." Fires also may kill most hardwoods and smaller cypress, but larger cypress usually survive. The occasional large fires are primarily responsible for the mosaic character of the wetland communities in the swamp, maintaining them in a dynamic flux of successional stages. It remains to be seen how important fires will be in future regulation of plant communities in the swamp.

Okefenokee, like many other wetlands, has been violated by naive attempts to derive wealth from seemingly worthless lands. Yet it endures. Will Cox, a former Swamper from Cowhouse Island, succinctly related what happened: "We did everything we could to destroy it. We skinned alligators until we like to drove every last one off. We killed the bears, otters, foxes, and almost got rid of them. We went after the cypress and cut down 3,000 acres of trees. I was a part of all that—we didn't know any better. But the old swamp came back. Okefenokee is God's work—man couldn't destroy it" (Presley 1984).

Shrub Bogs

Shrub bogs are wetlands dominated by shrubs (Wharton et al. 1976; Sharitz and Gibbons 1982; Ewel 1990). Although not true swamps since shrubs, not trees, are the dominant vegetation, they have many features in common with swamps. In Florida, shrub bogs total about one thousand square miles (about 2 percent of the state's area).

Shrub bogs occur mostly in north Florida, where they cover extensive areas within larger wetland systems. Examples can be found in Okefenokee Swamp and adjacent Pinhook Swamp, and in Sandlin Bay in Baker and Columbia Counties. Bradwell Bay Wilderness, covering about thirty square miles in Wakulla County, is another large shrub bog that, because of its large size and shape, can also be classified as a basin swamp (fig. 3). Tates Hell, in Franklin County, is also a large shrub-bog system that unfortunately has been severely altered by attempts to convert the wetlands to pine plantations. Several state and federal agencies have planned to purchase Tates Hell and to restore its wetlands.

Shrub bogs may have a high diversity of woody plants or may be dominated by a few species. Evergreen shrubs predominate, including titi, black titi, sweet pepperbush, large gallberry, wax myrtle, dahoon, and others (Wharton et al. 1976) (fig. 4A). Also common are shrubs belonging to the heather family (*Ericaceae*), such as doghobble, blueberry, staggerbush, fetterbush, and the azaleas (plate 15). Pond pine and slash pine may also be present. Soil in shrub bogs often consists of nutrient-poor peat deposits that overlay sand. Water levels are often high, although the surface dries during droughts. The frequency of fires in shrub bogs probably plays an important role in eliminating unadapted trees, as does the low nutrient content of the soil.

The abundance of fruiting shrubs in these bogs attracts many birds and mammals, including bears. In fact, one shrub is named bear gum because black bears eat its fruit. Although related to tupelo, bear gum is a head-high shrub, one of our few endemic wetland shrubs. Bear gum is known from only a few counties along the Apalachicola River (Clewell 1985).

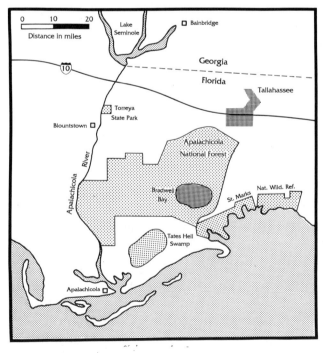

Figure 3. Map of Apalachicola River region of north Florida showing Bradwell Bay, Tates Hell, and Torreya State Park.

A

B

Figure 4. Cross sections of forested wetlands: A, Shrub bog—dominant plants are shrubs, bay trees, emergent aquatics, and pond cypress; B, Bayhead—dominant plants are bay trees and ferns and other herbaceous species growing on a deep layer of peat.

Panhandle shrub bogs are home to many rare species. One of these is the pine barrens treefrog, a one- to two-inch-long pastel green frog with gaudy yellow spots on its belly and under its legs and a purplish-brown line along each side from nose to feet. Even though it has a broad distribution, extending north to New Jersey, the pine barrens treefrog is rare because it occurs at a few small sites. In Florida, this frog lives only in shrub bogs in Santa Rosa, Okaloosa, and Walton Counties (Means 1976, 1992).

Other unusual biota found in shrub bogs (and the sometimes associated herb bogs) include nearly thirty species of insectivorous plants, including bladderworts, butterworts, pitcher plants, and sundews (Means 1990). Uncommon terrestrial orchids, such as the attractive white-fringed and spreading Pogonia, can also occur in shrub bogs. Habitats where these extraordinary species occur are rapidly disappearing because of improper land management.

Bayheads

Bayheads are so named because bay trees, including loblolly bay, swampbay, and sweetbay, predominate (fig. 4B). Bayheads are dominated by evergreen trees and shrubs and are one of the few forested wetlands in Florida where cypress are normally absent (Monk 1966, 1968; Wharton et al. 1976; Wharton 1977). Bayheads are usually small, a few acres in extent at most. They occur throughout the state, especially where there are depressions among sand hills as in Lake County in central Florida.

Bayheads receive sufficient seepage from adjacent uplands to keep their soils moist throughout the year. This constant saturation leads to the formation of peat, which may be up to six feet thick. Leaves, flowers, twigs, roots, and other organic debris don't fully decompose under these conditions. Bayheads are rarely flooded because surrounding sandy soils are porous and the catchment area is small. Following heavy rains, however, bayheads have so much water-soaked peat below them that they seem to float. The presence of moisture at the surface, even in dry weather, usually prevents bayheads from burning.

Because bayheads are fed by rain and seepage from nutrient-poor sandy soils, minerals for plant growth are scarce. Most of the nutrients are trapped in the peat. The absence of cypress in bayheads is perhaps a result of their isolation from surface flow, which is usually necessary to disperse cypress seeds.

Compared to some other types of swamps, bayheads are relatively uncommon. Altogether, they occupy only about 250 square miles in Florida (about 0.4 percent of the total area of the state). Yet bayheads provide a moist refuge for many animals and unusual plants and should be protected.

Cypress Domes

Cypress domes or heads are a common and widespread feature of the pine-dominated, flat landscape of Florida's coastal plain (Vernon 1947; Monk 1966, 1968; Wharton et al. 1976; Wharton 1977; Duever 1984; McPherson 1984; Duever et al. 1986). The domes have a characteristic profile because the pond cypress trees near the center are taller than those near the perimeter (fig. 5A). From the air, cypress domes can appear doughnut shaped because of the central pond where the water is deepest. Cypress domes and other cypress-dominated

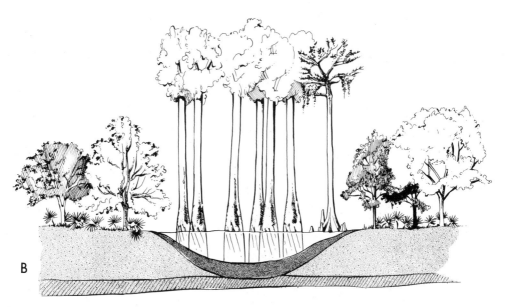

Figure 5. Cross sections of forested wetlands: A, Cypress dome—dominant plants are pond cypress, which are largest in wetter sites. Bromeliads and other epiphytes can be abundant. Pines and saw palmetto occupy uplands. A clay layer traps water in the dome; B, Gum swamp—dominant plants in wetter sites are swamp tupelo and bald cypress. Dwarf palmetto and red maple, elm, oaks, sweetgum, and other hardwoods live in drier sites. A layer of clay traps water, often forming a pond.

swamps are among the most numerous forested wetlands in Florida, occupying about 5 percent of the area of the state.

Cypress domes form in shallow, sandy depressions where the underlying soil is a relatively impermeable clay hardpan that traps rainwater (Wharton et al. 1976). Above the clay layer is generally peat, consisting mostly of the partially decomposed cypress twigs and needles.

The origin of cypress domes is unknown; there is evidence that the depressions were formed some twenty to thirty thousand years ago, when sea level was much higher, in marine lagoons similar to present-day Indian River Lagoon along Florida's east coast. Domes in south Florida also occur in limestone depressions that were formed by dissolution of the rock.

Because domes are relatively isolated from natural drainage patterns, they are almost entirely dependent on nutrient input from rain. Also, most of the woody plants (cypress being a notable exception) are evergreen and therefore do not add many leaves to the soil. Thus, cypress domes are poor in minerals and must conserve and recycle their scant supply. This is reflected in the small size of the trees, the open canopy, and the relatively low tree-species diversity. Nonethe-

Figure 6. Cypress dome habitat showing epiphytic bromeliads (cardinal wild pines) on pond cypress, with swamp ferns in the foreground. J. W. Corbett Wildlife Management Area in south Florida.

less, because much light reaches the ground, a rich understory of shrubs and a ground cover of ferns and herbs may develop. There are about twice as many shrub species in cypress domes as there are trees. Also, in south and central Florida, epiphytes including lichens, bromeliads, and orchids can be numerous, giving the trees a bristled appearance (fig. 6).

Hydroperiods in cypress domes are highly variable from one year to the next. In wet years, cypress domes may be flooded for months. In droughts they may be mostly dry, allowing upland weeds such as broom sedge and dog fennel to invade. But these weeds "drown" when water levels return to normal.

The vegetation in a cypress dome is often arranged in zones. Around the sunny outer margin grow short pond cypress. Showy flowers typical of moist pine flatwoods and associated prairies are often present. Marsh pinks usually are the most conspicuous, but many others can occur here as well, including yellow-flowered tall milkwort, meadow beauty, yellow-eyed grass, Catesby's lily, and Alligator lily (plates 8 and 9). Colorful terrestrial orchids also grow on the perimeters of cypress domes: snowy orchid, scarlet ladies'-tresses, grass-pink, yellow-fringed orchid, rose Pogonia, and spreading Pogonia are some of these (plate 10).

Within the dome, the pond cypress grow taller, and there are often other trees as well, including slash pine, red maple, swamp tupelo, and such shrubs as fetterbush and wax myrtle. Also common are swamp fern, Virginia chain fern, and various sedges and grasses. In addition, poison ivy, greenbriers, wild grapes, and other vines cling to the trees for support as they grow upward into the sunlight.

Near the center of the dome, where the water is deepest, the cypress are largest and there may be swamp tupelo and buttonbush. A variety of delicate ferns, mosses, liverworts, false nettle, and other moisture-loving herbs often form "collars," embracing the buttressed trunks and knees of cypress (fig. 7). The collars consist primarily of mosses, which grow near the average high-water level. Most lichens, being less tolerant of flooding, grow higher. Liverworts, resembling thin, short strips of dark green cellophane, grow near the ground where they remain moist.

In cypress domes with a persistent central pond, a variety of emergent or floating aquatic plants grow, including the lovely white water lily, the tall banana-leafed arrowroot, and the blue-spiked pickerel-weed—a nectar-rich favorite of swallowtail butterflies (plate 12). Also

Figure 7. Pond cypress trunk, with collar of moss and other plants indicating the high-water line and extent of seasonal flooding. Note the peat in the foreground, formed by cypress twigs.

visible because of their abundance may be the small flowers of yellow or purple bladderworts.

In the canopy of cypress domes, especially in southern Florida, epiphytic ferns, bromeliads, and orchids occur. Bromeliads dominate, with the most noticeable of these being the cardinal wild pine. This attractive plant has reddish bracts and a rosette of overlapping, stiff, pointed leaves more than a foot in length (plate 6). Because it produces offshoots at its base, several plants grow together around the tree, forming what appears to be a large green pom-pom. Less abundant are the orchids, the most common being the butterfly orchid. If you look very closely on the lower limbs of the cypress you may even see the tiny, leafless Harrisella orchid, one of Florida's smallest.

The vegetation in cypress domes is sensitive to rainfall and fire. Cypress growth is dependent on the hydroperiod. Trees in the center of the dome grow faster than those at the perimeter because the deeper peat retains moisture during the dry season (Duever et al. 1986). If the spongy peat gets too high and does not burn periodically, hardwoods may eventually become established and replace the cypress. How pond cypress first reach the depressions is not fully understood, but it seems most likely that mammals and birds disperse the seeds, since many cypress domes are located in areas where flooding rarely occurs.

The fauna in cypress domes is not rich, because food is scarce. Most trees and vines produce seasonal fruits for birds and mammals, but the low food value of their leaves limits the numbers of insects and their predators. Cottonmouth snakes may be common in cypress domes; however, they are most visible in spring when they congregate around drying pools. The one- to two-inch-long mosquitofish, and the even smaller least killifish, are among the few fishes to frequent the domes. They can be seen in the pools, searching at the surface for small insects that fall into the water. Any disturbance of the surface will attract them. During the dry season, frogs, salamanders, and snakes may hide in cypress domes where there is moisture. Many amphibians migrate to cypress ponds during wet periods to mate and lay eggs. Domes also provide roosting and nesting sites for birds, and daytime beds for larger mammals like deer and Florida panthers.

Cypress domes occur throughout Florida where the terrain is low, flat, and sandy and where there are shallow depressions lined by impermeable clay, marl, or limestone. Numerous cypress domes ranging in size from less than an acre to more than a square mile can be seen along the Florida Turnpike, in the Kissimmee Prairie area between Orlando and Fort Pierce, and in similar flat terrain in eastern Florida along Interstate 95. Cypress domes also occur in the Big Cypress region of south Florida.

Gum Swamps

Gum swamps are forested wetlands dominated by swamp tupelo trees, commonly called gums; cypress are often present but are scarce (Wharton et al. 1976; Wharton 1977) (fig. 8). Gum swamps are common in north Florida and in Georgia. They often occur around a permanent pond or along a blackwater creek. Water accumulates in these swamps, as it does in cypress domes and Carolina bays, because they usually occupy depressions that are lined by an impervious layer of clay (fig. 5B). There the trees grow at the lowest sites, where the peat layer is three or more feet thick.

As in bayheads, the thick accumulation of peat in gum swamps keeps the ground moist throughout the year. This moisture probably prevents most fires from killing the trees. Swamp tupelos often grow so thickly in the wetter areas of gum swamps, especially following logging, that few other plants can compete. Shrubs like buttonbush,

titi, fetterbush, sweet pepperbush, and Virginia willow live in areas with shorter hydroperiods.

Swamp tupelos are easily recognized by their basally swollen trunks (round in cross section). The trees often are hollow and have knot holes that are important to cavity-nesting birds like the prothonotary warbler and white-breasted nuthatch. In late summer the tupelos produce small, black, olivelike fruits that are eaten by many birds and mammals.

Small ponds in gum swamps are important breeding sites for amphibians. The clicking strains of chorus frogs are heard in gum ponds as early as January. Researchers in Georgia found that during a one-year period nearly four thousand amphibians of many species used a small gum-swamp pond (Wharton 1977). Some species, such as the sluggish mole salamanders, prefer ponds that regularly go dry because they contain fewer predators, such as fish. These salamanders take refuge in moist crayfish burrows and under tupelo tree roots during the dry season.

Carolina Bays

Carolina bays are a unique type of wetland found only in the southeastern coastal plain from Virginia to near the Florida-Georgia border (Wharton et al. 1976; Wharton 1977; Savage 1982; Sharitz and Gibbons 1982). Nearly a thousand have been located in Georgia, and many more are in the Carolinas. Their occurrence in Florida is uncertain; a few may be present in Hamilton, Madison, and Jefferson Counties, making them one of Florida's rarest wetlands. Carolina bays, named for the prevalence of bay trees in them, typically have an oval or teardrop shape on a long northwest-southeast axis. They range in size from less than an acre to several square miles and are frequently associated with lakes or ponds, many of which have been increased in size by small dams.

Many Carolina bays occur in south Georgia near Valdosta. Banks Lake National Wildlife Refuge, ten miles northeast of Valdosta, is one of the largest at three miles in diameter (fig. 2). It is a picturesque blackwater lake dotted with white water lilies and pond cypress whose swollen bases resemble huge, pleated hoop skirts. In April, the cypress are home to boldly colored songbirds like the great crested flycatcher and yellow-throated warbler. Many other large bay swamps are found nearby, including Grand Bay.

Carolina bays are clay-lined, peat-filled depressions up to thirty feet deep, located in otherwise sandy soil. Their origins are debated, but they may have been formed during the Pleistocene epoch by fierce northwest winds that scooped out the sediment, leaving a shallow, oval basin with a small berm on the southeastern side.

The vegetation in Carolina bays is highly variable and is often a mixture of plants common to cypress swamps, gum swamps, wet prairies, shrub bogs, and other wetlands. Besides bay trees and swamp tupelo, evergreen ericaceous shrubs like fetterbush are common in the nutrient-poor, acidic, waterlogged soil.

The fauna of Carolina bays is similar to that of other swamps. One unusual inhabitant is the round-tailed muskrat, a small and rare wetland rodent (Wharton et al. 1976; Humphrey 1992). The fauna of Carolina bays located near the Savannah River Ecology Laboratory in South Carolina have been studied in detail, especially amphibians and reptiles (Gibbons 1990). A total of twenty-two amphibian and twenty-two reptile species were noted in one study. During an October salamander breeding migration to a Carolina bay, more than five thousand marbled salamanders were counted in a single night (Cohn 1994).

River Swamps

River swamps occur throughout the Southeast wherever creeks and rivers regularly flood into adjacent floodplains (Wharton et al. 1976; Wharton 1977; Wharton et al. 1982). Swamps of varying sizes occur along most of Florida's seventeen hundred streams and rivers, and cover about a thousand square miles (about 2 percent of the state's area) (Wharton et al. 1976). These wetlands can be divided into two types, alluvial and blackwater, depending on vegetation, water chemistry, soils, and other factors.

Alluvial Swamps

The largest river swamps in the Southeast are alluvial. Such swamps are often called bottomland hardwoods because they are found on floodplains dominated by hardwoods. Seemingly limitless bottomland forests once stretched over the immense Mississippi Valley. Today most of that emerald forest is gone, having been converted to cropland. In Florida, alluvial swamps occur only along the Apalachicola and Choctawhatchee Rivers and to a lesser extent along the Ochlockonee, Escambia, and Yellow Rivers of northern Florida (Wharton et al. 1976; Wharton 1977; Wharton et al. 1982; Ewel 1990) (fig. 1). These muddy rivers have their headwaters in uplands where clay is prevalent. During periods of heavy runoff, the rivers erode this clay from the banks and deposit it over the floodplain downstream. In the Carolinas, alluvial swamps are referred to as red-river bottoms because of the color of the clay-laden rivers during flooding. Because of the vast watershed of alluvial rivers, which can extend over thousands of square miles, bottomland hardwood swamps can be flooded to depths of more than ten feet in the wet season.

The largest alluvial system in Florida is the Apalachicola River (more than 450 miles in length including the tributaries), which receives snow melt from the southern Appalachians by way of the Chattahoochee River. The Apalachicola has the third-highest discharge of rivers along the Atlantic and Gulf coasts.

Besides having the state's largest river swamp, which covers about two hundred square miles, the Apalachicola Basin is noted for its rare endemic biota. Many of these are relict species that have survived there perhaps since the last ice age, eighteen thousand years ago, while they were being extirpated in adjacent areas. Others evolved into the distinct species recognized today in the basin.

Botanist Andre Clewell (1977) has noted that more than a hundred unusual plant species live in the region, many considered endangered. Florida's Apalachicola Basin has been estimated to support nearly 350 species of vertebrates (including eighty-five freshwater fishes, forty-four amphibians, sixty-four reptiles, ninety-nine breeding birds, and fifty-two mammals) (Means 1977). Amphibians and reptiles are varied, with the upper basin containing the highest diversity of these animals in North America north of Mexico (Kiester 1971; Means 1977). This biotic richness is due in part to the position of the river near several faunal provinces and areas of endemism (Means 1977). Because of the unique natural heritage of the Apalachicola region, it must be given a high priority as an environmentally sensitive area.

In nearby southeastern Georgia, extensive bottomland hardwoods occur along the Flint and Altamaha Rivers. The largest swamps occur along the Altamaha and its two major tributaries, the Oconee and the Ocmulgee. In places, the riverine swamp exceeds four miles in width. Although smaller than the Apalachicola, the Altamaha is one of the major rivers of the Southeast. The rich supply of nutrients and leaf litter carried down to the sea by winter runoff enriches the lush "golden" salt marshes fringing Georgia's coast.

Alluvial swamps are among the most productive ecosystems known (Wharton et al. 1982). Huge oaks, cottonwoods, hickories, sycamores, and other hardwoods many hundreds of years old once grew in alluvial swamps throughout the Southeast, before widespread logging and land clearing occurred. The abundance of nutrients supplied by regular flooding, rapid decomposition of plant materials, absence of fire, and ample water provide near-ideal growing conditions for many trees. Unlike swamps in central and south Florida that are flooded mainly during the growing season, bottomland hardwood swamps are inundated primarily in winter and early spring when tree growth is least affected.

In comparison to depression and blackwater river swamps, which have an abundance of herbs and shrubs, alluvial swamps are relatively open and sometimes barren at ground level. In alluvial swamps the trees are large and widely spaced. The ground is covered by a thin layer of dead leaves; herb and shrub cover varies but is infrequent. Switch cane, a type of bamboolike grass, often forms isolated thickets known as canebrakes. The near-total absence of groundcover is perhaps due to the widely fluctuating water levels. Also, the absence of fire favors the development of trees rather than shrubs, with the dense canopy casting a deep shade over the forest floor in late spring and summer. Trees in alluvial swamps are mostly deciduous, the evergreen American holly being one notable exception. The prevalence of deciduous trees in alluvial swamps is in sharp contrast to the trees in nutrient-poor swamps like bayheads, where evergreens dominate.

Another distinctive feature of alluvial swamps is the absence of peat. Instead the soil consists of clay and silt—and sand, near point bars and on levees. The seasonally dry conditions and the low acidity of the water in these swamps favor complete decomposition, and floodwaters also remove leaves and other accumulated plant debris.

Because of their high productivity, bottomland hardwoods support many animals. Plentiful mast (nuts, fruit, and berries) provides birds and mammals with ample and nutritious autumn and winter food. Alluvial river swamps were formerly inhabited by the largest North American woodpecker, the ivory-bill, which is now extinct in the United States. These swamps also once supported large numbers of American swallow-tailed kites, which now occupy only a remnant of their former range. Other rare birds using bottomland hardwoods include Bachman's warbler, which is perhaps extinct, and Swainson's warbler, a dark brown ground-foraging warbler that fixes its nest to canes. Large numbers of black bears also used these forests, but are now mostly gone from the Southeast. Bats can also be plentiful. A variety of amphibians occur in alluvial swamps, including the bird-voiced treefrog and many salamanders.

Alluvial swamps are rich in tree species. In one study, forty-seven species of trees and shrubs were reported from the Apalachicola River floodplain (Leitman, Sohm, and Franklin 1983). The most numerous trees were water tupelo, Ogeechee tupelo or Ogeechee lime, bald cypress, pop ash, planer tree, and swamp tupelo or swamp black gum. Botanist Helen Leitman and coworkers found that tree diversity was greatest in the upper reaches of the river where topography was most varied. Although tree-species richness in alluvial swamps is high, generally only a few species are abundant at any one site (Wharton et al. 1976; Wharton 1977; Wharton et al. 1982).

Leitman, Sohm, and Franklin (1983) found that forest composition varied along the river and in relationship to the hydroperiod (fig. 9A). Sugarberry, possum haw, and American hornbeam occurred only in the floodplain of the upper river, whereas swamp tupelo, sweetbay, cabbage palm, and pumpkin ash were seen only along the lower river. Drier sites, inundated from 5 to 25 percent of the year, were dominated by sweetgum, sugarberry, water hickory, green ash, and three oaks: water, overcup, and swamp laurel. On wetter sites, inundated from 50 to 90 percent of the year, water tupelo, Ogeechee tupelo, bald cypress, and swamp tupelo grew.

Torreya State Park west of Tallahassee is a superb place to experience the rich ecosystem of the Apalachicola River floodplain and adjacent seepage slopes (fig. 3). Huge sycamores and poplars (four feet in diameter and a hundred feet high) and other hardwoods, as well as the Torreya and Florida yew, two rare conifers, grow in this magnificent forest.

Bottomland hardwoods are rapidly disappearing from the Southeast. All alluvial swamps have been affected to some degree. In Florida these wetlands are especially rare, representing less than 1 percent of the state's total area.

Figure 9. Cross sections of forested wetlands: *A*, Alluvial swamp—dominant plants in wetter sites are water tupelo and bald cypress. Dwarf palmetto and various oaks, ash, water hickory, American hornbeam, and other hardwoods live in drier sites;

B, Blackwater swamp—dominant plants in wetter sites are swamp tupelo, bald cypress, and pop ash. Laurel oak, red maple, swampbay, cabbage palm, and dwarf palmetto live in drier sites.

Blackwater Swamps

Blackwater swamps are found along the sluggish rivers of peninsular Florida and in coastal-plain areas throughout the Southeast (fig. 10). Named for their clear but coffee-tinted, organically rich waters, blackwater rivers carry little suspended sediment (Wharton et al. 1976; Huck 1987). Blackwater swamps are our most extensive forested wetlands, covering approximately 5 percent of the state.

Where river flow is weak in blackwater swamps, peat accumulates. The waterlogged peat is low in oxygen, stressing unadapted trees. Swamp tupelo and bald cypress often predominate in such conditions because their roots tolerate low oxygen levels (fig. 9B). Pop ash, swamp dogwood, swampbay, red maple, elms, and palms (cabbage palm, dwarf palmetto, and needle palm) are also common. Sweetgum and American hornbeam grow on higher ground. Near tidewater, extensive areas of swampbay and sweetbay may be present. The Ogeechee tupelo or Ogeechee lime is a small tree with burgundy-tinted, date-sized, sour but edible fruits. This tree often occurs in blackwater swamps from north Florida to South Carolina. Although not a tall tree, its trunk can reach a circumference of more than ten feet.

Figure 10. Blackwater swamp slough showing cabbage palms and various hardwood trees, with bald cypress knees in the foreground. Oklawaha River.

In Florida, the Hillsborough, Peace, St. Johns, Suwannee, and Withlacoochee (south) Rivers have extensive blackwater swamps (fig. 1). Along the St. Johns River south of Deland there are two state parks (Blue Spring and Hontoon Island) and a National Wildlife Refuge (Lake Woodruff) where there are blackwater swamps (fig. 11).

Along the Suwannee, extensive swamps dominated by tupelo, bald cypress, and red maple can be seen from the boardwalk at Manatee Springs State Park and at nearby Lower Suwannee National Wildlife Refuge, where there are a rich variety of wetland habitats. The Lower Suwannee wetlands are unusual among blackwater swamps because of the presence of water tupelo, which are mostly found in alluvial swamps.

Swamps in the Lower Suwannee once teemed with wildlife, including ivory-billed woodpeckers, bears, and panthers. Songbirds were plentiful, including Bachman's warbler. In March 1890, noted naturalist William Brewster accompanied Frank Chapman, an ornithologist, on an excursion up the river. At one point, Brewster boasted, he shot six Bachman's warblers in two hours! Brewster's 1890 journal re-

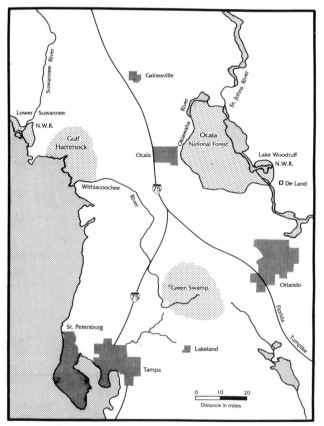

Figure 11. Map of west-central Florida showing location of Green Swamp, Gulf Hammock, Lake Woodruff National Wildlife Refuge, Lower Suwannee National Wildlife Refuge, and Ocala National Forest.

counted the first ornithological explorations of the Suwannee River, with a vivid portrayal of a scenic blackwater creek (Austin 1967):

It proved [to be] very beautiful, winding about through a fine forest of cypresses, sweet gums, red maples, and green ashes with palmettos along the banks. For the first mile it was broad with frequent large deep pools bordered by dense beds of bonnets but higher up it became so narrow that the trees arched over it inter-locking their branches for hundreds of yards at a stretch where the growth was of hardwoods or old cypresses, where of younger or more stunted cypresses and bay trees forming a nearly straight vertical wall on each side, the path of the stream looking in places like a narrow wood road walled in by straight cypresses hung thickly with dark Spanish Moss. In places the bay trees formed almost the sole growth. Their roots[,] washed clean by the over-flows or perhaps growing naturally above, instead of under, the surface[,] literally covered the ground so thickly that one could walk on them in slippers as on a dry floor. They resembled noth-ing so much as great beds of snakes lying stretched at full length in loose coils, or intertwined together in masses. Their general color was a plain stone gray mottled with darker very like that of a cottonmouth moccasin and their bark was in texture not unlike that of the skin of a large serpent. In fact the general resemblance, or perhaps I should say suggestiveness, was so strong that I could not walk on them without a shrinking sensation. It would be next to impossible to discover a real snake among them.

On the lower reaches of the creek I saw few large birds. A soli-tary Great Blue Heron, an Osprey sitting above its nest whistling shrilly and eyeing me suspiciously as I paddled past, a Red-shoul-dered Hawk, and a Kingfisher or two. Small birds were numerous, especially Prothonotaries of which I passed a dozen or more, several of them females. They haunted bushes which hung low over the stream where they flitted about among the terminal twigs, their yellow heads gleaming like gold among the foliage or showing in strong contrast against the dark water. I shot one fine orange headed male. Parulas and Yellow-throated Warblers were numerous as usual. Saw a pair of Crested Flycatchers as I was paddling slowly and silently across a broad pool where the sun-light brought out a sand bar beneath [and] with great distinctness I suddenly discovered a huge alligator gliding slowly under the canoe at nearly right angle. As I had not time to shoot ahead and escape him I suspended my paddle and sat perfectly still until he passed out of sight into deeper water on my left. His back must have nearly grazed my keel and he was not less than twelve feet in length with a bulk nearly equal to that of a small pony.

Florida's blackwater rivers and creeks are celebrated for their superb boating. Near the turn of the century, steamboat cruises up the Oklawaha River to Silver Springs were popular. This scenic central-Florida river was nearly ruined in the 1960s when the Army Corps of Engineers began construction of the Cross-Florida Barge Canal. Part of the river was flooded by Rodman Reservoir—"Lake Ocklawaha." Finally, environmentalists and state biologists convinced Congress that alteration of the river would be ecologically and economically unsound and probably would adversely affect the underlying aquifer (Carter 1974). Part of the Cross-Florida Barge Canal can still be seen from a high bridge on State Road 19, near Rodman south of Palatka.

Swamps also occur along the shores of many of Florida's seven thousand lakes, often marked by picturesque bald cypress with huge, swollen trunks. Swamp tupelo, pop ash, red maple, and other wetland trees occupy shallower sites. These fringing wetlands are similar to and often contiguous with those of the blackwater streams that feed the lakes.

River swamps and other riparian wetlands are integral parts of Florida's riverine system. In fact, these wetlands and rivers are interdependent, as was made obvious when the Kissimmee River was straightened. Alteration of riparian wetlands profoundly affects the river in the same way that changes in river flow affect the adjacent wetlands.

Strands

Strands are swamps unique to Florida (Wharton et al. 1976; Duever 1984; McPherson 1984; Duever et al. 1986). From the air they look like broad river swamps because they are elongated. Unlike river swamps, however, strands follow nearly level depressions over limestone or sand rather than tracing the course of a river or creek. Most of the area in south Florida where strands occur is so flat that creeks are best called sloughs because flow is so reduced. During periods of high rainfall, runoff in strands spreads into adjacent wetlands and flows

Figure 12. Cross sections of forested wetlands: *A,* Strand—dominant plants in wetter sites are bald cypress, pop ash, pond apple, and emergent aquatics. Cabbage and royal palms, laural and live oaks, red maple, and various ferns and other herbs live in drier sites; *B,* Hydric hammock—dominant plants are cabbage palm, live oak, southern red cedar, red maple, sweetgum, pignut hickory, loblolly pine. Saw palmetto occurs in uplands.

sluggishly, much as it does through the sawgrass prairies of the Everglades.

The origin of strands is not fully understood, but they apparently form when erosion and acids (carbonic acid from dissolved carbon dioxide and humic acids from plant decomposition) wear away exposed limestone (Duever et al. 1986). As depressions deepen, they accumulate cypress twigs and needles that decompose and produce additional humic acids, accelerating dissolution of the limestone and enhancing peat formation. Tree roots break apart the limestone, speeding the process. If the deepening peat does not periodically burn, it eventually raises the ground above the water table, allowing such hardwoods as red maple to invade and eventually replace the cypress.

Because the topography within a strand varies due to unequal weathering of the underlying limestone, a diverse mixture of trees, shrubs, and herbaceous vegetation is present, with varying tolerances to flooding (fig. 12A). Thus, strands can have wetland habitats ranging from those that are relatively dry, as in hydric hammocks (where

A

B

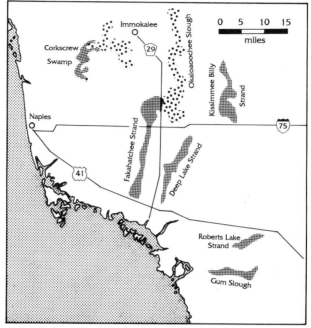

Figure 13. Location of the major strands in Florida. Redrawn from McPherson 1984.

cabbage palm, red maple, swamp laurel oak, and live oak are dominant), to those that have long hydroperiods, as in sloughs (where cypress, pond apple, and pop ash dominate).

Strands are found mostly in southwest Florida, around Big Cypress National Preserve. Some of the biggest are Deep Lake Strand, Kissimmee Billy Strand, Roberts Lake Strand, and Gum Slough (fig. 13). But Fakahatchee Strand is the largest, and it is unrivaled in its many unusual and rare plants and animals.

Hydric Hammocks

Hydric hammocks are hardwood-dominated forested wetlands that are surrounded by marshes, prairies, or pine flatwoods (Wharton et al. 1976; Craighead 1984; Huck 1987; Simons, Vince, and Humphrey 1989; Vince, Humphrey, and Simons 1989). The word *hammock* may be a corruption of the Seminole word meaning home, since the Seminoles frequently built their chickees in hammocks.

Compared to pine flatwoods, hammocks have a junglelike appearance caused by an abundance of vines, epiphytes, and palms. Also reminiscent of tropical forests is the "layering" in the canopy, in which trees, shrubs, and herbs grow to different heights.

Hammocks provide a necessary refuge for many species that cannot live in the drier prairies and pine flatwoods where fires are preva lent. In south Florida, hammocks are dominated by tropical hardwoods and palms and are rich in plants found nowhere else in the United States. In north Florida, hammocks have a high number of temperate tree species and may be the richest forests, on a per-acre basis, in the United States (Platt and Schwartz 1990). In central Florida, the flora is less diverse because these hammocks are located too far south for most temperate trees and too far north for tropicals. Some central Florida hydric hammocks are rich in shrubs, vines, and herbaceous plants, however. For example, even though Highlands Hammock State Park near Sebring supports relatively few tree species, it still has a wonderfully varied flora with more than seven hundred species of vascular plants (Stalter, Dial, and Laessle 1981; Walter Thompson, Florida Department of Natural Resources, unpubl. list, 1990; Daniel Austin, Florida Atlantic Univ., pers. comm., 1992).

Hammocks are used extensively by wildlife because they have many mast-producing trees, shrubs, and vines that provide a variety of such foods as acorns, other nuts and seeds, and fruits. Also, the old hardwood trees have plenty of nesting cavities.

Hydric hammocks are present throughout most of Florida (Simons, Vince, and Humphrey 1989; Vince, Humphrey, and Simons 1989). They often occur near streams, rivers, lakes, and even near salt marshes and mangrove swamps. Hydric hammocks were well developed along the Big Bend area of Florida's Gulf coast from St. Marks south to Crystal River, and along the St. Johns River, before extensive conversion to pine plantations in the 1970s. The largest remaining hammock is Gulf Hammock, south of Chiefland, which exceeds fifteen square miles in area (Simons, Vince, and Humphrey 1989) (fig. 11).

Hydric hammocks frequently occur along spring runs because of the high water table combined with infrequent flooding. For example, hydric hammocks border the Juniper, Salt, and Alexander Springs runs in Ocala National Forest. These scenic streams differ from blackwater streams in that their water is nearly colorless because of the absence of dissolved humic substances, and is alkaline because it has flowed through limestone. Spring runs are highly productive because sunlight penetrates the lucid waters to reach submerged aquatic plants. Apple and other aquatic snails feed on these plants and are abundant, providing food for limpkins. Nearby Indian kitchen middens filled with snail shells attest to the fertility of these streams.

Along spring runs in Ocala National Forest are the southernmost sites of the Atlantic white cedar, an increasingly scarce wetland conifer found from Maine to Florida. The moist but infrequently flooded peaty soils in these wetlands seem to be crucial to the survival of the white cedar, which is distinguishable from the more common red cedar primarily by its leathery cones.

Hydric hammocks have no unique tree flora (Simons, Vince, and Humphrey 1989; Vince, Humphrey, and Simons 1989). Nevertheless, they do have typical trees that frequently co-occur only in hammocks. These include cabbage palm, live oak, and southern red cedar, along with swamp laurel oak, sweetgum, loblolly pine, elm, red mulberry, persimmon, red maple, and pignut hickory (fig. 12B). Additional trees may be present farther north, or in southern coastal hammocks.

Vines (including wild grape, trumpet creeper, Virginia creeper, poison ivy, and peppervine) are abundant in hydric hammocks. The understory is rich in herbs, ferns, and shrubs such as wild coffee, beautyberry, and coral bean.

A variety of small tropical trees, including Eugenia, marlberry, and the exotically named paradise tree, have their northernmost distributions in coastal hammocks of eastern Florida. Here the nearby Florida Current (Gulf Stream) and the protective canopy of live oaks act like a greenhouse, moderating the effects of occasional subfreezing temperatures.

Hammocks often have a tropical ambience because of the richness of canopy-dwelling epiphytes. Ancient live oaks can literally bristle with lichens, ferns, bromeliads, and orchids; most plentiful is the resurrection fern. The largest epiphyte is the giant wild pine, whose gracefully arching two-foot-long leaves make it look like an overgrown pineapple top. This bromeliad has an unattractive green flower spike that reaches a height of four feet just before the plant dies, having expended all its stored energy on reproduction.

Palms are also present in hydric hammocks. Besides the frequent cabbage palm and saw palmetto, needle palm can also occur. This attractive palm resembles saw palmetto but has glossy, deeply cleft leaves; and its short trunk is armored by finger-long black spines.

Along the southern coasts of Florida where hydric hammocks abut mangrove swamps, the large blue land crab, reaching four inches across the carapace, burrows into the ground. The dark and water-filled burrows of this crab are also home to several other unusual animals, including the crab-hole mosquito. The adult mosquitos line the entrances of the crabs' holes during the day and swarm above them at dusk. The mangrove Rivulus is a small fish that can flip and slither between crab burrows, and that reproduces by self-fertilization (Taylor 1990). Rivulus deprived of water for a month can survive if kept moist; and they are also tolerant of low-oxygen conditions.

Hydric hammocks are rapidly disappearing. Of the approximately seven hundred square miles of hydric hammocks originally in Florida, only about half remain; of these, only about one-fifth are protected (Simons, Vince, and Humphrey 1989). Destruction of hammocks by development has been intense along the coasts and lake margins, where they are converted to home sites; yet many hydric hammocks are unsuitable as residential sites because they are seasonally flooded. Hammocks have rich soils and an abundance of moisture, and therefore have also been cleared for pastures, citrus, and other crops. In north-central Florida, hammocks are used for the commercial growing of decorative ferns, which require shade.

Besides directly destroying these hammocks, we have unknowingly introduced exotic plants and animals that further threaten them. The colorful, red-fruited peppertree (Brazilian pepper) is a major threat to the few remaining coastal hydric hammocks in the south. Its role as an invader is discussed in chapter 6.

An additional and potentially catastrophic threat to hydric hammocks is the rise in sea level. Because hammocks are mostly found at low elevations, often only a few feet above sea level, they will be significantly affected by a rising ocean (Simons, Vince, and Humphrey 1989). Hammocks of all kinds are unusual and valuable habitats that are imperiled.

 *2*

Getting Swamped
The Making of Forested Wetlands

A Window into the Past

Through geologic time swamps sometimes flourished—for example, during the Carboniferous period (three hundred million years ago)—as evidenced by thick deposits of coal left behind in many parts of the world. But those swamps, filled with giant lycopods, seed ferns, and tree horsetails, were nothing like the swamps of today. It was not until about fifty million years ago, during the early Tertiary period, that familiar wetland plants appeared. Tertiary swamps, forested with cypress, tupelo, and bay tress, were widely distributed over the Northern Hemisphere, when subtropical climates existed as far north as Greenland and Alaska. Alligators were top predators in some of those swamps, just as they are today.

But back then, Florida was still covered by shallow seas. It was not until the mid-Tertiary, some twenty-five million years ago, that Florida finally began rising from the sea. As the land emerged and became clothed in a mantle of green, it attracted many strange and wonderful animals, from sabercats to giant armadillos and horned camels (Webb 1974, 1990). For millions of years, Florida had a mild climate; at times it was even tropical. Grassy savannahs provided rich browse for horses and camels. Other grazers were quite unlike anything living today and included rhinolike rhinocerotids and long-necked giraffe-camels. Fossil remains of these and numerous other animals have been preserved in many central and north Florida springs, sinkholes, and rivers, among them the Crystal and Santa Fe Rivers and Brooks Sink.

Hardwood forests probably existed in Florida for most of those twenty-five million years, but there is little evidence of forested wetlands (Platt and Schwartz 1990; Webb 1990). Peat, associated with phosphate deposits in central Florida dating back fifteen million years to the mid-Miocene, suggests that wetlands did exist, but these deposits have not been well studied. Undoubtedly swamps existed near the coast, along rivers, and in other areas where depressions trapped water. In these wetlands, choruses of treefrogs sang during summer thunderstorms, swallowtail butterflies nectared at wildflowers, and the whine of mosquitos was omnipresent. Gators and cooters even basked along the riverbanks.

By the late Pleistocene (within the last one hundred thousand years), swamps had spread. Cypress trunks and knees, dated at about 18,000 B.P., have been recently unearthed along the Aucilla River in north Florida (S. David Webb, Florida Museum of Natural History, pers. comm., 1992). As familiar as these swamps might have been, you would have been startled to see a tapir or capybara plunge into a nearby river to elude a hungry jaguar. Giant armadillos as colossal as bulls and the elephantlike mastodons would also have caught your eye, as would the huge condors flying overhead.

This megafauna, as it is called by paleontologists, made the Florida of a hundred thousand years ago a very strange place. But much of it eventually went extinct. What precipitated these losses is unknown. Undoubtedly, rapid climatic changes, such as several ice ages (which reached their maximum extent between twenty and forty thousand years ago), and subsequent inundation by the ocean (between ten and sixteen thousand years ago, at the end of the Pleistocene epoch), and the presence of a newcomer, homo sapiens, who became a most effective predator and modifier of landscapes, were possible key factors. Florida has undergone many changes in its twenty-five million years of terrestrial history, but some species, such as cypress, have survived through them all. Thus, our swamps really are windows into the past.

Most of our present wetlands are relatively young. Following the great climatic changes near the end of the Pleistocene (about fifteen thousand years ago), it was not until some five thousand years ago that conditions favoring swamp development—high water tables and abundant rainfall—again allowed wetlands to proliferate throughout Florida and the Southeast.

Understanding the Present

Water

Water is crucial to all life, and without it in abundance, wetlands could not exist. Not only is water essential for growth and maintenance of wetland plants, it brings nutrients, disperses seeds, and prevents upland plants from invading. Water is also vital to wetland animals, especially many invertebrates, all fish, and most amphibians, whose life cycles depend on standing water for development of eggs and larvae.

Much of the southeastern coastal plain is covered by porous quartz sand, the eroded remains of the once much taller Appalachian Mountains. Rain quickly percolates through this sand. But where there is impermeable clay or limestone, water collects, forming wetlands. Most of Florida's wetlands occur in areas that were inundated by the ocean less than a hundred thousand years ago. As the ocean receded, it left behind relatively level deposits of sand and clay. Wetlands formed where there were clay-lined depressions.

Falling rain is the major source of water for most of Florida's wetlands. Rainfall throughout Florida, especially in the south, occurs mostly during brief but intense summer thunderstorms. During the winter, frontal storms of cold and dense arctic air sweep southward like huge atmospheric waves, easily pushing the lighter warm and moist air upward. As a result, heavy downpours occur along the front. These storms are most pronounced in north Florida and dwindle as they move south.

During the spring, as rainfall diminishes, water that has accumulated in wetlands either evaporates, is transpired by plants, or slowly percolates into the ground where it may seep into deep layers of permeable rock, forming aquifers. Rivers, streams, sloughs, and canals carry off much water, too. As we shall see, this natural cycle of flooding and drying is essential to the existence of swamps and other wetlands.

Life is impossible without water, but for some species too much can be just as harmful as too little. When water fills the pores between soil particles, it reduces the rate at which gases are exchanged with the atmosphere. Under these conditions, oxygen levels are lowered, while carbon dioxide and the toxic gas hydrogen sulfide (associated with rotten-egg odors) can accumulate. If this situation continues for more than about a week, most soil organisms—including plant roots—become stressed, leading to reduced growth or even the death of unadapted plants. Alcohol and acid can even build up in plant roots deprived of oxygen, adding further stress. On the other hand, wetland plants like bald cypress, water tupelo, cattails, and others that are adapted to long-term flooding can pump oxygen down from their leaves to the roots. In addition, specialized "adventitious" roots extending into the water, such as those of willows, can also absorb oxygen.

Plants are more tolerant of flooding in winter, especially if they are dormant. Summer flooding of south Florida's swamps places additional stress on unadapted plants because summer is the season when plants are actively growing and respiring, and it may be one reason for the lower diversity of swamp trees in that part of the state.

A cross section through a swamp such as a cypress dome (which is deepest toward the middle) shows differences in the distribution of plants along the water-depth gradient, depending on the plants' hydroperiod tolerance. Bald cypress, water tupelo, pond apple, swamp tupelo, pop ash and buttonbush are flood-tolerant species, and are the only woody plants to live where the hydroperiod is longest (Wharton et al. 1976; Duever et al. 1986). Cabbage palm is also relatively tolerant. Sweetgum and red maple are next in tolerance, followed by water hickory, slash pine, swamp laurel oak, live oak, and swamp chestnut oak. The latter three oaks are intolerant of prolonged flooding and usually grow in sites with brief flooding.

Small changes in topography can also affect this hydroperiod-dependent plant distribution. For example, red maples or even loblolly pines can grow surrounded by deep water because the microtopography in most swamps varies. Deeper sloughs, with long hydroperiods, may surround hummocks (mounds), which remain relatively dry. Trees can even form small hummocks by trapping sediment and debris with their roots. As a succession of trees grows from the mound, the hummock becomes progressively higher, and consequently drier.

Water is also crucial to wetland plants because it disperses their seeds. Seed dispersal is important because it enables plants to occupy new sites cleared by fires, storms, floods, or other natural disturbances. Some wetland trees such as ash, elm, loblolly bay, red maple, and sweetgum have relatively lightweight seeds that are carried a few yards by the wind. Willow seeds, embedded in a cottonlike fluff, are dispersed even farther, perhaps miles. Most of these tree types are "weedy" species that readily invade open ground. Other trees, such as cypress, oaks, swampbay, sweetbay, and tupelos, have relatively heavy seeds that are dispersed primarily by animals or flowing water. Cypress and tupelo seeds can float for two to three months or even longer, and thus could drift many miles (Schneider and Sharitz 1988). Even windblown seeds can be dispersed by water. Perhaps water transport is even more important than wind for wetland trees like red maple and American elm, which have water-repellent seeds.

Because of their dependence on water, wetlands are easily affected by drainage and overpumping from shallow aquifers. South Florida wetlands have suffered primarily from agricultural drainage schemes, whereas in north Florida, forestry practices are the primary agent of change. Examples of the latter are the attempts to convert Tates Hell and the Mallory Swamp–San Pedro Bay system into pine plantations. In a recent study done for the Suwannee River Water Management District (KBN Engineering and Applied Sciences et al. 1990), it was estimated that in Mallory Swamp in the 1950s to 1970s, wetlands and other habitats were converted to pine plantations at a rate exceeding nine thousand acres per year. Hundreds of miles of ditches were dug to build roads and to drain the area. By examining stream flow in the affected watershed, it was ascertained that runoff was greater after canal construction. In other words, the normal flood-retention function of the wetlands was partially lost. The overall impact on the region is not fully known, but attempts are now underway, with the help of cooperating landowners, to restore the hydrology to the pre-1950 levels (Robert Mattson, Suwannee River Water Management District, pers. comm., 1994).

Without sufficient water, wetlands lose their ability to benefit humans and the environment. As we are now finding out, it is extremely expensive to repair damaged habitats. Some impacts are unavoidable, but we must carefully balance the need to destroy wetlands against the possible long-term costs to the environment.

Fire

Fires profoundly influence swamps and, surprisingly, can even be vital to their maintenance. In sandy soil with little moisture-retaining humus, fires started by lightning can recur every two to three years

Figure 14. Fires
such as this one in
the Big Cypress
National Preserve
are vital to the
health of Florida's
wetlands.

Figure 14. Fires such as this one in the Big Cypress National Preserve are vital to the health of Florida's wetlands.

(fig. 14). In such situations, moist, herb-dominated prairies (often growing around the perimeter of cypress domes) contain small shrubs like St. John's-wort and sedges like white-top. Where fires occur less often, about every ten years or so, there may be cypress and gum swamps (Wharton et al. 1976; Duever et al. 1986). Basin swamps (such as the Okefenokee) appear to burn about every twenty years. In bayheads and alluvial swamps, fires are rare, occurring about once in a century.

In south Florida, freshwater swamps are dominated by three plant assemblages, depending on the time since a fire last occurred and on the intensity of the fire (Duever et al. 1986). Cypress and mixed hardwoods prevail in unburned swamps, while swamps that experience ground fires are mainly occupied by cypress, since most hardwoods cannot survive fires. Willows invade swamps where high-intensity fires have killed the cypress; however, if fires do not recur frequently, mixed hardwoods will eventually replace the willows.

Fires also affect marshes. Regular burning in marshes prevents the encroachment of trees. Willows are now invading parts of the Everglades and parts of the upper St. Johns marshes, probably because of lowered water levels and decreased frequency of fires. Another shrub, wax myrtle, also invades marshes that rarely burn.

In hammocks as in swamps, the frequency and intensity of fires are important factors in determining the composition of the plant community (Platt and Schwartz 1990). Where fires are prevalent, cabbage palms thrive in almost pure stands because they tolerate fire better than most trees. This is readily seen in the numerous cabbage palm–dominated hammocks that border the wide marshes along the St. Johns and Kissimmee rivers and in other areas of the state. Palm trunks in these areas are often charred from frequent fires.

Fires play a major and sometimes crucial role in the dynamic processes that form and maintain swamps and other wetlands. Because we have built such barriers to fires as roads and canals and have actively suppressed fires, we have altered the natural fire cycle. This is already affecting Florida's wetlands, resulting in an increase in swamps and hammocks, and a decrease in marshes and prairies. The decrease in fire frequency has also adversely affected other habitats in Florida, especially the endangered longleaf-pine biotic community. Fire plays a pivotal role in many of Florida's ecosystems, and without it there will be unwelcome ecological changes.

Nutrients

Besides fire and water, swamps are also greatly influenced by the availability of nutrients (Monk 1966, 1968; Wharton et al. 1976; Wharton 1977; Mitsch and Gosselink 1986). Alluvial swamps—Florida's most nutrient-rich swamps—are highly productive because they are fertilized by deposition of soil brought by periodic flooding. The rapid growth of alluvial-swamp trees means that large quantities of leaves, flowers, twigs, and seeds fall to the swamp floor. These decompose and, during flooding, provide food for aquatic invertebrates that are in turn eaten by fish, amphibians, reptiles, wading birds, and mammals.

Swamps along the blackwater rivers of the sandy coastal plain are lower in nutrients than alluvial swamps. The dark, amber-tinted waters in these nutrient-poor swamps result from the buildup of organic acids that are a by-product of the decomposition cycle. In swamps with long hydroperiods, plant debris decomposes slowly because fungi and bacteria are inefficient under acidic, nitrogen-poor, oxygen-starved conditions. Consequently, organic material collects, becoming peat. Nutrients trapped deep in the peat are unavailable to the plants. By contrast, in our upland forests, nutrients derived from decomposition are readily recycled back into the forest, so the humus layer is thin.

Swamps are complex but adaptable. They require an abundant source of water, but can also survive droughts and fire, as well as accommodate varying nutrient loads. Their stability lies in the adaptive responses of the many plants and animals that live in them. Swamps have existed in Florida for thousands of years and, with protection, will continue to provide many valuable services, such as flood attenuation, removal of pollutants, augmentation of stream flow, wildlife habitat provision, and climate alteration.

 *3*

Close Encounters

Swampwalking can be fun! Writer Jerry Howard (1988) vividly portrayed the experience in *Walking Magazine:* "I headed instinctively for the little swamp down the road and oozed directly into the mud. The merciful, tea-brown waters crept up to my thighs, bubbles tingling my legs. . . . Walking there was a matter of working with The Force: 'stuck' became an impossible state of mind, and 'forward' was where the swamp wanted me to go. . . . Eye to eye with frogs, circumnavigated by green darters and iridescent dragonflies, I was myself again, and at one with some long-forgotten primal force."

Writer James Gorman, another "swampophile," revealed his craving for swamps in *Audubon* (1992): "I like swamps. Not wetlands. Swamps. I like them dark and humid, with tea-colored water and snakes. Also frogs, alligators, and escaped convicts."

A vastly different, but nonetheless colorful and amusing view of swamp exploration was written by John James Audubon over a century ago when he described the haunts of the ivory-billed woodpecker (Audubon [1840–44] 1967):

> I wish, kind reader, it were in my power to present to your mind's eye the favorite resort of the ivory-billed woodpecker. Would that I could describe the extent of the deep morasses, over shadowed by millions of gigantic dark cypresses, spreading their sturdy moss-covered branches, as if to admonish intruding man

to pause and reflect on the many difficulties which he may encounter, should he persist in venturing further into their almost
inaccessible recesses, extending for miles before him, where he
should be interrupted by huge projecting branches, here and
there the mossy trunk of a fallen and decaying tree, and thousands of creepers and twining plants of numberless species!
Would that I could represent to you the dangerous nature of the
ground, its oozing, spongy, and miry disposition, although covered with a beautiful but treacherous carpeting, composed of the
richest mosses, flags, and water lilies, no sooner receiving the
pressure of the foot than it yields and endangers the life of the
adventurer, whilst here and there, as he approaches an opening,
that proves merely to be a lake of black muddy waters, his ears are
assailed by the dismal croaking of innumerable frogs, the hisses of
serpents, or the bellows of alligators! Would that I could give you
an idea of the sultry pestiferous atmosphere that nearly suffocates
the intruder during the meridian heat of our dogdays, in those
gloomy and horrible swamps! Nothing short of ocular demon-
stration can impress an adequate idea of them.

Fortunately, if you live in Florida (or unfortunately, if you believe
in Audubon's account), the beauty and wonder to be found in our
forested wetlands is close by. Swamps surround us. Wherever there is
a creek, a river, a spring or a lake, there is probably a swamp. But how
do you get to it and enjoy it without hurting it (or yourself)? The rest
of this chapter provides some general and specific guidance on where
to go and what to do when you get there.

Finding and Exploring Swamps

Parks are good places to get acquainted with swamps. There, boardwalks can provide easy access to wetland habitats, without wet feet.
Rangers also lead swamp "slogs" through wilder areas where you can
experience swamps more intimately. Many Florida cities, towns, and
counties have set aside wetlands—both to preserve the natural areas
and to give us opportunities to visit and learn from those areas without harming them. Check your local library and newspaper for information about nearby parks.

Maps are helpful in locating areas off the beaten track. One that I
highly recommend is the *Florida Atlas and Gazetteer* (available in

bookstores), which shows forested and wetland areas along with the back roads. More detailed are the U.S. Geological Survey topographic maps or "quads" (available by calling 1-800-USA-MAPS). *National Wetland Inventory Maps,* produced by the U.S. Fish and Wildlife Service (available by calling 813-893-3624), show the extent of all types of wetlands and are invaluable for locating swamps. The various Florida water management district offices also can provide maps of wetlands.

Two helpful books that list recreational areas, including those with wetlands, are *Florida Wildlife Viewing Guide* by S. Cerulean and A. Morrow (1993) and *Florida Parks: A Guide to Camping in Nature* by G. Grow (1993).

To make your trip safer and more comfortable in remote areas, here are a few suggestions. First, tell someone specifically where you will be. Second, take a compass. I prefer one that is worn like a wristwatch. Wear sturdy boots that support your ankles because the footing in swamps is often insecure. During the wet season, carry a head-high stick to give support and to probe the water where you can't see the bottom.

Move slowly when exploring a flooded swamp; cypress knees and windfall limbs can be hidden by dark water, and there may be deeper holes. In strands where there is limestone surface rock, there may be deep solution holes; watch for them. In backwaters of alluvial swamps, soft mud can make walking difficult.

Noting the kinds of vegetation can provide clues to potential water depth. For example, pond apple, bald cypress, pop ash, water tupelo, and swamp tupelo can grow where deep flooding occurs; so be careful when you are on foot near these tree species. On the other hand, sweetgum, maple, and most oaks grow where the water is usually shallow. Where there is an open canopy, aquatic vegetation like water lilies and arrowroot indicate the deeper water.

Avoid wading during floods: water levels in river swamps can be many feet above normal. If you see fronds of saw palmetto surrounded by water, the nearby swamp could be flooded by several feet.

The soil in swamps can be either firm (sandy), or soft (muddy or peaty), or both, so watch your footing. In blackwater river swamps and around the perimeters of cypress domes, the soil is generally sandy with some peat. In bayheads and in the centers of domes, thick layers of soft peat may be present. Alluvial river swamps can have sloughs with soft, muddy bottoms; strands may have rocky or softer peat-covered soils.

One of my favorite ways to explore swamps is by canoe. Not only do your feet stay dry, but in a canoe you can easily carry photographic equipment, lunch, and a cooler of cold drinks—a real luxury in swamp travel. Also, travel by canoe is relatively silent, making it easier to see wildlife than when you travel on foot; and it may be the only way to entice a reluctant spouse into a distant wetland.

There are many swamps and hammocks that can be seen by paddling. Some of my favorites are Alexander and Juniper Springs runs, and the Oklawaha, Wekiva, Tomoka, and Withlacoochee (south) Rivers, to name just a few. In southeast Georgia, I enjoy Banks Lake near Lakeland, Ebenezer Creek northwest of Savannah, and of course, the Okefenokee Swamp. For Florida canoeing, I highly recommend getting both volumes of *A Canoeing and Kayaking Guide to the Streams of Florida* by E. Carter and J. Pearce (1990). For Georgia routes, I recommend *Southern Georgia Canoeing* by B. Sehlinger and D. Otey (1980). These books provide helpful descriptions of canoe routes, points of access, best seasons to travel, possible difficulties, and things to see. I must warn you, however, that once you learn to paddle silently into backcountry swamps rich with wildlife, you will lose your appreciation for the sounds created by airboats and motorboats.

Avoiding the Pestiferous Atmosphere

Swamps do have some noxious critters—a "pestiferous atmosphere," as Audubon termed it. The worst are biting insects, especially mosquitos and yellowflies. And, yes, there are venomous snakes. Six potentially dangerous species occur in Florida: the eastern diamondback, the timber or "canebrake" rattlesnake, the copperhead, the cottonmouth, the pygmy rattler, and the eastern coral snake. But most of these are uncommon or rare in wetlands, and they seldom attack, even when provoked. Given the opportunity, most snakes will try to escape rather than attack. Yet snake bites do occur, especially around homes, where children pick up or tease venomous snakes. If you are bitten, immediately seek medical attention.

Eastern diamondback and timber rattlesnakes, as well as cottonmouths, usually are not aggressive. But they are potentially dangerous because they have large quantities of powerful venom. Generally, when threatened they will posture—rattlesnakes in a coil with rattling tails, and cottonmouths usually uncoiled, displaying their gaping white mouths. Unlike rattlesnakes, which have a typical S-shaped strike posture with the head raised, cottonmouths often pose stretched out, with their heads near the ground and bent back where they can best strike upward (Dundee and Rossman 1989). Some other snakes, such as the brown water snake, are pugnacious but nonvenomous. Snakes are fascinating. They often have attractive and unusual color patterns. And snakes are ecologically important as both predator and prey; we should learn to live with them.

Our most pestiferous critter must be the mosquito (see chapter 7). The yellowfly is another aggressive biting insect you might encounter. It appears in late spring and is present throughout the summer. Yellowflies are about three-eighths of an inch long. The body is mostly buff yellow; the large eyes, which cover most of the head, are a bright metallic blue-green. Being swift and silent fliers, they can inflict a painful bite before being noticed. And as in the mosquitos, only the female bites. She flies in circles, often striking several times before landing and inserting her razor-sharp proboscis. Yellowflies are prevalent near rivers, streams, and swamps where their aquatic larvae live (Fairchild and Weems 1973). Long pants, a long-sleeved shirt, and a hat with neck flap help to ward off these flying pests.

Protection from biting insects in the form of repellents or head nets is a necessity in Florida's wetlands during the warmer months. The most effective repellents contain DEET (N,N-diethyl-meta-toluamide) as their active ingredient (Schwartz 1989). The higher the percentage of DEET, the longer the repellent is active. Although DEET keeps the bugs off, if it gets in your eyes or other sensitive areas, it will burn; thus it should be applied with caution—especially on your face. DEET also dissolves plastic (like watch crystals), and it's oily, making it difficult to handle a camera. For people who don't like to use DEET, Avon's Skin-So-Soft bath oil is a widely used repellent, although not so effective. If you don't want to apply any repellent directly on your skin, you can wear a head net and spray repellent only on your clothing. Either way, be prepared for biting insects when you visit a swamp; they'll be waiting for you!

Swamp Photography

Swamps are photogenic, but it can be a challenge to take good pictures in the dense shade that is one of the pleasures of swamp exploration. A tripod will help, and using your camera self-timer will reduce vibration. For exposures of one second or longer, open up the iris by one to two f-stops to compensate for reciprocity, a problem that occurs with long exposures. A more subtle problem with swamp photography is the bright light-gaps in the canopy, which produce uneven exposures when you are using a wide-angle lens. To reduce this high contrast, position the camera so that the sky is not in view; or try this type of photography in winter when more light is reaching the ground.

For close-ups, an electronic flash is invaluable (fig. 15); most animals are too active for you to use a tripod. A high-powered flash is best because it allows shorter exposures. If possible, use one that is dedicated to the camera (termed TTL) so that the light produced by the flash is automatically controlled by the camera. Using a diffuser over the flash will reduce unwanted reflections from waxy or damp subjects, so often found in swamps.

Use the slowest film that will produce the quality of image you want. I prefer slow-speed slide films (Kodachrome 64, Fujichrome 50 and Velvia, and Kodak Elite 50 or 100) because they have accurate colors and are fine-grained. Higher-speed films allow faster shutter speeds, which can be important in the dimly lit forest; however, there may be some loss of image quality because of the coarser grain.

The choice of lenses depends on the subject. I mainly use three lenses. A 50-mm macro lens with extension tubes is ideal for close-ups of flowers and inactive insects. For active subjects like many butterflies, snakes, and birds, a longer 70- to 200-mm macro zoom is

Figure 15. The author photographing in a wetland; note the diffuser on the flash.

best. For habitat photos, I prefer a 21- to 35-mm wide-angle zoom lens.

Swamp photography is a rewarding way to share your swamp experiences with others. Because of the great variety of plants and animals to be found in Florida's wetlands, exploring swamps can provide many surprises and memorable experiences for you to record on film.

 *4*

Wet and Wild

Treks in Florida's Swamps

This chapter is about some of the memorable swamp trips Kathy and I have made; these are the kinds of experiences you can expect when you make your own treks.

Some Swamps along Blackwater and Spring-Run Creeks

Alexander Springs Run

December is a perfect time to canoe Alexander Springs Run in Ocala National Forest. Golden and flame-orange maples contrast sharply with the cloudless blue sky. Brown limpkins flecked with white forage among water-lettuce, pickerelweed, and floating pennywort; and occasionally their strange, mournful cries echo down the river, reminiscent of sound effects in an old Tarzan movie.

During one canoe trip along Alexander Springs Run, Kathy and I paddled over to the shore to watch a young gator with glassy eyes the size and color of walnuts. It sat frozen, with its tire-black tail resting on the sandy bottom. Overhead, noisy robins and yellow-rumped warblers feasted on the fire-engine red fruits of dahoon holly and the black fruits of swampbay. As we scanned the shore, our attention was drawn to two small masked bandits plodding along the bank. The pair of juvenile raccoons waded long-legged into the shallow water and began feeling with sensitive fingers for crayfish and mussels. Red-shouldered hawks cried harshly from the treetops. Farther along, sprawling clumps of purple aster climbed high over a tangle of woody vines and limbs. A few showy yellow bur-marigold blossoms remained in areas where just two months ago they had emblazoned the streamside with banks of gold.

Charlie Bowlegs Creek

At Highlands Hammock State Park in central Florida, Charlie Bowlegs Creek flows languidly through a lush blackwater swamp. Cypress and sweetgum dominate the creek, where a boardwalk meanders among the stout trunks. A resident gator often lounges on the margin of the sky-reflecting pool. Once, only a few yards from the boardwalk, we found a beautiful pale green Luna moth "sleeping" atop the knobby spire of a cypress knee. In a nearby area, called the Fern Garden because of the abundance of sword ferns, there is a pop-ash swamp luxuriant with water lilies and pickerelweed. From March to May, colorful and graceful swallowtail butterflies busily search through the swamp, seeking the nectar-rich white-flowered Virginia willow bushes.

In May, the delicate and fragrant spider lily blooms in the swamps of Highlands Hammock (near the Cypress Swamp Trail and Fern Garden Trail). The spidery blossoms display long spokelike sepals that radiate beyond a central corolla. A single, waist-high flower stalk bears two large flowers. Each fragile corolla is pure white and about two inches in diameter. The long style, and six anthers tipped with orange pollen clusters, protrude several inches from the corolla, poised ready for pollination by large moths.

Three Important Swamp Systems

Green Swamp

Green Swamp is one of the largest swamp systems in Florida, encompassing an area of about eight hundred square miles (fig. 11). Located in west-central Florida near Orlando, it covers parts of Lake, Pasco, Polk, and Sumter Counties. Approximately two-thirds of the area is in a natural state, with about one-third of this as forested wetland (Thomas 1976; S. L. Brown 1984; Southwest Florida Water Management District 1985). There are two major swamp communities: cypress domes and blackwater-river cypress and mixed-hardwood swamps. The largest contiguous wetlands in the Green Swamp system are blackwater-river swamps along the Withlacoochee and Hills-borough Rivers (where swamps reach a mile in width), and Devils Creek Swamp (covering about three square miles) near State Road 471 in Sumter County.

The Green Swamp system sits in a large basin. Most of the water that is trapped moves into the atmosphere by evapotranspiration (about 77 percent); some seeps into the rivers (about 15 percent); and the rest percolates through the ground and into aquifers (about 8 percent) (S. L. Brown 1984). By retaining runoff, the region is valuable as a flood-detention area, and seventy square miles have been designated for this purpose.

The headwaters of four major rivers (Hillsborough, Peace, Oklawaha, and Withlacoochee) are in Green Swamp. The Withlacoochee River (south) drains most of the area. Owing to its relatively high elevation, Green Swamp also provides a pressure head for the Floridan Aquifer (Pride, Meyer, and Cheery 1961). The variety and extent of forested landscapes in Green Swamp provide habitat for more than 250 species of vertebrates—some of which are rare and imperiled (Southwest Florida Water Management District 1985).

Because Green Swamp is important for water recharge, flood prevention, and as a major wildlife habitat, the state has classified over half of it as an Area of Special Concern. Unfortunately, only about one-tenth of the land is in public ownership, and concerns have been raised about unregulated development within the swamp.

Part of Green Swamp is within the Richloam Wildlife Management Area of Withlacoochee State Forest. There, primitive camping sites and good hiking trails can be found along part of the extensive Florida Trail System within the forest. The many miles of blackwater rivers provide leisurely canoeing through extensive and diverse hardwood and cypress swamps.

Kathy and I made our first trip into Green Swamp one September. What impressed me most about Green Swamp was its vastness, and of course the lush vegetation—it was indeed green. Water levels were low because of below-normal rainfall, and most of the area was dry. We hiked along the sugar-sand banks of the Little Withlacoochee. Scraggly gray skeins of Spanish moss hung from bald cypress, as if drying. Ancient live oaks with fissured bark were overgrown with resurrection ferns. Nestled amid the ferns were Bartram's wild pine bromeliads and green-fly orchids. Three Boy Scouts in a cherry-red canoe slowly paddled up the amber-tinted river. Overhead, a small flock of tufted titmice busily searched for insects in a flat-crowned cypress, and the "whooo-oh" call of a barred owl reverberated down the river.

Scant, but recent, rain had stimulated fungi to fruit; mushrooms were everywhere. Black earthstars had erupted from the moist sandy soil, and brown-and-orange–banded variegated bracket fungi grew in ranks from the trunks of dead oaks. Orange-winged gulf fritillary butterflies hungrily nectared at pale purple elephant's-foot flowers, while lazy Palamedes swallowtails fluttered by—searching for mates, or for swampbay on which to lay eggs. As we hiked back to the car, we saw queen butterfly larvae, garbed in gaudy black, yellow, and white stripes, munching on the leaves of a climbing milkweed vine that sprawled over low shrubs.

Arriving at another part of Green Swamp, in the Richloam Area off State Road 471, we explored some of the cypress domes that are abundantly scattered over most of the region. In some of the wettest areas, miniature "island gardens" of ferns, mosses, liverworts, and other moisture-loving plants grew like living collars around the cypress knees.

Another cypress dome was surrounded by scattered slash pine. Nearer the dome was a zone of sedges that led into an area of small cypress, both pond and bald. The trunks of these trees were embellished with mosses, leafy liverworts, and lichens, the baton rouge being the most obvious of these last. Two types of narrow-leafed bromeliads were present, Bartram's wild pine and the cardinal wild pine. Butterfly orchids also adorned the cypress trees, although these orchids were noticeably smaller than those I have seen on live oak.

Cypress domes in Green Swamp are often luxuriantly carpeted with Sphagnum moss. Thick peat deposits wick moisture up from below, keeping the soil damp even during dry weather.

At another area, Kathy was fascinated by the abundance of butterflies nectaring at pickerelweeds in a roadside ditch. A steady stream of yellow and black eastern swallowtails, brown Palamedes, blue and black spicebush swallowtails, a few smaller orange-colored gulf fritillaries, and a lone yellow-and-black-banded zebra longwing came foraging for nectar at the royal-blue flowers. A green treefrog resting inconspicuously on a pickerelweed leaf watched with drowsy eyes as the parade of colorful wings drifted lazily among the flowers. Later we spotted a mixed flock of Carolina chickadees, northern Parula warblers, yellow-throated warblers, white-eyed vireos, and blue-gray gnatcatchers searching for insects in sweetgums and red maples bordering the road. A few birds descended into a nearby pool and bathed, returning immediately to sunny perches to dry off and preen.

I wandered off into a moist forest on the opposite side of the road. Few plants were present except cypress, although there were a few five-foot-tall clumps of royal fern. As I walked around the edge of a pond, I saw a cooter turtle that had just been killed. Going closer to investigate, out of the corner of my eye I saw something move—a SNAKE! A three-foot-long cottonmouth was coiled in front of a cypress, only a few short feet from where I stood. Its dusky coloration, with a faint diamond pattern on its back, made it nearly invisible amid the semidecomposed cypress twigs. The cottonmouth remained motionless, so I stepped closer to take some photos. Without moving its body, it shot out its moist, forked, pink tongue—tasting the air. After a few minutes, it slipped silently into the water and disappeared.

I walked on, wondering what had killed the turtle. Suddenly I was startled by a crash, then a splash. My first thought was a gator. I looked around. Peeking from behind a cypress trunk appeared a small furry head, slicked back and wet. Inquisitive brown eyes watched me. We stared at each other. Then in an instant the otter was gone and only ripples remained.

Another day, just after Thanksgiving, we canoed along the Withlacoochee River not far from Rutland, off State Road 44. The water was low, and the riverine forests of swamp tupelo, red maple, pop ash, and bald cypress were exposed. In places, herbs and seedling trees were growing over the russet-colored forest floor, forming green patches. Browsing on the tender vegetation was a magnificent buck with a huge ten-point rack. Curious, he moved along the shore, following us. We paddled on, passing golden patches of bur-marigold.

A barred owl called from around the next bend, so we hurried off to find it. On a small island ahead were two large bald cypress trees, likely places for the owl. We pulled our canoe ashore and searched the first tree. Sure enough, on one of the "lower" limbs, about forty feet up, sat the owl. Without moving its body, it twisted its head around and stared down with big owl eyes. We tried getting a good look at the owl but somehow a limb or a wisp of Spanish moss always interfered. At first, as we moved around under the tree, the owl watched us intently; but soon it lost interest and began to doze.

Reluctantly we left the sleepy owl. Moving on, we spied small flocks of white ibis foraging along the edges of the swamp, where they poked their long curved bills deeply into the peaty soil to capture inverte-brates. Limpkins in drab brown attire lazily basked on fallen logs or actively searched amid water lilies, probing for snails, the mainstay of their diet.

Paddling on, we ducked our heads just in time: on a leafless button-bush limb overhanging the water, brown-and-yellow-banded Polistes wasps crept over their fist-sized, papery nest. The wasps were warm-ing themselves in the winter sun. When a wasp returned to the nest, the others would greet it with their palpating antennae. By building their nest over water, the wasps may avoid ants that often eat the lar-vae. Later, we saw another, smaller wasp nest built under a folded grape leaf—a perfectly dry and inconspicuous home.

Green Swamp is invaluable. One writer compared it to a vast reser-voir more than one hundred feet deep and covering eight hundred square miles—enough to flood Florida with over a foot of water. The swamp is also home to countless wildflowers, birds, frogs, snakes, bears, and other wildlife.

Fakahatchee Strand

Located in Collier County, in southwestern Florida, is the largest cy-press and hardwood strand in the United States—Fakahatchee Strand State Preserve (fig. 16). When combined with the adjacent Big Cypress National Preserve, the Florida Panther National Wildlife Ref-uge, and the Everglades National Park, it forms a premier wetland system over four thousand square miles in extent—larger than the states of Delaware and Rhode Island combined. For anyone interested in natural history, Fakahatchee is a captivating and a wild place.

Nowhere else in the continental United States can you see anything that so closely resembles the rain forests of the neotropics. When I first saw the masses of Guzmania bromeliads ornamenting the limbs and trunks of pop ash and pond apple trees in the dark sloughs of Fakahatchee Strand, it reminded me of a similar sight in the tropical rain forests of Belize (fig. 17); only there, the Guzmania grew from the trunks and imposing buttresses of Pterocarpus trees.

Fakahatchee Strand is recognized as a unique natural area contain-ing one of the highest densities of rare plants in Florida (Luer 1972; Austin, Jones, and Bennett 1990). The Strand also has the greatest di-versity of epiphytic ferns, bromeliads, peperomias, and orchids in the continental United States.

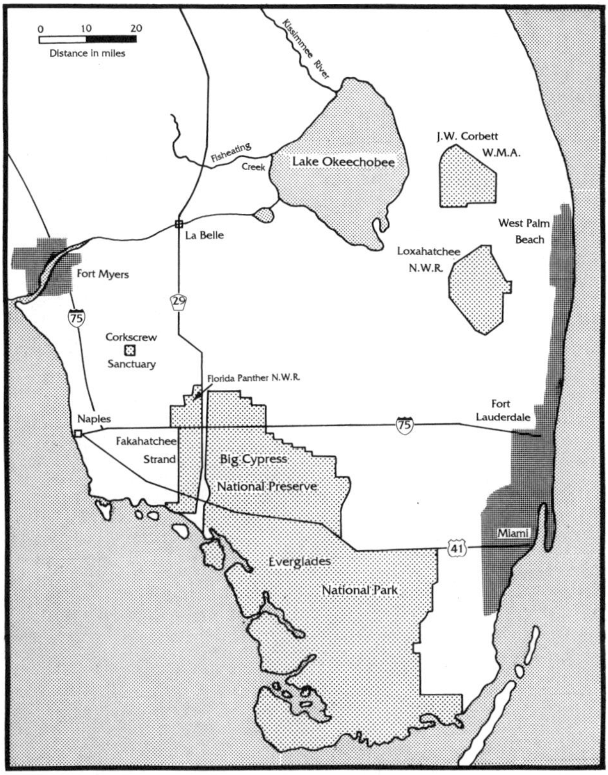

Figure 16. Map of southwest Florida showing location of Big Cypress National Preserve, Corkscrew Swamp Sanctuary, Everglades National Park, Fakahatchee Strand State Preserve, and Florida Panther National Wildlife Refuge.

Fakahatchee Strand is a rich mosaic of wetland plant communities. Professor Daniel Austin and his students at Florida Atlantic University have studied its flora for many years and have recorded nearly five hundred species (Austin, Jones, and Bennett 1990). Pop ash, swamp laurel oak, red maple, and second-growth bald cypress dominate. Rotten stumps and charred snags are all that remain of the once-majestic forest giants—the virgin stands of bald cypress, which were cut by loggers less than fifty years ago. A meager remnant of the original forest can still be seen at an isolated site near Indian Village along the Tamiami Trail. The site, called Big Cypress Bend, has a boardwalk that winds among ancient cypress giants whose sparse gray limbs are bedecked with colorful cardinal wild pines. Several of these patriarchs are being slowly destroyed by the ever-tightening grip of strangler figs.

About thirty miles to the northwest of Fakahatchee Strand is Corkscrew Swamp—the last sizable stand of virgin bald cypress in Florida, some of which may be more than seven hundred years old (Thomas 1976; Duever, Carlson, and Riopelle 1984) (fig. 16). Its seventeen square miles, preserved by the National Audubon Society, are a major

Figure 17. Fakahatchee Strand is notable for its exceptional variety and abundance of epiphytes. In one area known as Guzmania Gardens, pop ash trees bristle with Guzmania bromeliads.

nesting area for endangered wood storks, and an important roosting area for the rare swallow-tailed kite (Millsap 1987).

Fakahatchee Strand State Preserve covers about 125 square miles, extending north from the mangrove-lined Ten Thousand Islands region to Alligator Alley (Interstate 75), and east to State Road 29. Augmenting the Strand is the newly acquired forty-square-mile Florida Panther National Wildlife Refuge, just north of I-75, plus Corkscrew Swamp and adjacent lands purchased by the South Florida Water Management District. We hope that adjacent areas will also be preserved.

Located on the western edge of the twenty-five-hundred-square-mile Big Cypress Swamp system, Fakahatchee Strand is at the southern end of the nearly forty-mile-long Okaloacoochee Slough, a major subdrainage system of the Big Cypress (fig. 13). During heavy rainfall, runoff flows south in sawgrass glades near the Devil's Garden area in Hendry County, through Fakahatchee's pop-ash sloughs, and finally empties into the muddy, mangrove-lined waters of the Gulf of Mexico near Everglades City.

The Strand was little explored before this century. Its swampy, inhospitable, junglelike terrain and hordes of hungry mosquitos kept out all but the most intrepid. This made it an ideal refuge for Seminole Indians, who hid there to avoid government troops during the Seminole Wars. The presence of earlier Indians in the Strand is indicated by mounds, possibly used for camping by the Glades Indians (Austin, Jones, and Bennett 1990).

A few daring naturalists like J. G. Cooper explored the area as early as 1860 and exclaimed about its unusual flora. Later, when the threat of destruction became imminent, concerned citizens like Daniel Beard and Melvin Finn tried to save it. Like most swamps, however, Fakahatchee was valued only for those resources that could be exploited, not for its intrinsic beauty or as habitat for wildlife. In the late 1940s and early 1950s, loggers came and cut five million board feet of bald cypress, much of it probably over five hundred years old. The trees were dragged, using skidders and long cables, from where they fell to the logging train on tracks built on raised tramways. In the process, other trees, shrubs, ferns, and herbs were ripped loose, and the soft peat was torn up. Once the protective canopy was gone, the ground dried, allowing surface fires to spread. Melvin Finn (1965) described the destruction, as witnessed by two National Park Service biologists, as a "'green hell' where a million years of natural miracle was being systematically and unmercifully destroyed. They 'counted' over ten thousand royal palms amidst the human-wrought devastation. When the cypress fell, into the water plunged the crowns of orchids, some specimens so large as to require the room of an entire car to carry one away."

That the Strand recovered from this ecological near-devastation is amazing. I can only wonder what the virgin swamp must have been like, and how many species disappeared as a result of the logging and the fires that followed it. Opening of the protective canopy must have eliminated many delicate plants like the rare, filmy fern *Trichomanes*, which requires shade and high humidity.

Later, once highways were built, providing easy access, hunters used swamp buggies to pursue white-tailed deer, turkeys, fox squirrels, bear, and feral hogs. These large-tired vehicles left gaping wounds in the loose marl soils of the fragile glades surrounding the Strand. Many of these deep-rutted trails are still visible and will persist for years. In addition, cabins were built on the high ground or put on pilings above the water. Orchid collectors came too, looting many of the older plants that had miraculously survived the logging and subsequent fires.

More recently, another threat loomed. In 1966, an unscrupulous development company, Gulf American, bought the Strand from J. C. Turner Lumber Company. Carter (1974), in his informative book *The Florida Experience,* wrote that Gulf American planned to sell small parcels of the Remuda Ranch Grants, as it was called, as recreational or investment property. The lots, which sold for $1,000 per acre, were mostly unsurveyed, inaccessible wetland—some of which was rarely dry. Fortunately, unlike Golden Gate Estates—a similar area to the west that was ditched and diked, forming 170 miles of canals and eight hundred miles of roads—Fakahatchee escaped this destruction: in 1974, the state acquired most of the area.

Yet despite being publicly owned, Fakahatchee's problems are not over. The Fahka Union Canal system (built by the developers of Golden Gate Estates to drain the area) has lowered the water table (Swayze and McPherson 1977), resulting in several wildfires in the 1970s, including one conflagration that covered nearly a quarter of Collier County and burned a large portion of the Preserve (Carter 1974). Noted Florida naturalist Archie Carr (1973) referred to this canal as "not just a lesion in the body of the land, but a human tragedy."

In June, Janes Memorial Scenic Drive can be dry and dusty. And hot! The clear skies and high temperatures have sucked the moisture from everything; the cooling thunderstorms of summer are weeks away. Sweat beads my face, and my back is soaking wet. Even early in the morning, it's already uncomfortably warm and oppressively humid. I roll up my car windows as pickups roar past, the dust flying. Squadrons of dragonflies patrol the road for flying insect prey. Although dragonflies consume countless mosquitos, enough still remain to make this place unbearable for unprotected humans. Along Janes Drive, dragonflies easily maneuver around slow-moving cars; but on the highway, the sharp thud of chitin against steel and glass suggests that their reactions are no match for our high speeds.

In the prairielike glades along Janes Drive, the tall white flowers of swamp lilies stand out among gray-green grasses, rushes, and sedges (plate 4). The waist-high blossoms beckon, but are isolated by stand-ing water and soggy ground. In areas where springtime fires have temporarily burned away the groundcover, Alligator lilies—spidery, sweet-smelling, and with long golden anthers above delicate white corollas—push forth from bulbs buried deep in the charred soil.

This year the rains are late. Most of the tea-colored water is gone, and only the deeper holes in the swamp remain filled. The water level now has dropped two feet or more in some places. Without the dark water, some of the Strand's beauty and mystery is gone. Countless beer cans lie strewn about in roadside ditches; some have even floated far out into the swamp. Is there any place in Florida not violated by our trash?

Janes Drive is a focal point for many animals. Most abundant are the large and fearless lubber grasshoppers. During the summer these three-inch-long insects cross the road by the hundreds looking for mates or places to deposit eggs. Many are crushed, and their chitinous corpses litter the road.

Down the road a mile or so, raccoons amble across and fade into the undergrowth. If you are lucky you might see a black, long-tailed apparition—a sleek otter—darting across the road and disappearing into the dark waters; if you missed it, all that remains are a few muddy footprints and drops of water on the dusty road. Once, not far off the drive, I watched an otter splashing and playing with a "toy"—a large crayfish.

Brick-red viceroy butterflies often use Janes Drive as a flight path. Males dart out from their sunny positions on roadside willows to in-vestigate passersby, looking for a receptive mate or to chase intruding males. Other butterflies use the open road differently: after rains, many swallowtails perch near roadside puddles, probing the moist earth for minerals.

Inquisitive white-tailed deer with big brown eyes are frequently seen along Janes Drive. During high-water periods, deer frequent East Main, one of the old railroad trams used to haul cypress from the swamp. One February, Kathy and I walked far up the tram (fig. 18). Deer were plentiful. At one spot, we heard several splashing through the waist-deep water. Three does and a spotted fawn emerged from the swamp fifty yards ahead. The leading doe stared intently at us, her long ears held erect, her tail nervously twitching. Trying to intimidate us, she pawed at the ground and stamped her front feet; and, once, even stood up on her hind legs. The others watched, unconcerned,

Figure 18. Kathy crosses a log bridge along the East Main tram in Fakahatchee Strand.

then just milled around. Finally, snorting and with white tails raised, they bounded up the tram and vanished into the swamp.

Bobcats are frequently seen in the Strand, too. Once while I was walking up East Main, one came walking toward me. I stopped and watched, hoping that it would come closer, but it either saw me or smelled me and bolted into the forest. Later I got closer to another bobcat because I was downwind and had approached it from behind some tall sword-fern thickets along the tram. Getting within thirty yards, I watched the young cat lying relaxed in the sun, licking itself. Its coat was auburn above, its lighter belly was spotted, and its ears were tipped with long, white hairs. After a few minutes, it sauntered up the grassy path and vanished.

There are still some Florida black bears in Fakahatchee too, and Kathy and I have seen their tracks near Janes Road. Former Fakahatchee Strand biologist Charles DuToit said that bears were repopulating the Preserve after being nearly hunted out; but hunters are pressuring the state to reopen bear hunting there.

Perhaps the rarest and most elusive of Fakahatchee's inhabitants is the Florida panther. DuToit told me that one female definitely had a home range in the Strand. A mature male had a territory within the Strand, but was killed along State Road 29. This adult male (named Panther no. 37 by the state when it was radio-collared in January 1990) had a large home range that included the Bear Island area in the northern part of Big Cypress National Preserve (Charles DuToit, Florida DNR, pers. comm., 1990). It was the first panther photographed while using the newly constructed I-75 wildlife underpass.

Unfortunately, Fakahatchee's panthers are not as healthy as those in the more productive Bear Island region just to the northeast. By closing the Preserve to deer hunting, the Department of Natural Resources hopes to increase the deer population, which will lead to healthier panthers.

After you drive about seven miles north along Janes Drive, tall and stately Florida royal palms emerge from the canopy. One expects to see these majestic, hundred-foot-tall trees lining an avenue in Coconut Grove rather than growing in a tangled swamp. Like Grecian stone pillars, they rise high above the shorter canopy of hardwoods and second-growth bald cypress. Their smooth gray trunks look more like cast concrete than wood. Huge twelve-foot leafy fronds jut from the crown. Fakahatchee is one of the few areas where these palms still grow in the wild; they are especially numerous along the trams.

My first trip to the Strand was memorable, not for what I saw, but for what I didn't see. It was not at all what I expected. It looked forbidding! Along the road, a green wall of vegetation concealed the swamp except in a few places where the water depth had prevented the rampant growth of vines, shrubs, and small trees. Off the road, a tangle of greenbriers as tough and sharp as barbed wire radiated outward, and clumps of razor-sharp sawgrass ten feet high made walking difficult and sometimes painful. Also intimidating was the black water of unknown depth, and the possibility of running into a cottonmouth or an immense gator. All these thoughts quickly faded, however, when those tiny dipteran arthropods called mosquitos let me know that I had something they wanted enough to die for—my blood! What they lacked in size they made up for in numbers and ferocity. The mosquitos in Fakahatchee bite with a special vengeance.

Perhaps they are trying to repay us for the destruction we inflicted upon their home.

The abundant bromeliads in the Strand make ideal nurseries for *Wyeomyia* mosquitos, which bite during the day. And, since the Preserve is near the coast, salt-marsh mosquitos probably move into the Strand and attack deer, bear, raccoon, and humans as well. Phil Lounibos, a mosquito ecologist at the Florida Medical Entomology Laboratory in Vero Beach, pointed out some of the potential breeding sites for mosquitos one day as we scrambled out of the swamp followed by a virtual cloud of blood-suckers.

Little by little, though, I discovered when to go, where to look, and how to get around in the Strand; and began to ignore the constant whine of mosquitos. Slowly, the Preserve revealed some of its beauty and secrets. The more I see and learn about Fakahatchee, the more I realize how little I have seen or understood of this inhospitable but intriguing place.

Highlands Hammock

Highlands Hammock State Park is vastly different from Fakahatchee Strand. It is a mature forest with stately live oaks that are centuries old. It has the sedate beauty of an old arboretum, and lacks the unkempt wildness of Fakahatchee; but it is no less fascinating.

Highlands Hammock is six square miles of forested wetlands and drier sand scrub located in central Florida near Sebring. The park is fascinating for several reasons. First, it contains one of the oldest hydric hammocks in the state, with huge live oaks nearly a thousand years old and over thirty feet in circumference. Their giant limbs spread one hundred feet outward, and support vast aerial gardens of ferns, bromeliads, and orchids (Stalter, Dial, and Laessle 1981). Second, the park has a diverse flora comprising seven hundred vascular plants (Walter Thompson, Florida DNR, unpublished list, 1990; Daniel Austin, Florida Atlantic Univ., pers. comm., 1992). Besides a live oak/cabbage palm–dominated hammock, there are bayheads, a pop-ash slough, and a blackwater cypress swamp along Charlie Bowlegs Creek. All of these areas are only a short walk away via an extensive system of nature trails and boardwalks, making the natural environment accessible to nearly everyone (the new cypress-swamp boardwalk is wheelchair accessible).

Wild Orange Grove Trail led Kathy and me to a lush bayhead containing forty-foot-tall sweetbays with smooth gray trunks and waxy-green leaves. Their thick tan roots arched upward from the damp soil like the coils of some giant subterranean reptile. Cinnamon ferns grew in dense patches, their reddish-brown spore-bearing fronds just uncoiling at waist height. Large swamp tupelos, two feet in diameter, grew among the sweetbays, their swollen trunks making them easily recognizable. A small footbridge crossed a sluggish rivulet ornamented with pickerelweed and lizard's-tail. This is the site of the elaborate nuptial dances of dark-winged damselflies (see chapter 7).

But soon the character of the swamp changed, even though the terrain was just a few inches higher. The bay trees were replaced by larger sweetgums and somewhat smaller red maples. Ferns—swamp, Virginia chain, and cinnamon—were plentiful, covering the ground to the nearly complete exclusion of other herbs. Then we reached the hydric hammock. There the trees were more diverse—cabbage palm, live oak, swamp laurel oak, red mulberry, American elm, sugarberry, and pignut hickory. The understory was mainly wild coffee, beautyberry, needle palm, and coral bean; ferns were rare, but epiphytic strap ferns grew in large clumps on the rough trunks of the giant oaks. Mushrooms were plentiful, indicating recent rains. Predatory Euglandina snails and herbivorous manatee snails crawled over trunks of nearby trees. A thumb-sized, reddish-brown giant palm weevil—an insect whose larvae bore into the growing tips of cabbage palms—crept over the trunk of a nearby palm, its long snout and clubbed antennae making it look ridiculous. This strange insect is one of the largest weevils in North America.

Near the road, and in other more open areas of the hammock, the small circular webs of spiny orb-weavers were scattered among the larger tattered webs of the golden-silk spiders, whose amber-hued webs spread conspicuously more than six feet between shrubs. A heavy-bodied female golden-silk spider vibrated her web as I came close. Her puny mate, a mere fraction of the size of the three-inch-long female, was barely visible at the edge of the web on the opposite side. As I gazed at the spiders, a single long "whooo-oh" from a barred owl resounded through the quiet hammock. A few seconds later, the call was answered by the mate with a "who-cooks-for-you?" The owls hailed each other several more times; then only the buzzing of nearby mosquitos remained in the air.

When we reached the Cypress Swamp Trail, we met park ranger Kyle Mason, who was using his lunchtime to observe fall warblers that were migrating through the park. He told us that birding was excellent and guided us toward a red-shouldered hawk that he had just seen. We had walked only a short distance when suddenly the hawk flew across the trail and landed in a nearby cypress tree. It silently scanned the flooded swamp below. Then, effortlessly, it jumped from the tree, glided outward about a hundred feet, and swooped down to grasp a tiny animal—possibly a frog—from near the ground. We were amazed that the raptor could see such small prey at that distance.

On another trip one June, I was walking from the Hickory Trail to the Fern Garden Trail when I was surprised to see a red-shouldered hawk standing on the ground. It jumped and flapped, trying to carry away something heavy. It laboriously moved several yards, then stopped behind a cabbage palm. I slowly approached from behind the trunk, and saw the hawk tearing at something—a small mammal. Spying me, the hawk spread its wings to hide its prey, and erected its head feathers as a warning. The hawk's impressive talons clutched a juvenile nine-banded armadillo (its body plates were white instead of the dark brown of the adult). The armor of the young armadillo had not yet hardened, allowing the hawk to tear the flesh from between the soft plates. I crept closer. Gradually, the hungry raptor became unafraid of me, and I was able to inch closer still. Mosquitos buzzed around the hawk's moist head; sometimes it would brush them away with a wing. Metallic blue blowflies hovered around the armadillo corpse, trying to lay eggs. Not far away, another red-shoulder called, then flew by, chased by blue jays. The feeding hawk watched from the ground as the other birds fled through the canopy; then resumed feeding. I was awed by this intimate encounter with the majestic bird with intense brown eyes.

Next to the Fern Garden Trail is a pop-ash slough. A boardwalk provides access to the swamp without disturbing the flora and fauna. The trees here are short, their clustered trunks are dappled with reddish baton-rouge lichens, and their limbs hold small butterfly orchids with grape-sized pseudobulbs.

When Kathy and I were there in the fall, several kinds of floating plants grew lavishly in the still water near the boardwalk. The smallest and most numerous of these were water spangles, an aquatic fern with hairy leaves about the size of a fingernail. Larger, quarter-sized frog's-bit, with heart-shaped leaves, also covered much of the surface. Scattered about were the much larger, attractive white water lilies, along with the ubiquitous pickerelweed. On this October day, three kinds of swallowtail butterflies hungrily probed at the blue wands of the latter, taking little notice of nearby observers.

Arched gracefully over the boardwalk were arrowroots ten feet tall. Their small flowers, which look like twisted purple crepe paper, attracted brown bug-eyed skipper butterflies that noisily buzzed from flower to flower, probing for nectar with their tubular mouthparts. Below, on the big bananalike leaves of the arrowroots, were telltale signs of where the skipper caterpillars had spent the summer— munching away until some leaves were reduced to green skeletons. Other leaves, eaten when they were tightly rolled up like Cuban cigars, lay open, exposing rows of perforations resembling sheet music for a player piano. Here and there, green treefrogs slept on emergent leaves, their camouflaged forms barely visible as they clung tightly to the leaves. A lime-green anole basked in a ray of sunlight on a wax myrtle branch, its eyes scanning the nearby leaves for insects. Walking on, we reached the end of the boardwalk, where the still-moist scat of a bobcat lay in a large scrape. The cat must have just stopped there, and then silently faded into the thick vegetation.

Life abounds in this and other Florida swamps wherever one looks closely enough to see it. The remaining chapters look more closely at the plants and animals that live in our forested wetlands.

 *5*

Swamp Seasons

An Alligator's Almanac

Spring

Florida's swamps are dynamic natural systems where considerable changes occur with the seasons. Not only is this variation crucial to the plants and animals that live there; it also makes swamps more fascinating.

Florida extends from the temperate into the subtropical zone, so the timing of flowering and fruiting for a specific plant can vary by more than a month at opposite ends of the state. Spring comes early to central and southern Florida. Willows are among the first to flower: in January, their golden, sweet-scented catkins attract swarms of hungry bees, wasps, and butterflies. Most noticeable of these are the rather tame hairstreak butterflies with postage-stamp-sized wings, which land on the catkins and leisurely sip nectar, rubbing their tailed hind wings together all the while.

Red maples bloom early, too, with some trees flowering in December. Their small but profuse reddish flowers attract a variety of insects and birds, including flocks of yellow-rumped warblers and pairs of northern cardinals. Warblers can pollinate these flowers by carrying pollen on their bills and feathers. Far more obvious than red maple flowers are the scarlet masses of two-winged seeds or samaras that appear a few weeks after the flowers but before the leaves. Such prominence suggests that birds disperse them, and the extinct Carolina parakeet indeed fed on the seeds, perhaps spreading them. The samaras are a crucial early-spring food of the wood duck, being plentiful when winter supplies of acorns and other hard mast have already been consumed.

Another early sign of spring are the small, flat seeds of American elms, which are produced in prodigious numbers. The green seeds are inconspicuous except when being blown en masse across the dark waters of a blackwater stream by the blustery winds of January.

In February, the drooping cream-colored "bottle brush" blossoms of lizard's-tail first appear in southern swamps, attracting butterflies and bees to the fragrant wands. Hidden in the shadows of bayheads are the green-hooded cups of jack-in-the-pulpit, which emerge from deep layers of leaf mold. In cypress domes flooded by early spring rains, rosy-hued bells resembling heather flowers line the branches of fetterbush. In March, the white racemes of Virginia willow perfume the air with their musty scent. These nectar-rich flowers are eagerly visited by newly emerged swallowtail butterflies.

Spring may have just reached north Florida by March. Willows can still be naked, but red maples are scarlet with flowers and seeds. At this time, several colorful and fragrant wetland azaleas and rhododendrons bloom, especially in the Panhandle. The Florida azalea and the Pinxterbloom azalea both flower before putting out leaves, which helps them attract pollinators in the early-spring woods.

Slowly, as the days lengthen and spring advances, a flush of verdure spreads across the bare limbs of winter trees. By April, the longer and warmer spring days have stimulated the southern Florida swamps into activity, and the lovely cream-colored flowers of sweetbay perfume the air with a sweet, lemony aroma. Near the end of April, look closely at the Spanish moss. Search among the dangling tips of the long gray tassels for a few tiny, three-petaled greenish flowers. Though puny, they can be highly fragrant and probably attract nocturnal moths. Slowly, their capsules swell with the developing plumed seeds, which will be dispersed by next winter's winds until they lodge on rough bark with the aid of hooklike hairs.

Wetland birds begin to court and nest in spring. In March, the melodious singing of Carolina wrens is heard throughout swamps and hammocks. In May, the "sweet-sweet-sweet" notes of prothonotary warblers ring out in our northern swamps as the birds busily forage in cypress and tupelo for caterpillars and other insects to feed their hungry young. The prothonotary is delightful to behold, glossed in a fluorescent yellow headdress punctuated by brilliant black eyes. In contrast to his flash of gold in the shadows, look overhead for the graceful swallow-tailed kite soaring on long wings.

In April and early May, nonresident birds that have overwintered begin to leave, temporarily replaced by a steady procession of migrating songbirds passing through our forests on their way north. Insects are plentiful in spring, grazing on the lush new plant growth low in toxic chemicals that make older leaves less palatable. The bounty of caterpillars, leaf-hoppers, moths, bugs, and beetles provides the migrant birds with the energy they need to begin a family farther north.

Clear skies, warm temperatures, and an absence of rain characterize May weather in Florida. The increased evaporation and transpiration rob wetlands of remaining surface water. The water table recedes, sometimes going below the root level. This can be a harsh time for aquatic life, but for some animals the drying ponds become bountiful feeding troughs. As pools shrink, predators like cottonmouths, egrets, great blue herons (plate 32), wood storks, alligators, raccoons, and otters gather to gorge on the concentrated prey. Near a drying gum-swamp pond, I once found nine bowfin fish skulls—the leftover dinner of one or more otters. Surprisingly, predators may aid the long-term survival of aquatic species by reducing competition for the low levels of oxygen present in drying pools (Kushlan 1990).

By June, lightning-started fire reasserts its influence on the landscape. The air is thick with the sweet aroma of burned foliage, as black smoke billows high and fires consume the dried vegetation. But soon the cumulus clouds, thirsty for moisture and driven by heat, begin reaching skyward each morning, like upthrusting snow-capped mountains. By late afternoon, the sky is a study in gray and white, as if it had been drawn with charcoal on a white canvas. Huge, menacingly dark, anvil-shaped clouds bring life-giving rain to the parched land.

The response to rain is rapid. The once dry and brown or burned-black prairies become verdant and dappled with pink, yellow, and white wildflowers. Minerals, released from organic material exposed to air or liberated from burned vegetation, now enhance the new growth.

The coming of rain signals amphibians to find a mate and lay eggs. Late spring evenings resonate with the varied songs of calling frogs. Daytime refrains may include a variety of croaks, quacks, and quonks. Any change in humidity or barometric pressure, or the rumble of thunder, or rain tapping the vegetation, can stimulate countless tiny jade-green treefrogs to sing. The result is an exultant rain chorus—a froggy rhapsody—spreading through the swamp like a song.

Summer

Florida summers are oppressive. Temperatures range into the upper 90s, and the air is thick and hazy with water vapor. Biting critters are plentiful: mosquitos, yellowflies, chiggers, ticks, and "no-see-ums," among others. In coastal swamps, black clouds of whining mosquitos arrive to greet human visitors. Yellowflies relentlessly pursue their victims, circling constantly; then without warning, they swiftly land on exposed skin and draw blood with a scalpel-sharp proboscis.

But summer is a special time, with spectacular light shows brought on by passing lightning storms. Summer is the time when swamp life is most exuberant. As the water rises, aquatic plants like the beautiful white water lily, four-petaled duck potato, and royal blue pickerel-weed bloom. Occasionally you find waist-high cardinal flowers, whose scarlet blossoms lure ruby-throated hummingbirds into shady swamps (plate 11). Where there is deep water, you can hear the booming, machine-gun grunts of male pig frogs, proclaiming territories.

Summer nights are a perfect time to explore swamps. After the sun sets, the cooler air is filled with pleasant scents, and with interesting chirps, buzzes, and other night sounds. And in the twilight, bats fly erratically around swamp perimeters, darting high and low in their search for aerial prey.

One July evening, I explored the rich bottomlands of the Altamaha River in south Georgia. The air was heavy with the sweet smell of wil low, which grew abundantly along the river. Fireflies drifted lazily through the air, flashing their green beacons. By 9 P.M., the canopy resonated loudly with insect and frog calls. The unmistakable whistle calls of bird-voiced treefrogs came from the willows. One male would whistle, then another, and their din would rise and then fade into silence, only to be taken up again. Shining a light toward the nearest frog, I revealed the bulging white throat of the impassioned songster (plate 26). Searching, I found many others. Occasionally a gray treefrog would briefly trill, followed by another. Suddenly, lightning flashed overhead and a loud crack of thunder jolted me. Rain drops fell on the leaves; it was time to go.

Autumn and Winter

The wind is wearing a wistful hint
of autumn perfume today;
And the sweet gum tree on her green leaf gown
Has pinned a scarlet spray.
–Lucy Cherry Crisp (Green 1939, 245)

As the days grow shorter, the pace of life in Florida swamps slows. Life seems to coast, resting from all the spring and summer activity. Autumn and winter bring an abundance of fruits for birds and mammals. Like competing billboards, the fruits advertise, "Come eat me!" Colorful purple berries appear on the aptly named beautyberry; red and orange berries appear on holly, wild coffee, and on some greenbriers; and black or dark blue fruits appear on holly, swampbay, water tupelo, swamp tupelo, greenbrier, and muscadine grape. Sweetbay and other magnolias produce cones that, when dry, release black seeds covered by a thin waxy fire-engine-red pulp known as aril (plate 16). These attractive fruits hang on elastic threads, making them visible to birds. In subtropical south Florida, pond apple fruits, as big as mangos, ripen and turn greenish-yellow at summer's end. When ripe, they drop into the water where their black seeds are dispersed. A variety of other waterborne fruits and seeds include those from water tupelo, Ogeechee tupelo, oaks, and cypress, which are dispersed by winter floods. Wood ducks, our only species of waterfowl that nest primarily in swamps, feed heavily on this floating mast. The attractive plumage of the drake wood duck no doubt prompted its poetic Latin name, *Aix sponsa:* "A water bird in a bridal dress."

By November, the short days and cooler temperatures bring a wash of warm colors to the emerald-tinted landscape. These fiery shades slowly spread south. Beginning in Canada in September, they don't peak in Florida until late November or December. Then, maple leaves turn scarlet and yellow, adding a beauty reminiscent of northern hardwood forests to our bottomland hardwoods. The leaves of the sweetgum become dark burgundy or gold, and those of hickory, mustard yellow. Cypress needles turn brown or reddish brown, and twigs with attached needles begin to drop. By this time, most of the other trees have also lost their leaves.

The open winter canopy allows light to reach the forest floor. If water levels are not too high, seeds germinate and grow. The russet-colored swamp peat becomes green and alive with fresh growth. Tiny cypress seedlings retain their long, radiating needles, which look like high-tech antennae. These seedlings lead a tenuous existence between drought and flood. Most will perish in the winter floods or spring droughts, or after being submerged by summer rains. Enough survive in most locations to replace aging trees, however.

By December, cold fronts begin bringing blasts of frigid arctic air into Florida. With surprising speed, the air is chilled and invigorated. The resultant blue skies and lowered humidity make these special days—some of the best times to explore our wetlands. The yearly cycle in our swamps has come full circle—a year of exuberant life and enchanting beauty.

 *6*

The Emerald Kingdom
Plants with Wet Feet

Florida's swamps and hammocks have a rich and varied flora. This richness comes from our many forested wetlands, which offer a wealth of specialized niches. As already mentioned, such factors as hydroperiod, nutrients, prevalence of fire, and climate all influence plant life. The varying combinations of these factors in Florida have resulted in a high diversity of plants that have become adapted to particular habitats.

Just how many plants inhabit Florida's forested wetlands is unknown, but if we include fungi even though they are not true plants, the number is in the thousands (there are approximately four thousand green plants and two thousand fungi in Florida). In this chapter, I will mention only a few of the many fascinating and beautiful plants that make Florida's swamps so alluring.

Fungi

Imagine a world where "plants" are white, brown, red or blue, but few are green; where they don't need sunlight, but some can produce their own light; and where they feed off plants and animals, both living and dead, rather than using sunlight to make food from carbon dioxide and water. They lack roots, stems, and leaves, and never produce flowers or seeds. Instead of "oak" or "rose," their names are earth-tongue, dead-man's fingers, elf cap, devil's urn, and stinkhorn. These seemingly alien forms are the fungi.

Fungi are not true plants; they are perhaps more closely related to animals. Lacking chlorophyll, they are dependent on organic matter for energy. Although they are simple, fungi occur in an amazing variety of colors and shapes. They are made of slender filaments called hyphae. Specialized hyphae, appearing as whitish, hairlike masses under piles of rotting leaves or in decaying logs, secrete enzymes over and through their food so it can be absorbed. Fungi are one of the few groups of organisms that can digest cellulose, the main component of wood.

Fungi are perhaps the dominant organisms in woodland soils (Barron 1992). Their biomass can equal the weight of a small car per acre, and they may spread over several acres. Fungi are primarily responsible for recycling organic matter and returning essential nutrients to the soil where they can be used by green plants. Most of this recycling goes unnoticed. It is only when a fallen oak becomes covered with bright-orange sulfur shelf fungi, or turkey tails, or other fruiting fungus bodies (mushrooms), that we realize what is happening, unseen, within the wood.

Strangely, many fungi live in a mutually beneficial (symbiotic) relationship with plant roots. This relationship is known as mycorrhiza. Mycorrhizal fungi aid in nutrient uptake by tree roots, and are so essential that many plants could not exist without them. In turn, the fungi are supplied with sugars derived from the green plants' photosynthesis.

Some fungi feed on bacteria, or even on live animals! Because wood is difficult to digest and of low food quality, it is no wonder that some fungi have turned to richer food sources. Bacteria and microscopic animals such as nematodes (roundworms) are exceptionally plentiful in soil and rotten wood, and are a rich source of protein. Some fungi, such as the turkey tails, have rootlike hyphae that seek and digest masses of bacteria. Other fungi, such as the oyster mushroom, which decomposes wood, can release paralyzing toxins that immobilize nematodes. Hyphae then enter the worm through its mouth and digest it (Barron 1992). In this way the oyster mushroom obtains nitrogen and phosphorus, which are scarce in wood.

The colorful and varied forms of mushrooms that appear on dead trees or on the ground are the spore-producing organs essential for propagation of the fungal species. Each mushroom is merely a mass of hyphae that forms when sufficient food has been stored to initiate reproduction. Spore production is dependent on several factors, particularly temperature and moisture. That is why mushrooms often appear following a rain. The overnight emergence of mushrooms is possible because the cap and stalk are formed underground or in dead wood, and rapid elongation of the stalk pushes up the mushroom.

Once produced, mushrooms are usually short-lived. They are quickly eaten by insects, snails, slugs, box turtles, mice, squirrels, and other animals. Some are even attacked by other fungi; others simply dry up. Generally, mushrooms have some way of avoiding being eaten until the spores mature. Some emerge at night and are mature by morning. Others may be inedible until ready to release their spores. And others, such as truffles, which remain hidden below ground, release odors upon maturation to attract animals that dig them up and eat them.

Fungal spores are produced in immense numbers by mushrooms. Dispersing spores look like a faint mist that can be seen by shining a flashlight on the underside of a mushroom at night. Animals spread spores by eating the fungi and then defecating the resistant spores. Also, flies attracted to fungi can transport spores on their feet. Some fungi even use rain to disperse spores, such as when a raindrop falls into the "cup" of a tiny bird's nest fungus: a splash-gun reaction shoots packets of spores several feet. Spores are highly resistant to drying, heat, and cold; and, like seeds, they only germinate when conditions are ideal.

Fungi are classified into two major groups: mushrooms and their allies (collectively called club fungi), and sac fungi. Mushrooms and allies, with about twenty-five thousand species worldwide, comprise most of the familiar gilled fungi with umbrella-shaped caps, such as the white Agaricus mushroom commonly purchased in supermarkets. Mushrooms can also be bracket-shaped, corallike, or saclike as in the case of puffballs.

Sac fungi (except for those associated with algae, forming lichens) represent about thirty thousand species and are mostly small. They include molds, mildews, and yeasts. Some large sac fungi are fingerlike, and some even have a cap; but generally they are not parasol-shaped. Sac fungi may be ecologically significant, but little is known about them. Because of their inconspicuousness in swamps, sac fungi will not be further discussed here.

One of our most distinctive mushrooms, the column stinkhorn, is found in hammocks and pinelands in winter (plate 1). This reddish-orange fungus is about two inches high and has several arched columns that are fused at the apex. Within the cavity formed by the arches is a spongy material covered by a slimy black spore mass. The fruiting body of the stinkhorn forms in the ground in a whitish "egg" that erupts above the surface. Few observers, however, will venture sufficiently close to see this detail because stinkhorns emit a rotten-cheese odor that is repulsive even at five yards' distance. The stench, and perhaps the flesh color, attract flies, which crawl within the arches and feed on the sticky spore mass, thereby dispersing the spores that stick to their feet.

Another readily identified mushroom is the Magnolia coincap. It is neither smelly nor conspicuous. In fact, it is small and dingy, with only a coin-sized cap, and looks like many other tiny, parasol-shaped mushrooms. It would certainly go unnoticed except that it is the only mushroom that regularly decomposes Magnolia cones.

One of the more unusual kinds of organisms found in swamps are the slime molds (Mycetozoa). But they are neither club fungi nor sac fungi. In fact, they appear to be intermediate between plants and animals and are now classified with the protozoa rather than the fungi. Slime molds have two distinct stages in their life history, a motile, amoebalike "plasmodium" stage (seldom seen because of where they live), and an immobile, sporangia or "mold" stage that produces spores (fig. 19). In the plasmodium stage, slime molds forage for bacteria by creeping amoebalike in such dark, humid places as beneath the bark of rotting logs or in moist soil.

Slime mold sporangia are highly variable in shape. The chocolate-brown, hairlike sporangia of the slime mold *Stemonitis* are often visible on fallen logs. Slime mold spores are carried by the wind and can develop into another plasmodium stage under proper conditions.

Florida's damp woods have many strange and interesting fungi. Unfortunately, most are not easily identified; however, they can still be appreciated for their unusual forms, attractive colors, and exotic odors! Fungi are an ecologically important group that should be better known. Until a mushroom guide is written for Florida, the best field guide for our area is *Texas Mushrooms: A Field Guide* by Susan and Van Metzler (1992).

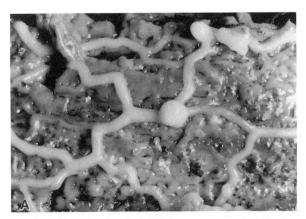

Figure 19. Stemonitis slime mold (*Stemonitis* sp.) is just one of the many fungi found in swamps: A, motile—plasmodium stage; B, immobile—sporangia or mold stage.

Lichens

A walk through any forest will bring you close to many lichen species. Over 150 macrolichens (the larger species) have been reported from Florida (Moore 1968), and many other smaller species are present, but remain little known. Some fourteen thousand species are known worldwide. On tree trunks, lichens appear as colored blotches, or as small crustose or leafy plants attached to bark (fig. 20). Lichens are not individual plants, but are a partnership—or symbiosis—between a sac fungus and a green alga (or more rarely a bacterium). The fungus—the more obvious part of the association—provides the alga with a protective covering, and absorbs water and minerals. The alga is photosynthetic and provides the carbohydrates, amino acids, and other foods necessary for both partners. This symbiosis has proved imminently successful, as evidenced by the abundance of lichens and their broad, worldwide distributions.

Figure 20. Lichens are plentiful and diverse in swamps, growing both in the canopy and on tree trunks. *Parmotrema* sp. (A) and *Ramalina* sp. (B) are two common canopy lichens.

In southeastern swamps, one of the most obvious lichens is the "baton rouge" or "bubble-gum" lichen. It resembles reddish-pink watercolor spots (one to twelve inches in diameter) on the trunks and limbs of trees (plate 2). This lichen has a pink center and a darker red rim. It gets its distinctive color from a red bacterium.

Many other forms of crustose lichens are more abundant than the baton rouge, but because of their drab coloration are less conspicuous. Lichens take various shapes. For example, old-man's beard resembles a loose tangle of green or black fibers hanging like beards from tree limbs. Other species, such as *Usnea strigosa,* may resemble miniature antlers or small trumpets.

Lichens vary in their tolerance to flooding. Generally, pale species are less tolerant than darker species. This results in a "lichen line" on some swamp trees. Such a line is a good indicator of past flooding events, since lichens grow slowly.

Lichens can only reproduce asexually—by fragmentation or by

propagules containing fungal hyphae and pieces of the alga. Where conditions are optimum, such as in the southeastern United States, lichens can grow relatively quickly. But in icy polar and alpine areas, and in parched deserts, growth is measured in millimeters per century. Lichens are eaten by a variety of animals, including snails and slugs, insects, and various mammals—even humans. Lichens are easily killed by pollutants like sulfur dioxide and thus are sensitive indicators of both the degree and distribution of airborne pollution.

Mosses and Liverworts

Mosses and liverworts are small leafy green plants that lack roots and conductive tissues and thus must absorb minerals and water directly through their leaves. Mosses usually have reproductive organs of both sexes on the same plant, although some are either male or female. For reproduction to occur, the sperm must swim through a film of water to a female reproductive organ, or be carried by splashing raindrops. Therefore, mosses are most common in damp environments and are dependent on rain for both nutrients and reproduction. Spores are produced in tiny capsules that develop on short, hairlike stalks. Because mosses are so small, they are not easily identified, and consequently few have common names. Yet more than one hundred species are known from Florida (Breen 1963).

Mosses are especially noticeable after a rain, when they swell and add an attractive range of greens and varied textures to tree trunks and rotten logs. One of the most obvious species is the carpet moss, a pale green moss that forms thick, firm, carpetlike masses around the bases of cabbage palms and among old "bootjacks," the brown supports left by fallen palm fronds. Two other mosses are also commonly found on cabbage palms. The green-tuft moss looks like microscopic dark green scouring pads when dry. It can form distinctive patches in areas where water runs down the palm trunk. A larger species, the silvery star moss, resembles small clusters of stars because of its relatively large radiating leaves.

Mosses also live on the ground. For example, Sphagnum moss forms green and red carpetlike mats in some wetlands such as Okefenokee. In colder climates it can fill lakes and other depressions, forming Sphagnum bogs.

Liverworts are small, mosslike plants that also live primarily in moist habitats. Although easily overlooked, there are over one hundred liverwort species in Florida and they can be quite abundant (Breil 1970). Reproduction in liverworts is similar to that in mosses, but the spore capsule of liverworts often splits into four parts when the spores are released (in mosses, the capsule only opens at the top).

Liverworts are divided into two groups, leafy and ribbonlike. Leafy species have two rows of tiny flattened overlapping leaves; and often a third row (which distinguishes them from mosses) occurs below the upper two. Ribbonlike liverworts lack distinct leaves.

Ribbonlike liverworts can be common at the bases of trees, on rotten logs, and on the ground where they remain moist. They resemble layers of translucent, green cellophane ribbons, and can cover areas of several square feet. The cellophane-ribbon liverwort is one of the most common ribbonlike liverworts and can be recognized by its distinctive midrib and dark green color.

The leafy liverworts are more abundant than ribbonlike liverworts but because of their small size are less apparent. Two common genera, *Frullania* and *Lejeunea,* attach to bark and resemble minute, flattened mosses. Sometimes these liverworts are so numerous that a single tree may have thousands of them tightly creeping over the bark. The largest common leafy species in our area is *Porella.* It is most noticeable on the trunks of tupelo and cypress along alluvial rivers, where it forms large dark green to black mats just below the seasonal high-water mark. This dark band is often referred to as the Porella line. When dry, Porella is nearly black; when wet, the delicate leaves uncurl and become translucent green.

Ferns and Their Relatives

Ferns are a prominent part of our swamp flora. Vast green meadows of sword fern, cinnamon fern, royal fern, swamp fern, Virginia and netted chain ferns, and others grow throughout the state in moist forests where the hydroperiod is short.

Florida is rich in ferns, with more species than any other continental state (Small 1932; Lakela and Long 1976). About half of the 130 or so ferns in Florida live in hammocks and swamps. As is true for other groups of Florida's plants, the richness of fern species is partly due to the presence of both temperate and tropical species.

Although ferns lack flowers, their varied forms make them appealing. When fertile (producing spores), the intricate patterns formed by the sori (spore clusters) on the underside of the fronds are amazing, and are best appreciated when magnified. The shape of the sori is a useful characteristic in fern identification.

Most ferns are moisture-loving plants, inhabiting humid environments like hammocks and swamps where water is plentiful. Some species are epiphytic and live in trees. Wherever there are old live oaks, for example, you are sure to find resurrection ferns covering the tops of larger limbs. Resurrection ferns also live on other trees, and can even grow on the ground. These ferns conserve water by curling tightly in dry weather. Once they become wet, they uncurl and appear "resurrected."

Other common tree-dwelling ferns are the shoestring fern and the golden polypody. These ferns frequently grow on cabbage palms in south and central Florida, where they attach to the trunk or to old bootjacks. The shoestring fern is an atypical fern because it has narrow, dark green shoestring-like fronds an eighth of an inch wide and up to two feet long, which are crowded into hanging clumps. Being tropical, it often dies back in winter following freezing weather. Surprisingly, mature (sporophyte) stages of this fern were found on a cliff face in northeast Georgia near Augusta, and possible immature (gametophyte) stages exist as far north as Ohio (Farrar 1978).

The golden polypody is a more typical fern, with broad drooping fronds nearly two feet long (fig. 21). Although this species is called golden, its furry rhizome is covered with rusty or chestnut-colored scales. It is also called the serpent fern because the rootlike rhizome, which often winds through the bootjacks of cabbage palms, extends several feet in length, and is about the diameter of a finger. It stores water and food for the new light green fronds that appear following early summer rains. Hontoon Island is a good place to see this fern, since most of the tall palms there are embellished with attractive specimens arching gracefully from the bootjacks sixty feet up.

Another fern often seen growing from cabbage-palm bootjacks is the sword fern. "Boston fern" is a mutant variety of the sword fern that is often grown as a houseplant. Sword ferns can also be terrestrial in hydric hammocks in south Florida, where the head-high swords can form extensive undergrowth in sunlit gaps. On the ground, sword ferns can grow to remarkable size. Botanist John K. Small, in his book *Ferns of Florida* (1932), reported measuring fronds twenty-seven feet in length! Florida is the northernmost limit for this tropical fern.

Figure 21. The golden polypody is the most common large epiphytic fern growing on cabbage palms. Note the conspicuous sori, which contain the reproductive spores.

The hand fern is the most peculiar fern growing on cabbage palms. The stalked fronds are rounded at the base and have flattened "fingers" that droop from the free end, making them resemble a hand (plate 3). Spores are produced by knobby, club-shaped structures that grow from the leaf stalk. Although rare over most of Florida, and considered endangered by the state, the hand fern still prospers in a few south Florida swamps like Fakahatchee Strand.

The variety of ferns and mosses that prefer to live on the cabbage palm suggests that this palm must have existed a long time for such associations to have developed. And, indeed, ancestors of the cabbage palm lived in North America and even in Europe for more than fifteen million years (Zona 1990).

Some epiphytic ferns also grow on other trees. The common strap fern attaches to many kinds of trees, stumps and windfalls, but rarely lives on palms. Strap ferns are tropical, and only the common strap fern lives as far north as central Florida, where it can be seen at Highlands Hammock. Several other strap ferns, such as the narrow strap fern and the tailed strap fern, are found in swamps and hammocks in extreme south Florida, especially in Fakahatchee Strand. As their name implies, strap ferns are long, broad in the middle, and pointed at both ends.

Psilotum, or whisk fern, is a curious fernlike plant that is sometimes seen growing on trees, but more often lives on dead stumps and other sites where humus has collected. The whisk fern belongs to an ancient group of fern allies known as the Psilophyta. Their close relatives, some of the first vascular plants to appear on land, lived 350 million years ago (during the Devonian period), and no fossils of these plants have been seen in more recent deposits.

Whisk ferns have conductive tissues like higher plants but lack roots and leaves. Unlike true ferns, whisk ferns produce spores in swollen chambers along their broomlike branches. In his interesting book about Bulow Hammock, naturalist David Wallace described the whisk fern as an "an odd plant, leafless, a spray of wiry green stems with bulbous, pea-sized structures at the joints" (Wallace 1989). Psilotum occurs sporadically in swamps and hydric hammocks throughout Florida and north to South Carolina. Although clumps can grow to be several feet in diameter, they often go unnoticed because they look like leafless green twigs about ten inches high.

Numerous terrestrial ferns also inhabit Florida's swamps and hammocks. The largest are the leather ferns, whose fronds reach lengths of ten feet. Two species are found in swamps of central and south Florida, but are most abundant in salt marshes and mangrove swamps of southern Florida where they can cover extensive areas. They are also plentiful in similar tropical habitats around the world.

The cinnamon fern is one of our most common ferns. It lives in hammocks and in the drier parts of swamps. It is easily recognized because of its size (about waist high) and the color of its distinctive fertile fronds. The attractive spore-producing fronds are four feet high and covered with reddish-brown hairs, which give the fern its name. When flecks of sunlight illuminate the fertile fronds, they seem to glow like embers. The graceful green photosynthetic fronds encircle the taller spore-bearing fronds.

Most terrestrial ferns cannot stand lengthy immersion. An exception is the delicately branched royal fern, a close relative of the cinnamon fern, which grows in swamps where hydroperiods are long. Its fibrous, water-resistant black root-clumps elevate the plant by more than a foot. Cinnamon ferns also form prop-root clumps, but they are generally shorter, and therefore live in drier situations. (Because the rusty red roots of cinnamon ferns are relatively resistant to decomposition, they are used as a growing medium for orchids and other moisture-loving greenhouse plants.)

Other ferns can live in deeply flooded swamps by attaching themselves to cypress trunks and knees or to fallen logs. One of these is the netted chain fern. It is a widespread, medium-sized fern (with fronds about a foot long) that grows on damp ground or on cypress knees. The netted chain fern has erect fertile fronds that produce spores. A related, but quite different species, the waist-high Virginia chain fern, is regularly found growing in cypress domes and other wetlands. Chain ferns have a chainlike pattern of veins in the leaflets that can be seen with a hand lens on the underside of the leaves. In the Virginia chain fern, sori grow over these veins in obvious, elongate, chestnut-colored clusters that alternate on each side of the midvein. This fern can also be recognized by its dark, purple-black stem.

Another prevalent wetland fern is the swamp fern. It grows in a variety of moist habitats and is tolerant of flooding. Like the Virginia chain fern, it is about three feet high and grows from an underground rhizome, enabling it to form large patches. The swamp fern has unscalloped leaflets opposite one another along the stem. The sori form two distinct, cinnamon-brown rows along each side of the midvein of the leaflet.

Most of these plants are easily recognized as ferns, but there are several atypical ferns in wetlands, too. "Water spangles" and the smaller, button-sized mosquito fern live floating in masses on the surface of ditches, ponds, sluggish rivers, or lakes. The mosquito fern has tiny leaves arising from a short, branched stem. The dime-sized water spangles have two rounded leaves covered with stiff, branched hairs.

Cypress Trees

"Its majestic stature is surprising, and on approaching them we are struck with a kind of awe at beholding the stateliness of the trunk, lifting its cumbrous top towards the skies, and casting a wide shade upon thye ground, as a dark intervening cloud, which, for a time, precludes the rays of the sun. The delicacy of its color and texture of its leaves, exceed everything in vegetation." These are the words chosen by William Bartram ([1791] 1955) to describe the bald cypress, certainly the best known tree of southeastern swamps.

Almost anywhere in the coastal plain of Florida, Georgia, the Carolinas, Louisiana, Alabama, Mississippi, and even in a few areas northward to Delaware, Indiana, and Illinois, where there are cypress trees, there is a swamp. Patriarchs six hundred to nine hundred years old and seven feet in diameter once were common in southeastern swamps. Recent studies have identified ancient cypress along the Black River in North Carolina that are over fifteen hundred years old (Earley 1990). Cavities in these trees once provided nesting sites for ivory-billed woodpeckers and for roosting Carolina parakeets. Now the ivory-bills, the parakeets, and most of the old-growth cypress are gone.

Cypress are conifers or evergreen trees, but they are unusual because they shed their needle-bearing twigs in winter. Where water levels remain high or vary considerably, the trunk is often swollen into a bulging base ten feet or more in diameter (fig. 22A). Such swelling, or "buttressing," also occurs in other swamp trees including tupelo, pop ash, and elm, and may be a way of increasing stability in wet soil where shallow roots provide little purchase (fig. 22B).

There are two kinds of cypress in the Southeast, bald cypress and pond cypress. Whether they are distinct species is still debated. Bald cypress, reaching heights of 130 feet and diameters of twelve feet or more, is the larger. It has flat needles growing from both sides of a drooping feather-like twig (fig. 23A). The smaller pond cypress, usually reaching heights of less than one hundred feet and often only a foot or two in diameter, has shorter scalelike needles arranged in a spiral over the twig (fig. 23B). These twigs are often pointed upward instead of drooping. Also, the knees of pond cypress are rounded whereas those of bald cypress tend to be pointed.

Bald cypress usually occur along rivers, in lakes, and in swamps next to rivers where the hydroperiod is long and the peat soil is deep

Figure 22. Wetland tree adaptations: *A*, Bald cypress (*Taxodium distichum*), has large, fluted butresses for stability; *B*, Ogeechee tupelo (*Nyssa ogeche*), has snakelike surface roots for stability and oxygen uptake.

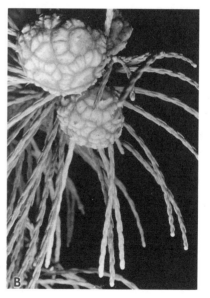

Figure 23. Comparison of cypress needles: *A*, Bald cypress (*Taxodium distichum*), has needles arranged perpendicular to the twig; *B*, Pond cypress (*Taxodium ascendens*), has needles bent toward the twig; note seed balls.

(Duever, Carlson, and Riopelle 1984). In contrast, pond cypress generally grow in relatively isolated wetlands such as cypress domes, but they can grow elsewhere. Pond cypress often live where soils are poor and highly acid and the peat layer thin. Also, pond cypress often occur where fires are prevalent.

A dwarf form of pond cypress occupies habitats where nutrients are especially scarce and water is seasonally limited. These oddly shaped trees, resembling hat racks, are often two hundred years old but less than ten feet high; the bark is gray and noticeably sunbleached. The Big Cypress National Preserve, a region northwest of the Everglades, includes extensive wetlands called dwarf cypress scrub or cypress savanna (Duever 1984; Duever, Meeder, and Duever 1984; McPherson 1984; Duever et al. 1986). In similar habitats in the Panhandle, a number of rare pitcher plants, such as the attractive white-top, occur.

The typical pond cypress, with its few green twigs, has lush foliage compared to the dwarf pond cypress. This latter stunted growth form is probably the result of poor growing conditions. The marl soils in the Big Cypress are deficient in some minerals. And, in the dry season, the roots of the dwarf pond cypress suffer from water stress because they are unable to reach groundwater that is isolated below the relatively impermeable layer of marl.

In both bald and pond cypress, male and female cones occur on the same tree. Male cones appear during the winter and spring. They are present longer to ensure that ample pollen is available to fertilize female cones. In spring, green female cones appear, and after being pollinated, mature before the end of the year. The mature seed balls, about the size of a golf ball, contain about fifteen seeds (fig. 23B). The balls either open while still on the tree, allowing the seeds to fall, or drop to the ground, eventually releasing the seeds (C. A. Brown 1984; Schneider and Sharitz 1988). The seeds are dispersed primarily by water, but animals may be important too, and that may explain how pond cypress appear in wetlands isolated from flooding.

Cypress seeds are eaten by a variety of animals including wood ducks, Florida sandhill cranes, and squirrels (Duever et al. 1986). In addition, the Carolina parakeet probably was a major seed eater, and may also have dispersed the seeds.

For germination to occur, cypress seeds must soak for one to three months (C. A. Brown 1984). Seedlings will die, however, if submerged too long or if they get too dry. Because conditions are rarely ideal for germination and seedling growth, only a small fraction of the seeds will germinate and survive beyond the critical seedling stage (Gunderson 1984). Relatively dry summers with low water levels provide ideal conditions for cypress germination. In 1993, the scant rainfall over much of the Southeast allowed cypress and tupelo seedlings to germinate and grow in profusion.

Cypress knees are formed when the roots arch upward above the ground. Each tree can grow several hundred knees. Knees add a novel charm to cypress swamps. Like steep-sided Lilliputian mountains sculpted by forest sprites, they seem to be part of the unseen world underlying the swamp. Ornithologist Frank M. Chapman remarked, "the strange cypress knees shoot up from the ground like roots excelling at their humble position" (Austin 1967). In Palmdale, Tom Gaskin once operated a museum devoted solely to the cypress knee. Although picturesque, cypress knees are a mystery, and their functional significance still puzzles scientists. Usually, however, the height of knees is related to water depth; and knees are often absent where cypress are rarely inundated, such as those at the edge of a cypress dome.

Because of the scarcity of oxygen in water-saturated soils, early researchers theorized that cypress knees were snorkels, functioning similarly to the roots of mangroves. Cypress knees show little ability to absorb oxygen, however. Also, unlike the specialized gas-conducting roots of mangroves and water tupelo, which have corky wood with large air spaces, the wood in cypress knees is too dense for gas transport (C. A. Brown 1984). Another theory is that cypress knees provide structural support to the trees by strengthening the root system. This seems more likely, as evidenced by the still-standing cypress trees surrounded by numerous fallen hardwoods in South Carolina swamps that were ravaged by Hurricane Hugo in 1990. Regardless of their function, cypress knees are a captivating aspect of our swamps.

Cypress has been described as "the wood eternal" because well-preserved logs have been uncovered that are centuries old. This resistance to decay makes the wood ideal for outdoor construction; not surprisingly, hollow cypress logs were once used as water pipes.

Cypress was once difficult to harvest because of its size and weight. Before the advent of mechanized logging, the trees had to be girdled one year and cut the next to ensure that they were sufficiently dry to float. The logs were floated out during high-water periods (Sargent 1947). The early loggers took only the best trees. Hollow trees, some of which still survive, were left and now provide much-needed homes for wildlife.

Cypress are ancient trees that once had an extensive worldwide range in the Northern Hemisphere. Fossilized cypress twigs have been recovered from a Miocene lake deposit in western Idaho (Gould 1992). This discovery was exciting because scientists extracted DNA from the twenty-million-year-old twigs that was nearly identical to the DNA of modern bald cypress. Cypress have existed for millennia. If swamps are protected, cypress could be around for a long time to come.

Palms

Palms are conspicuous in Florida's wetlands; most of the twelve native species can be found there (Pritchard 1978). Needle palms grow in hydric hammocks; dwarf palmettos inhabit blackwater and alluvial swamps; paurotis palms are found in brackish wetlands and wet savannas in south Florida; royal palms are endemic to strands and hammocks in southernmost Florida; and cabbage palms are nearly ubiquitous in Florida, especially along the coast.

Our most familiar palm is the cabbage or Sabal palm, Florida's state tree. Few other Florida trees are as distinctive; its columnar trunk and hemispherical crown make it unmistakable. Its name is derived from the edible "heart of palm"—a cabbage-like tissue at the base of the fronds. Florida black bears also relish palm hearts and will remove them from young palms. Found abundantly over most of the state, except in the western portion of the Panhandle and inland north of Jacksonville, cabbage palms also grow along the coast to North Carolina, and in the Bahamas (Brown 1973).

In early summer, mature cabbage palms produce long, flowering panicles, some reaching nine feet in length and bearing thousands of straw-colored, sweetly fragrant flowers. The tiny blossoms attract multitudes of nectar-seeking bees, wasps, flies, and butterflies. In winter, glossy pea-sized black fruits develop. These sweet but thin-fleshed fruits are relished by a host of birds including northern cardinal, American robin, yellow-rumped warbler, fish crow, pileated woodpecker, and blue jay, as well as by mammals like the raccoon and Florida black bear (Zona 1990). Kathy and I have watched small flocks of wintering cedar waxwings feeding on the fruits in February, after most other fruits are gone. The fruits were also an important seasonal food of Florida's Indians, and white settlers ate them fresh or made them into syrup.

Bootjacks are the leaf sheaths remaining on cabbage-palm trunks after the fronds are shed. The degree to which the jacks remain attached to the trunk is highly variable. Some trees retain many jacks; some retain a few; and others are quite bare except for the most recent jacks.

Bootjacks provide ideal habitat for small animals like treefrogs and skinks, which are frequently heard rustling amid the brittle sheaths, searching for insects. During cold weather, frogs and lizards seek shelter under the jacks. The decomposing jacks also serve as substrates for epiphytic ferns, and can protect the rhizomes of ferns, such as the endangered hand fern, from squirrels and other herbivores, and perhaps even insulate them from ground fires and icy weather.

Relatives of the cabbage palm have been present in North America for some time. The palm *Sabalites,* perhaps the ancestor of our cabbage palm, existed in north Florida in the mid-Miocene, about fifteen million years ago (Berry 1916). It was also widespread in Europe at about the same time (Zona 1990).

The largest and most majestic of Florida's native palms is the royal palm, listed by the state as endangered (fig. 24). These stately trees reach more than a hundred feet high and have huge arching fronds more than twelve feet long. Along Janes Memorial Scenic Drive in Fakahatchee Strand State Preserve, their distinctive crowns rise high above the surrounding canopy. Royal palms apparently were once more widely distributed in Florida than they are today: in 1774, William Bartram found them growing along the St. Johns River in Volusia County—two hundred miles north of their present location. Since then, however, they have been restricted to south Florida by occasional hard freezes.

Florida royal palms occur primarily in Fakahatchee Strand and also in smaller numbers in the Everglades. In the years before the Great Depression, mature Florida royal palms were so valued for landscaping that corduroy roads were built in south Florida swamps so the massive trees could be removed (Ward 1979).

Royal palms produce flowers that, like those of the cabbage palm, are highly attractive to nectar-seeking insects. Several months after flowering, numerous dark blue olive-sized fruits appear. Given an abundance of moisture, the seeds readily germinate. In Fakahatchee Strand, young royal palms grow on stilts formed by stout roots that

Figure 24. Florida royal palms (*Roystonea elata*), such as this one in Fakahatchee Strand, are native only to south Florida.

elevate the plants above the water. Growth is rapid, as evidenced by the mature specimens up to sixty feet or more in height now growing along the forty-year-old logging tramways.

The Florida royal palm appears to be doing well. In a 1980 status survey, Daniel Austin of Florida Atlantic University estimated that the Strand contained about five thousand royal palms. However, there is some concern that royal palms near urban areas may be hybridizing with the widely planted and closely related species from Cuba (David Martin, USFWS, pers. comm., 1993). How such hybridization might affect Florida royal palms is unknown.

Aroids

Aroids, or arums, are common wetland herbs with dark green leaves and unusual blossoms. These consist of a pencillike central spadix composed of numerous tiny male or female flowers, often surrounded by a hooded spathe (a modified leaf). One of our most common aroids is the green arum, which has arrow-shaped leaves similar to duck potato. The white spadix of the green arum is nearly obscured by its green and white spathe. The green arum frequently grows in swamps and is tolerant of shade.

The golden club is a small aroid with a colorful yellow-tipped spadix about the size of a large pencil (plate 5). It grows in ditches, lakes, and sunny areas in swamps and other wetlands. It is abundant in parts of the Okefenokee and in blackwater panhandle streams, where its attractive sulfur-yellow spadix appears in March. Another aquatic aroid, water lettuce, is appropriately named because it resembles a head of floating Bibb lettuce. In south Florida, canals, sluggish streams, and small ponds called lettuce lakes can be covered by this unusual plant.

Jack-in-the-pulpit is a widespread aroid that frequently grows in hydric hammocks and hardwood swamps in central and north Florida. It is abundant in Highlands Hammock, and in hydric hammocks along Alexander Springs Run where it grows nearly waist high. Its name comes from the shape of the blossom. The spadix—the jack—is surrounded by the green-and-white-striped, hooded spathe—the pulpit. A related but less common aroid, the green dragon, has a whip-like spadix extending far beyond the spathe. This species is mostly found in north Florida; it is plentiful on the shaded seepage slopes along the east side of the Apalachicola River at Torreya State Park.

As described in the interesting and beautifully illustrated book on aroids by Deni Brown (1988), *Arisaemas* (jack-in-the-pulpit and related species) have an atypical sex life. Unlike most other flowering plants, arisaemas may lack sex chromosomes; thus they can change sex, depending on their nutritional state.

Producing fruit requires energy. In the deep shade where arisaemas grow, it may be difficult to produce sufficient food to bear fruit. Because of this, female Arisaema flowers are produced only when food reserves are high (Bierzychudek 1982; Doust and Cavers 1982). When reserves are low (such as in small plants or when growing conditions are poor), a male flower is produced instead.

When flowering does occur from January through April, Arisaema pollen is carried to the female flowers by small fungus gnats that may mistake the spadix for a mushroom where the gnats normally lay their eggs and the larvae develop (Bierzychudek 1982). Gnats frequently get trapped in the female flowers, especially after the fruits

Figure 25. A fungus gnat is trapped in the spathe of jack-in-the-pulpit after being lured to the mushroomlike spadix. Gnats have fertilized the flowers, which are now developing into berries at the base of the spadix.

begin to swell (fig. 25). Pea-sized red berries appear in summer and autumn on the female spadix; these are relished by catbirds, thrushes, and other fruit-eating animals.

Grasses, Sedges, and Rushes

Of Florida's herbaceous wetland flora, the grasses, sedges, reeds, and similar plants are perhaps the most diverse and abundant, occurring in almost bewildering variety. Besides the familiar grasses, sedges, rushes, and cattails, there are bald-rushes, spike-rushes, beak-rushes, fringe-rushes, lake-rushes, bulrushes, nutrush, nut-grass, sawgrass, and bur-reed (fig. 26). Although a few of the more than a hundred species of grasslike wetland plants are easily distinguished, most can only be identified by close examination of flowers and seeds. I will discuss here only a very few that are to be encountered in or near some swamps.

Sawgrass is a ten-foot-high sedge with three rows of razor-sharp teeth. It covers hundreds of square miles in the Everglades. Although primarily a species of the glades, sawgrass also frequents sunny openings in swamps throughout the state.

Switch cane is a bamboolike grass with thin, woody stems that occasionally reach lengths of nearly thirty feet. It frequently grows in river swamps and other wetlands in north Florida where under-

Figure 26. Sedges of the genus *Carex* are among the common grasslike plants living in swamps.

ground runners enable it to cover large areas known as canebrakes. Switch cane is readily recognized by the stiff bristles that radiate from the leaf petioles.

Two species of wild rice, Indian rice and southern wild rice, which reach about ten feet in height, grow in our wetlands. Indian rice often lives along the sunny margins of spring runs, whereas southern wild rice is found along the banks of larger rivers.

White-top, a sedge, has several distinctive green and white bracts surrounding small flowers at the top of its two-foot-high stem. Seen from a distance along a ditch or on the edge of a shallow marsh, the white-top stands out like a true flower among the green grasses. Only upon closer inspection do you discover that it is "only" a sedge. Two useful references to wetland grasses, sedges, and rushes are Godfrey and Wooten's *Aquatic and Wetland Plants of the Southeastern United States: Monocotyledons* and Dressler et al., *Identification Manual for Wetland Plant Species of Florida.*

Epiphytes

Perhaps the most distinctive feature of Florida's swamps is their exceptional variety of air plants, or epiphytes. No other area in the continental United States has such a richness of tree-growing plants.

There are more than sixty species of vascular epiphytes (ferns plus flowering plants) in Florida. These include: one club moss, one whisk fern, fourteen true ferns, seventeen bromeliads, twenty-nine orchids, one cactus, and five peperomias (a type of succulent often grown as a houseplant because it tolerates low light levels). Many other smaller and more numerous nonvascular epiphytes—mostly lichens, liverworts, and mosses—are more widespread.

Forested wetlands in Fakahatchee Strand contain most of the flowering epiphytes known from the United States, including fourteen bromeliads, twenty-three orchids, and four peperomias (Austin, Jones, and Bennett 1990). In fact, this single swamp probably contains the largest number of different vascular epiphytes of any place in the Western Hemisphere, north of Cuba!

Many epiphytes are killed by frost, drought, and being blown from the canopy. In addition, the arboreal roots and shoots of epiphytes usually have no protection from fires. Epiphytes are also damaged by such animals as the lubber grasshopper, white-tailed deer, and various rodents, especially squirrels (Craighead 1963; Butler 1974). A new threat to bromeliads is a Central American weevil that kills mature plants. Epiphytes are sensitive to many environmental factors, but they are adaptable and usually persist; however, once their habitat is gone, they may never recover.

Bromeliads

Also known as wild pines, bromeliads are the most abundant flowering epiphytes in Florida. They are found throughout the state, but are most diverse in the south. Although some species, such as the ball moss, occur in many habitats (even in dry sand-scrub areas and on power lines), most bromeliads prefer humid habitats like swamps and hammocks.

Bromeliads grow slowly, flower, and then sometimes die after their stored carbohydrates are used in flowering and to form seeds. The giant wild pine, our largest bromeliad, may live as long as fourteen years before producing seeds and dying (Frank and Curtis 1981).

Most of our bromeliads bloom in late spring and summer. In our most diverse genus, *Tillandsia*, with thirteen species, individual flowers are small, tubular, and usually bluish. The cardinal wild pine is notable for its flamboyant reddish bracts, produced in spring. Bromeliad flower stalks vary greatly in size. Some are only a few inches high, as in the fuzzy-wuzzy air plant; others can reach a length of six feet, as in the giant wild pine.

In the Neotropics, hummingbirds are important bromeliad pollinators, but most of our bromeliads are probably self-pollinated. After pollination and seed maturation, the capsules open, releasing hundreds of plumed seeds to be carried by the wind until they lodge on bark.

"Air plants" would seem to survive only on moisture and nutrients obtained from the air, but actually it is rain that provides both of these necessities. Epiphytic bromeliads, like all epiphytic plants, absorb water through their leaves; the wiry roots serve only for anchorage.

The way in which bromeliads obtain water and minerals separates them into two ecological groups, the "atmospheric" and the "tank" species (Benzing 1980). Atmospherics, such as Spanish moss and ball moss, obtain water and minerals directly from falling rain. Most atmospherics are small, possibly because they trap little water and few minerals.

Tank species, such as the giant wild pine, the cardinal wild pine, and the attractive Guzmania, get more minerals and water by funneling rain into a "tank" formed by a rosette of broad, overlapping leaves. Dust and plant and animal debris also accumulate in these tanks, making a dilute "nutrient soup."

In the humid Neotropics, tank bromeliads reach extraordinary sizes. Our largest tank species traps about a quart of liquid (Frank and Curtis 1981), but some tropical bromeliads may hold several times this volume. It has been estimated that in one acre of Colombian cloud forest, bromeliads contain more than thirty thousand gallons of water—enough to fill a swimming pool (Benzing 1990).

These herbaceous reservoirs provide ideal, albeit temporary, habitats for aquatic organisms. Because sizable predators like fish are absent, these basins become relatively safe, private ponds for insects, frogs, and other small animals. In fact, nearly five hundred species of aquatic biota have been reported from neotropical bromeliad tanks (Frank 1983). Bromeliad tanks can be miniature ecosystems supporting entire food chains, from plants to predators; however, most of the animals feed on organic detritus accumulating in the tanks. Bromeliads benefit from their resident biota because nitrogen, phosphorus, and other minerals from animal wastes are deposited in the tanks.

A few bromeliads have gone one step beyond forming aquatic impoundments: they have become insectivorous. Biologist Durland Fish discovered that the powdery Catopsis, a bromeliad from south Florida and Central America, apparently lures insects, which become trapped in its tank (Ward and Fish 1979). This vase-shaped bromeliad has waxy flakes on the inner surfaces of its leaves that may attract flying insects. In one study, twelve times as many insects were found in Catopsis tanks as were found in those of other bromeliads (Frank and O'Meara 1984). Once enticed into a tank, an insect apparently slides down the waxy flakes and drowns in the basin. Digestion of the captive insects and release of minerals are accomplished by bacteria living in the tank. Thus Catopsis, which lives in a nutrient-poor environment, has become carnivorous like pitcher plants.

Spanish moss, our best known and most widespread flowering epiphyte (occurring from Virginia to Argentina), is in many ways the least typical. Not only does it normally lack roots (roots are usually seen only on Spanish moss that grows from seeds), but it consists of loosely clinging small plantlets in long, dangling chains that break apart and are dispersed by wind. The destructive windstorm or "blizzard" of March 1993 blew down vast quantities of the moss, and although many plants died, some undoubtedly were aided in dispersal.

Although Spanish moss produces flowers, as all bromeliads do, the match-head-sized blossoms are few and inconspicuous. From April to June, the dainty, fragrant blossoms appear near the tips of the tassels (fig. 27). Following pollination, a few plumed seeds are produced the following spring when the dry capsule splits (Garth 1964).

Spanish moss is silvery gray when dry because of minute trichomes, scalelike structures that coat its surface like a cellophane fuzz. Trichomes are most visible in the atmospheric bromeliads like ball moss and Spanish moss, but they are found on the leaves of all epiphytic bromeliads; they aid in the absorption of water and nutrients (Benzing 1980).

Abundant, soft, resilient, and easily gathered, Spanish moss was used by Indians to make garments. Later it was collected to stuff mattresses and furniture cushions—a multimillion-dollar industry that reached its peak in 1936. The plants were collected using long hooks and put in piles or trenches where the outer tissues decomposed, leaving the tough, inner black fiber. Spanish moss may have been responsible for the great Jacksonville fire of 1902, which started in a moss-drying shed and burned more than two thousand buildings

Figure 27. Spanish moss (*Tillandsia usneoides*), a bromeliad, produces a few minute, three-petaled flowers in April and May. The coiled stems of each plantlet are coated with silvery scalelike trichomes that absorb rainwater.

(Wood 1989). Although Spanish moss is still being harvested, synthetic materials have largely replaced it for commercial use.

Humans were not the first animals to find Spanish moss useful for bedding. Birds use it as nesting material, and some, such as the swallow-tailed kite, the Acadian flycatcher, the northern Parula and the yellow-throated warbler, construct their nests almost entirely of it (Bent [1937] 1961; Sprunt 1954). Also, the northern yellow bat and the Seminole bat roosts and rear their young in clumps of Spanish moss (Jennings 1958).

Orchids

Orchids are an engaging and alluring family of plants, the most familiar of which is the garish hybrid Cattleya often warn as a corsage. But our native species would look very much out of place on a lapel, since many are not showy, being small and subtly tinged brown or green.

Epiphytic orchids originated in the tropics, and for the majority of our species Florida represents but a tiny outpost at the northernmost limit of their range. This makes these plants extremely sensitive to habitat loss. And, in fact, some species probably are already extirpated from Florida, and others may be represented by just a handful of plants.

Orchids are a spectacular family of plants because of their appealing flowers. This appeal is directed toward one purpose—reproduction. Orchids are pollinated primarily by insects, especially bees and moths, so their flowers must be attractive. Orchid pollen is unusual in that the grains adhere to one another, forming masses called "pollinia." This allows the pollen to be easily carried by insects from one plant to another for pollination. Most orchids are dependent on this out-crossing; however, some orchids can self-pollinate if insects are lacking. In Florida, self-pollination may be fairly common because insect vectors may well be absent.

The butterfly orchid is the most abundant epiphytic orchid in southern Florida hydric hammocks and swamps. It occurs as far north as Daytona Beach, and in the Bahamas, but it is most numerous in the southern half of the state. Flowering occurs in late May and June when a long shoot and panicle of showy flowers, up to three feet long and with twenty-five or more flowers, is produced. The quarter-sized blossoms are greenish-yellow to yellowish-brown, with a pink-to-lavender blotch on the white lip. Color patterns vary, with some flowers having a pure white lip. Orchid biologist Carlyle Luer observed small bees pollinating this orchid; the bees were probably attracted by the sweet fragrance, which is most noticeable in the afternoon (Luer 1972).

The butterfly orchid is an adaptable species, living in a variety of habitats and growing on many kinds of trees. It is most common, however, on live oak where it sometimes forms large masses with fifty or more pseudobulbs, each reaching several inches in diameter. Unfortunately, these attractive plants, which may be fifty years or more in age, are rapidly disappearing because of collecting, habitat destruction, wind damage, and other factors. The Christmas freeze of 1989 nearly devastated the butterfly orchids in central Florida.

Even though some of this mortality is related to man's activities (especially loss of habitat), there is considerable natural mortality of butterfly orchids. Large colonies perish because they live primarily on old limbs, which eventually fall. Young plants suffer even higher mortality because they easily become desiccated.

The green-fly orchid grows farther north than any other epiphytic orchid in the Western Hemisphere and is the only one in the continental United States that ranges outside of Florida (fig. 28). It is found near the coast from North Carolina to Louisiana, and also on the east coast of central Mexico. For most of the year, this small orchid remains hidden amid the resurrection ferns covering the upper surfaces of ancient live-oak limbs. From summer to winter the green-fly or-

Figure 28. The green-fly orchid (*Epidendrum conopseum*) is the only epiphytic orchid found in Florida that ranges into neighboring states. The flowers vaguely resemble insects.

chid produces attractive one- to two-inch-long sprays of small, greenish flowers. Seen up close, each flower vaguely resembles a small flying insect—a green fly.

The ghost orchid, Polyradicon, is a beautiful and curiously leafless epiphyte that lives in Fakahatchee Strand and a few other swamps in south Florida. Its flower is one of the largest of our native orchids. For most of the year, the ghost orchid consists only of obscure greenish-gray roots tightly clasping the lichen-mottled trunks of pop ash, pond apple, and other swamp trees. When the orchid blooms in June and July, the large ivory-colored flower is striking amid the shadow-filled half light of pond apple sloughs (fig. 29). Donovan Correll (1950), a noted orchid biologist, described the flower as a "snow-white frog suspended in mid-air." This unique orchid in its native south-Florida habitat so impressed Carlyle Luer that he began an epic search to photograph and study every orchid species native to the United States

Figure 29. The ghost orchid (*Polyradicon lindeni*), found in Fakahatchee Strand and a few other similar swamps, is one of Florida's rarest epiphytic orchids.

and Canada, and eventually wrote two beautifully illustrated books (Luer 1972, 1975).

My first encounter with Polyradicon was in Fakahatchee Strand one June. It was my first trip beyond the road and I quickly learned how important a compass can be: after only a short distance, the thick canopy obscured the sun and there were no landmarks. I found that travel was easiest when I followed the meandering sloughs of pond apple and pop ash. Here the water was deeper and mostly free of other vegetation, and I could avoid the razor-sharp sawgrass. Walking knee-deep in the dark water was a refreshing and pleasant experience, once I became confident that the footing was secure and that large gators and snakes were either not present or not interested in me. I knew that the ghost orchid grew on pond apple and pop ash, and that it should be flowering. As I explored, I found several orchids attached to the trees. The most spectacular was a large clamshell orchid, which had several foot-high bloom spikes. Each flower had a dark purple–veined lip below which were five yellow sepals and petals (plate 7). From a distance, the flowers seemed to dance like puppets.

As the day wore on and I became less conscious of potential hazards, I nearly stepped on the biggest cottonmouth that I had ever seen! The dark brown snake, longer than my arm and about the same diameter, was basking on a fallen palm frond. Although I was only a few feet away, the lazy and confident cottonmouth merely bent its head back and opened its large, cotton-white mouth, revealing its sizable fangs. I left the old snake to its sun bath and continued my quest.

Finally, in one of the deeper sloughs, I at last saw ahead in the shadows something so white that I knew it could only be a flower. As I approached, wading through the tannin-stained water, I could see that it was a Polyradicon. I was amazed that such a large and elegant flower could come from such a puny mass of radiating roots. Leaning closer, I detected a pleasant perfume. The lovely, nearly hand-sized blossom seemed quite out of place there in the Strand, but that is where it survives and is infrequently pollinated by some large and unknown moth.

In Florida, the ghost orchid is restricted to the southernmost swamps, with the largest population probably in Fakahatchee Strand. It is also found in Cuba and in the Bahamas. Because of its limited range, as well as lack of data on population sizes throughout its range, it is essential that this beautiful and intriguing species be protected.

Insectivorous Plants

Insectivorous plants—pitcher plants, sundews, butterworts, and bladderworts—are common in Florida's wetlands, especially in the Panhandle, where twenty-nine species occur. The largest of these are the six species of pitcher plants, which occur in savannalike wetlands of the Panhandle. One of the tallest is the trumpet pitcher plant, nearly waist high, which resembles long green pipes with wine-colored lids (fig. 30). Another tall pitcher is the colorful white-top, which has knee-high trumpets whose upper portion and hood are pigmented snowy white with burgundy veins. Good places to look for pitcher plants and other insectivorous plants are Apalachicola National Forest, areas around Pensacola Bay, and in Okefenokee Swamp.

In the Okefenokee, insectivorous plants are abundant. One of the most conspicuous is the hooded pitcher plant, which thrives in open shrub bogs where Sphagnum moss a foot or more thick blankets the damp ground. It has pitchers over one foot tall, colored apple green

Figure 30. The trumpet pitcher (*Sarracenia flava*) is one of the many insectivorous plants found in Florida's wetlands. Insects are attracted to nectar produced around the lip of the trumpetlike leaf.

and rusty red, with white "windows" over the back of the hood (plate 13). Clumps of hooded pitcher plants grow beside the three-quarter-mile-long boardwalk near the Suwannee Canal (on the east side of the swamp).

Fascinating adaptations enable pitcher plants to be insect eaters (Schnell 1976; Slack 1979; Folkerts 1982). The hooded pitcher plant absorbs nutrients from insects that are digested in its hollow, water-filled, pitcherlike cavity, which is actually a modified leaf. Insects are attracted to the pitcher by nectar produced by the rim of the colorful overhanging hood. Ants, the primary prey, are attracted to the slippery ledge and fall into the watery tank below (Fish 1976). Insects are prevented from escaping by downward-pointing hairs lining the cavity. Eventually the ants drown and are digested by enzymes produced by the plants, which then absorb the nutrients. The success of this scheme can be readily seen in the bottoms of old pitchers, which contain the black chitinous remains of thousands of ants.

Carnivory in plants may have evolved in response to a shortage of nitrogen in acidic soils. Such soils are also deficient in essential trace elements like molybdenum, so the scarcity of these minerals may have led to insectivory (Folkerts 1982).

Amazingly, a variety of insects and mites purposely inhabit pitcher plants to either feed on the attracted prey or to eat the pitchers. These arthropods include larvae of mosquitos, flies, and moths; an aphid; and mites. Fourteen of these arthropod species are totally dependent on pitcher plants and live nowhere else (Folkerts 1982).

Bladderworts are widespread and common carnivorous plants that live in swamps, roadside ditches, ponds, and lakes throughout the South. The largest is the yellow-flowered floating bladderwort, which floats on a rosette of air-filled leaves arranged like wheel spokes. It absorbs nutrients from small aquatic invertebrates that, after touching sensitive hairs on submerged "trap leaves," are sucked into tiny saclike chambers and digested alive (Schnell 1976; Slack 1979). Several smaller bladderworts with grasslike leaves also grow terrestrially.

Two other groups of insectivorous plants frequent Florida's wetlands. These are butterworts and sundews. They live primarily in open sunny areas where a disturbance such as fire prevents a canopy of trees or shrubs from growing. Roadside ditches and power-line rights-of-way are other good places to see them. The prevalence of carnivorous plants along roadsides has led to the recent popularity of botanical "ditch trips."

Butterworts have a rosette of overlapping prostrate leaves an inch or two in length that curl inward at the edges. The pale-green or purple leaves have a pebbled texture from numerous secretory glands, which make the leaves feel greasy—hence the species' Latin name, *Pinguicula*, which comes from *pinguis*, meaning fat. Small insects are trapped and later digested by a sticky secretion produced by the glands.

Sundews also have a rosette of leaves that can be either prostrate or erect. The dark green leaves, which range from less than an inch to over a foot in length, have a narrow petiole or stalk, and usually a paddlelike blade. The blade is visibly studded with numerous red, hairlike glands that produce a sweet but sticky secretion that traps and digests insects. *Drosera*, the species' Greek name, refers to the dewlike drops at the tips of the hairs.

Vines

Vines are both plentiful and diverse in Florida's swamps. One of the most frequent is the greenbrier, represented by over ten species. Greenbriers are tough, sometimes finger-thick vines that may be armed with spines. They ramble through forested wetlands throughout Florida, especially in sunny areas. Poison ivy is another very common vine that grows in both sunny and shaded areas and is tolerant of flooding. Various grapes, Virginia creeper, and supple-jack are woody vines that climb high into the canopy and whose stems can reach diameters of several inches. All of these species produce fruits that are relished by birds and mammals.

Showy flowering vines found in swamps and hammocks include the early-spring-blooming yellow jessamine, whose colorful and fragrant flowers attract hungry swallowtail butterflies. Higher in the canopy are the tubular reddish flowers of the spring-blooming crossvine and the summer-blooming trumpet creeper, both of which are pollinated by ruby-throated hummingbirds.

One of the more unusual plants in our swamps is the climbing heath. Although it grows like a vine, it is actually an ericaceous shrub that climbs more than forty feet inside the bark of pond cypress and Atlantic white cedar. The climbing heath is especially common on pond cypress in the Okefenokee Swamp, where the racemes of small white flowers appear in winter.

Another atypical vine is the climbing aster. The profusely

branched, woody stems form fifteen-foot-high tangles in sunny swamps and along rivers and streams. The colorful purple and yellow flowers are produced in profusion in late summer.

In addition to these, there are even several vinelike ferns in Florida. Lygodium, for example, is an exotic climbing fern found in hammocks and swamps throughout the state.

With the possible exception of poison ivy, most vines are worth a closer look; and their generally tangled appearance adds much to the ambience of the swamp. To learn more about the woody vines of at least part of the state, see Godfrey's *Trees, Shrubs, and Woody Vines of Northern Florida and Adjacent Georgia and Alabama* (1988).

Shrubs

Trees may form the bulk of the plant biomass in swamps, but shrubs can be more diverse and numerous, and in shrub bogs they are the dominant woody plants. Shrubs comprise more than sixty species in north Florida's wetlands alone. Hollies, Viburnums, hawthorns, St. John's-worts, and members of the heather family (Ericaceae) are the most common and most various.

Perhaps the most abundant and widespread wetland shrub in Florida is the wax myrtle. This large shrub or small tree with aromatic leaves grows nearly everywhere, especially in disturbed sites. In fall, female wax myrtles produce clumps of tiny waxy fruits along the outer limbs, where they are eagerly eaten by such different species as yellow-rumped warblers and Florida black bears. Wax myrtle is also a prized landscaping shrub because of its adaptability. It can grow in nutrient-poor soil because it can fix atmospheric nitrogen—a trait usually found only in legumes.

Shrubs are most abundant in sunny wetlands like shrub bogs and cypress domes. Many species, such as ericaceous shrubs in the genera *Gaylussacia, Leucothoe,* and *Lyonia,* do well in peaty soils with low nutrients, and thus are common in shrub bogs and other rain-fed wetlands.

Shrubs are also important in hammocks. One of the most attractive is wild coffee, with its glossy red winter berries. Two species grow in south Florida hammocks. The glossy-leafed wild coffee has waxy leaves and produces small clumps of shiny, burgundy-red berries; the dull-leafed wild coffee has dull green leaves and produces more numerous reddish-orange BB-sized berries (plate 14). Wild coffee was contemplated as a substitute for coffee during World War I, but was never used because it may be poisonous.

Beautyberry is another ubiquitous and colorful hammock shrub. It has attractive clusters of pale pink flowers appearing from April to July. Later in the year, showy clumps of vivid purple berries surround the stems near the leaves. Catbirds, northern cardinals, brown thrashers, and many other birds eat the berries. Fruits from beautyberry and other shrubs are also important foods for Florida black bears (Maehr and DeFrazio 1985).

Shrubs are also beneficial to insects. The globelike flowers of buttonbush are important nectar sources for swallowtail butterflies. Other shrubs, mostly those with racemes of white flowers, including titi, black titi, sweet pepperbush, and Virginia willow, also attract butterflies and bees. Azaleas are enjoyed by both butterflies and people. The pale pink, fragrant flowers of the wild azalea seem to glow amid the more somber browns and greens so prevalent in our swamps on those cool rainy days in March. The coral-to-white bells of ericaceous shrubs like dog-hobble, fetterbush, and staggerbush lure bees, offering nectar in spring and early summer. Two helpful sources of information on shrubs are Godfrey's *Trees, Shrubs, and Woody Vines of Northern Florida and Adjacent Georgia and Alabama* and Foote and Jones's *Native Shrubs and Woody Vines of the Southeast.*

Hardwood Trees

Hardwoods generally are the dominant plants in swamps, especially river swamps. More than a hundred species of hardwoods and large shrubs live in Florida's forested wetlands. In fact, some blackwater swamps are called mixed-hardwood swamps because hardwoods such as tupelo, pop ash, maple, and sweetgum predominate. Gum swamps often contain nearly pure stands of even-aged swamp tupelo; bayheads contain sweetbay and loblolly bay (fig. 31). Even in cypress swamps, hardwoods such as water and swamp tupelo frequently outnumber the cypress. Although hardwoods are plentiful in swamps, the greatest richness appears to be where soils are neither too wet nor too dry, such as in moist sites of other wetland types like hydric hammocks. Wetlands often have a higher tree diversity than adjacent uplands.

Perhaps the most common and widely distributed hardwood in our wetlands is the familiar red maple. Found in swamps from Maine

Figure 31. The sweetbay (*Magnolia virginiana*) is a common wetland tree that produces large, fragrant white flowers in April and May. It can be dominant in depressional wetlands known as bayheads.

to south Florida, it is one of the few temperate trees adapted to the subtropical climate of southern Florida. One reason for its success may be its ability to cope with Florida's unpredictable winter weather, which features sudden cold fronts alternating with warmer periods. These variable conditions provide conflicting temperature cues, which are responsible for triggering dormancy or growth. Somehow, red maples adapt to these confusing signals, with each tree seeming to have its own rhythm: some maples are seen with seeds in January, while others, quite close by, have flowers, or are bare!

Three hardwoods that grow in wetlands need to be mentioned just because of their unusual bark or trunk ornamentation. These are water locust, river birch, and sugarberry. The water locust has long, branched spines jutting outward from the trunk on short stems. River birch has rusty colored, papery bark that peels off in sheets. Sugarberry (hackberry) has thick, corky growths on the trunk, ornamenting the bark of older trees. The pea-sized orange sugarberries produced in autumn are relished by wildlife.

To those just learning the diverse Southeastern tree flora, the inconsistency in tree names makes it a difficult task. Common names are the worst, with swamp tupelo being called "gum," "black gum," "swamp black gum," or even "tupelo gum." Swamp tupelo as "black gum" could easily be confused with black tupelo, which is also called "black gum." Even the scientific names are confusing, since some botanists treat swamp tupelo as a valid species—*Nyssa biflora*—while others view it as a variety of black tupelo—*Nyssa sylvatica* var. *biflora*. If you are not confused yet, Brown and Kirkman (1990) point out in *Trees of Georgia and Adjacent States* that "black gum" is a misnomer since the trees produce neither gum nor latex! Botanist Daniel Austin says that the gums were named for the frequent presence of bee hives (gums) in hollow tupelos. Perhaps it is just easier to remember that tupelos all belong to the genus *Nyssa*—the river nymph.

Another wetland tree, the familiar sweetgum, does, however, produce a true gum from its inner bark. It is eaten by sapsuckers, which drill numerous rows of holes around the trunk. Early white settlers gave the sweet sap to their children to help them swallow bitter-tasting medicines. During the summer, sweetgum leaves release a fragrant oil when crushed.

Hardwood trees are essential to the swamp ecosystem, providing food and shelter for a variety of animals. Their green leaves are eaten by numerous insects. Later, when the dead leaves fall and become flooded, they are colonized by fungi and are soon eaten by aquatic insects. The energy-rich sap is tapped by many birds and insects. Mast, made up of fruit, acorns, nuts, and seeds produced by the trees, is relished by deer, bears, and numerous birds, especially wild turkeys. The decaying wood is consumed by termites and a variety of fungi, which are in turn eaten by boring insects and rodents.

Trees also provide shelter to animals ranging from mosquitos to wood ducks. They also furnish a three-dimensional substrate colonized by epiphytes including algae, fungi, lichens, ferns, bromeliads, and orchids. In addition, trees benefit swamps in less obvious ways. For example, their leafy canopy moderates changes in temperature and humidity, keeping the swamp climate relatively stable. Trees also provide the ingredients for much of the peaty soil in swamps.

Trees serve many functions in forested wetlands, and many of these are just now becoming known. Some alien trees, however, are threatening the very framework of our wetlands. Two of the worst of these are Melaleuca (punk tree) and the peppertree (Brazilian pepper or Florida holly).

Melaleuca was introduced to south Florida from Australia in the early 1900s to "forest the Everglades" and to serve as an ornamental plant. Plant collectors gathered seeds from trees growing in areas of Australia that had a climate similar to that of south Florida. Now an estimated six billion (yes, *billion*) Melaleuca trees cover parts of south Florida, including the Everglades, where Melaleuca has invaded more than forty-five hundred square miles. Melaleuca is highly tolerant, living in sites that alternately flood and dry and frequently burn (Myers 1984; Ewel 1986). Droughts and fires have benefited this pest, which has thick layers of fire-resistant bark. In fact, fires stimulate the opening of ripe seed capsules, releasing millions of wind-blown seeds. Perhaps the most significant factor in the spread of Melaleuca has been the large-scale draining of south Florida, which has been compounded by Melaleuca's high transpiration rate, leading to further water losses.

Efforts are underway in the Everglades and Loxahatchee National Wildlife Refuge, as well as elsewhere in south Florida, to eradicate Melaleuca. Herbicides are the primary tool, but it is hoped that biological controls such as herbivorous insects and parasitic fungi may someday be effective.

Another exotic plant invading large areas of south Florida is the peppertree (Ewel et al. 1982; Ewel 1986). Like Melaleuca, it was deliberately introduced into Florida. The peppertree requires better-drained soils than Melaleuca, but is more tolerant of shade, enabling it to invade hammocks and other woodlands. However, it does best in disturbed areas, and quickly spreads along roads, fire trails, ditch banks, and power-line rights-of-way. Like Melaleuca, peppertrees can form dense thickets, crowding out native plants. In addition, they may produce a toxic substance that prevents even shade-tolerant species from growing close by.

During the late summer, peppertrees produce masses of tiny white flowers that are readily pollinated by bees and wasps. In winter, thousands of small red berries form. These are relished by robins, catbirds, opossums, raccoons, and bears—all of which scatter the seeds widely. This species is so widespread in south Florida that organized efforts are needed to control it.

Obviously Melaleuca, peppertrees, and a host of other exotic wetland plants such as water hyacinth, wild taro, and Hydrilla are now major components of our biota. Botanist Daniel Austin estimates that nearly one-third of the vascular plants in Florida are exotic (Daniel Austin, Florida Atlantic Univ., pers. comm., 1992). Exotics are in Florida to stay; we can't change that. If we act now, however, we may be able to mitigate their negative impact on natural areas.

 7

Creepy Crawlers and Flashy Fliers

An abundance of food and water and a relatively stable environment provide nearly ideal conditions for many animals in Florida's swamps. Butterflies, birds, and frogs are among the most noticeable swamp animals, but they are vastly outnumbered by scores of species of small insects, and by even greater numbers of tardigrades, rotifers, ostracods, nematodes, and sundry other microscopic animals that lurk in the dark water, creep over submerged vegetation, or crawl through moist soil. In this chapter you will meet some familiar and some not-so-familiar swamp critters.

Mollusks

Snails, slugs, and even freshwater clams are some of the many invertebrate animals that live in wetlands. About eighty species of terrestrial mollusks occur in Florida, with snails dominating. In swamps, most snails are small and drab and therefore go unnoticed, but a few snails are large and colorful. Tree snails are the most arresting. One of these is the brightly banded Florida tree snail, or "lig," which lives in tropical hammocks of southernmost Florida (Deisler 1982). The two-inch-long, conical snails can be ivory white or banded by green, yellow, brown, or pink. Many distinctive color varieties have been described, but eager shell collectors have decimated some populations. Color variants are a result of genetic differences established by isolation in individual hammocks. Using their rasplike tongues, ligs graze micro-scopic plants from smooth-barked tropical hardwoods (Voss 1976).

Most of our other tree snails are less colorful, but they are nonethe-less absorbing. One of these is the manatee snail. It has a one-inch-long, thin, nearly transparent shell with brown markings similar to tortoise shell. One June evening, I was exploring a blackwater swamp in Bull Creek Wildlife Management Area near Melbourne, Florida. Under the dense hardwood canopy it was dark, and large raindrops began falling. Soon the tree trunks trickled with water, and then I noticed the manatee snails beginning to creep about. They glided effortlessly over the moist, multicolored mosses and lichens encrust-ing the trunks of maple and sweetgum, grazing the crusty vegetation (fig. 32). The snails' pale gray bodies were fully extended some two inches. During droughts, the manatee snail secretes a protective plug that covers its operculum (the cover for its shell opening), reducing water loss.

Another woodland snail native to Florida is Euglandina. Its spindle-shaped, pinkish to orange-brown shell is from one to two

Figure 32. A half-inch-long manatee snail (*Drymaeus dormani*) grazes lichens, fungi, and algae from the trunk of a red maple in a central-Florida swamp.

inches long. The extended, flesh-colored foot and head are also about one inch long. Euglandina's upper fleshy lip is drawn out laterally, forming a pair of curled, tentaclelike "mustaches." Like other land snails, it also has two pairs of smaller tentacles.

Euglandina lives in moist woods where it is a nocturnal predator of slugs and snails up to twice its size (Chiu and Chou 1962; Auffenberg and Stange 1986). During its one- to two-year life span, a Euglandina will eat more than three hundred prey. It swallows small mollusks whole; to eat larger snails, it sticks its mouth into the shell aperture and consumes the animal alive.

This snail was released in Hawaii, Tahiti, Bermuda, and elsewhere to eliminate the giant African snail, an exotic vegetarian pest. Unfortunately, Euglandina preferred instead to eat native tree snails and thus became an unwanted exotic pest itself.

One of our largest snails is the apple snail. The brownish golf-ball-sized shells are common along the shores of rivers or lakes and on the dry bottoms of sloughs and ponds. The apple snail is primarily tropical, occurring only as far north as southernmost Georgia. It lives in swamps, ponds, lakes, streams and rivers, where it browses on submerged vegetation. If its pond dries up, the apple snail burrows into the mud, where it is protected from desiccation by slime and its thin but strong and impermeable shell.

Apple snails survive in water with little oxygen by climbing a leaf or twig to the surface and extending a two-inch-long snorkel into the air. The snail then pumps air into a "lung" and returns to deeper water and resumes feeding. It also has gills that are adequate when the water is well oxygenated. Apple snails reproduce by laying clumps of twenty to thirty pearl-sized, calcified eggs. These cream-colored egg clusters are placed above the high-water line on emergent aquatic vegetation including cypress trunks and knees, where they are quite conspicuous.

Because apple snails are large and easily captured, they are eaten by many animals, including alligators, the endangered snail kite (or Everglades kite), limpkins, boat-tailed grackles, and probably raccoons and river otters. Apple snails were also consumed in large numbers by the Calusa Indians, who inhabited south Florida for several thousand years before the Spanish reached America.

Slugs are shell-less mollusks closely related to snails. Three slugs are native to Florida, and several others have been introduced (Stange 1978). The most common is the two- to four-inch-long brown or dark gray Philomycus, whose slime trails are sometimes apparent on the trunks of trees in damp forests. Although common, Philomycus is seldom seen because it lives high in trees where it feeds mostly at night (Ingram 1949). After a daytime rain it can sometimes be found crawling lower along tree trunks. Slugs are hermaphroditic, which enables them potentially to mate with every slug they meet—a distinct advantage if mates are rare. Eggs are laid on the soil or hidden in crevices. Young slugs begin feeding soon after hatching.

Surprisingly, clams also occur in our swamps. The most numerous are the tiny fingernail clams, which have thin shells. Fingernail clams can be especially abundant in backwater pools left by receding waters in alluvial river swamps. Several species of much larger freshwater mussels also live in our rivers and streams. These bivalve mollusks are eaten by a great variety of predators ranging from fish to otters, and were an important food for southeastern Indians. Throughout the Southeast, these mussels are imperiled by habitat loss and pollution.

Crustaceans

Crustaceans are crabs, shrimp, crayfish, pill bugs, and related species. Although a few live on land, most are aquatic, and most are microscopic. Tiny, but numerous, copepods swim through the water; others, such as ostracods, creep over the flooded forest floor. Larger crustaceans like pill bugs live under moist debris. Our largest terrestrial crustacean is the blue land crab, which digs six-inch-diameter holes in coastal hammocks and mangrove swamps in southern Florida. Smaller, but more plentiful, are the fiddler crabs that excavate finger-sized burrows along tidal river swamps. The larvae of these crabs develop in the ocean and migrate back up the river.

Of our larger wetland crustaceans, crayfish are the most diverse and widespread. In Florida there are fifty crayfish species, thirty of which are endemic (Franz and Franz 1990). Those crayfish that live in swamps are primarily nocturnal. During the day, they retire to burrows that are surrounded by a characteristic "chimney"—a cone-shaped mound of soil up to six inches high made from marble-sized soil balls. These burrows form important moist refuges for many animals, including fish, salamanders, an unusual frog called the crayfish frog, and snakes, which may even hibernate in them (Wharton et al. 1981).

Crayfish are most numerous in productive alluvial swamps, where

Plate 1. Column stinkhorn fungus (*Linderia columnatus*) emerged from the ground.

Plate 2. Baton rouge lichens (*Chiodecton rubricintum*) on the trunk of a cabbage palm.

Plate 3. Hand fern (*Ophioglossum palmatum*) growing among bootjacks of a cabbage palm.

Plate 4. Swamp lilies (*Crinum americanum*) flowering near a hammock in the Big Cypress.

Plate 5. Golden club aroid (*Orontium aquaticum*) flowers and leaves.

Plate 6. Cardinal wild pine bromeliad (*Tillandsia fasciculata*).

Plate 7. Clam-shell orchid (*Encyclia cochleata*) flower.

Plate 8. Meadow beauty (*Rhexia* sp.) flowers.

Plate 9. Catesby's lily (*Lilium catesbaei*) with lynx spider.

Plate 10. Yellow-fringed orchid (*Platanthera ciliaris*) flowers.

Plate 11. Cardinal flower (*Lobelia cardinalis*) spike.

Plate 12. Pickerel-weed (*Pontederia cordata*) flower spike.

Plate 13. Hooded pitcher plant (*Sarracenia minor*) pitchers and flowers.

Plate 14. Glossy-leafed wild coffee (*Psychotria nervosa*) leaves and berries.

Plate 15. Fetterbush (*Lyonia lucida*) flowers.

Plate 16. Red fruits of sweetbay (*Magnolia virginiana*) hanging from "cone."

Plate 17. Black and yellow Argiope spider (*Argiope aurantia*) on decorated web.

Plate 18. Polyphemus moth (*Antheraea polyphemus*) eyespots and antennae.

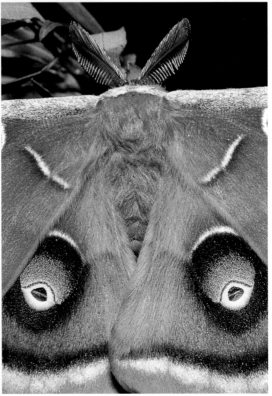

Plate 19. *(right)* Spicebush swal-lowtail caterpillar (*Papilio troilus*).

Plate 20. *(below)* Ruddy daggerwing butterfly (*Marpesia petreus*).

Plate 21. *(left)* Caterpillar of the ruddy daggerwing butterfly (*Marpesia petreus*).

Plate 22. *(below)* Viceroy butterfly (*Basilarchia archippus*) on button-bush flowers.

Plate 23. *(above)* Red-banded hairstreak butterfly (*Calycopis cecrops*) on sweet pepperbush flowers.

Plate 24. *(left)* Lubber grasshoppers (*Romalea microptera*) mating in a saw palmetto.

Plate 25. Southern spring peeper (*Pseudacris crucifer bartramiana*) with X on back.

Plate 26. Bird-voiced treefrog (*Hyla avivoca*) singing with air-filled throat pouch.

Plate 27. *(right)* Green treefrog (*Hyla cinerea*).

Plate 28. *(below)* Yellow rat snake (*Elaphe obsoleta quadrivittata*) basking.

Plate 29. Male green anole (*Anolis carolinensis*) displaying reddish dewlap.

Plate 30. Florida redbelly turtle (*Pseudemys nelsoni*) close-up of yellow-striped head.

Plate 31. Limpkin (*Aramus guarauna*) family along Alexander Springs Run. Photo by Kathy Larson.

Plate 32. Great blue heron (*Ardea herodias*).

they feed on plant material, detritus, and small invertebrates. A number of larger animals eat crayfish, including fish, snakes, alligators, turtles, white ibis, barred owls, red-shouldered hawks, raccoons, mink, otters, and humans (Wharton et al. 1981). In Louisiana, where crayfish are highly esteemed, they form a multimillion-dollar fishery. They are also farmed in the Southeast in swamps where the hydroperiod and organic detritus are manipulated to increase productivity.

Spiders

In summer and autumn, Florida's hammocks and swamps are ornamented with gossamer webs of diurnal orb-building spiders. The most spectacular is Nephila, the golden-silk spider, which constructs a large amber-tinted web. A mature female Nephila can spread nearly across one's palm. The abdomen of the female is yellowish-orange above and cinnamon below. Her legs have black tufts of furlike hairs. The male, which lives with the female (but on the other side of the web), is tiny in comparison—only about one inch long and one one-hundredth of the female's weight. (Comstock 1948; Weems and Edwards 1978).

Unlike most orb-web spiders, which build a new web daily, Nephila makes its web to last. The web is also large, extending six feet in diameter and reaching outward twenty or more feet for support. Along roads, these spiders often build their webs between power lines, and thousands of spiders may occur per mile, forming a giant aerial insect net. Nephila's web must be strong to capture large prey like dragonflies and cicadas. The normal prey are smaller insects like bees, flies, and small lepidoptera, but small birds may sometimes become trapped in the webs as well. In South Carolina, Alexander Sprunt, Jr., found several unfortunate yellow-throated and yellow-rumped warblers caught in these webs (Griscom and Sprunt 1957).

In his captivating book about spiders, John Henry Comstock (1948) wrote that "the silk of the spiders of the genus Nephila surpasses in strength and in beauty that of the silkworm." He further reported that Nephila spiders in Madagascar were reared especially for their silk, the threads being drawn "from each of a considerable number of [living] spiders at the same time; and . . . twisted into a single larger thread, by a mechanical twister, from which it passes to a reel." This process was shown at the one of the Paris Expositions, and a complete set of bed hangings made from Nephila silk was exhibited (Comstock 1948).

The strong silk of Nephila is also used by Polynesians for nets and bags (Weems and Edwards 1978). Furthermore, the Polynesians eat female Nephilas, which have a flavor described as "like peanut butter without the sticky consistency." Perhaps we may someday eat "McNephila" under the golden arches!

Nephila females grow quickly. First visible in late winter, they become conspicuous by March and April, and by June some are already more than one inch in body length. By summer's end, they are plump with developing eggs. The young spiders hatch from a silk-covered egg sac deposited under the bark of a tree or in a similar hiding place.

When you come upon the web of a Nephila, look closely around the edge for small Argyrodes spiders, which have a silvery, triangular abdomen. These kleptoparasites feed by pirating small prey from the web. Apparently, if they become too numerous the female Nephila will leave and build another web elsewhere (Weems and Edwards 1978).

Another spider that makes prominent webs in swamps and hammocks is the strange Gasteracantha—the spiny orb-weaver. Although its web is two to three feet across, with support threads extending two or three times this distance, the spider is puny—less than half an inch across (Edwards 1988). As with Nephila and many other spider species, Gasteracantha males are smaller than the females.

Despite being small, the female Gasteracantha is showy: her carapace is spiked with a halo of reddish "thorns" that frame the flattened, bean-shaped abdomen, which is cream-colored on top and black beneath. Her name is appropriate: *Gasteracantha* translates as "spiny stomach." If you look closer, you can see a "face" on the abdomen, made by a series of black dots that resemble chunks of charcoal studding the head of a snowman. Because of its winsome grin, this happy-faced spider is one of Kathy's favorites.

The web of Gasteracantha can be readily identified even without the spider. That's because a series of whitish tufts or decorations are stitched onto some of the support threads and around the rim of the web. These tufts reflect ultraviolet light, which might attract UV-sensitive insect prey (Craig and Bernard 1990). Alternatively, because these decorations are mostly on support threads, they may advertise the web to birds, mammals, and larger flying insects that could damage it (Eisner and Nowicki 1983). Unlike Nephila's webs, those of

Gasteracantha are rebuilt daily, and the spider recycles the old web by eating it.

Two related spiders occurring in swamps are the arrow-shaped Micrathena and the spined Micrathena. Like Gasteracantha, they are less than one inch long and have spines on their abdomens. The Micrathena has two long black spines protruding rearward from its lemon-yellow abdomen. These spines and its small head give the spider its arrow shape. The spined Micrathena has a thick, irregularly shaped black-and-white abdomen with small reddish spines. As in Gasteracantha, the Micrathena males are half the size of the females.

Another of Kathy's favorites is the small, clown-faced *Leucauge,* which has an orange-lipstick smile and eyes like M&Ms. These colorful markings on the underside of the pea-sized abdomen highlight this greenish spider in its dark surroundings. Leucauge lives in many habitats, and it hangs upside down on its elaborate horizontal web, with its smiling face turned skyward. Perhaps the orange markings lure small insects into its web.

Around the margins of swamps is another orb weaver, the black and yellow *Argiope* (plate 17). This fairly large spider, about two inches long, generally builds its web on low vegetation, often over water. Its thorax is covered with short, silvery hairs, making it appear coated with mercury. These silvery hairs may keep the spider cool by reflecting sunlight. The abdomen is coal black, with sulfur-yellow and silver markings. Perhaps this bold pattern mimics that of the hornet—one insect that is avoided by birds.

Argiope's web is noticeable because it often has one or more whitish vertical bands of silk, thickly woven in a crisscross or zigzag pattern, that radiate from the center of the web. This decoration, or stabilimentum, reflects ultraviolet light and may lure insects into the web (Craig and Bernard 1990). (Flying insects are sometimes attracted to UV because they use it to find open spaces in the forest. Many flowers also have UV-bright patterns to entice insect pollinators.) The decorations could also serve to make the webs more visible to vertebrates, which could avoid them. They may also serve to make the spider less conspicuous as it sits over the decoration. The stabilimentum may have many functions, but, contrary to its name, it probably does not make the web more stable (Foelix 1982).

Swamps are also home to spiders that do not build webs, such as the fishing spiders. These are also called nursery-web spiders because their young hatch within an elaborate, specialized web or "nursery."

Fishing spiders are related to wolf spiders, which feed by pouncing on prey. They detect prey visually, or can sense the vibrations caused by insects flying or walking nearby. This was amply demonstrated one night in Belize, when I unknowingly held a fluttering silk moth near a large, hairy, black Cupiennius wolf spider. Suddenly the spider jumped a considerable distance toward me and the vibrating moth, which I instantly dropped and the spider grabbed!

Fishing spiders walk on water by means of special hairs on their feet that prevent the surface tension from breaking. Some fishing spiders can even dive, clutching an air bubble that supplies oxygen while they are submerged.

The largest fishing spider in Florida, and one of the largest spiders native to the United States, is the four-inch-long Okefenokee Dolomedes—a richly marked, dark brown spider that frequents the trunks of swamp trees (fig. 33). These big spiders are capable of capturing sizable prey. For example, Carlyle Luer photographed one with a captured crayfish (Luer 1972). Dolomedes has even been seen feeding on minnows in the St. Johns River (Barbour 1944). Thomas Barbour (1944) wrote: "A tiny flash of silver caught my eye, and I looked again, to see a spider carrying a small dead fish, perhaps an inch long, across a wide leaf to the dark interior of a large [water] lettuce cluster. I thought that possibly the spider had found a dead fish by chance and I relit my pipe, when about six feet away in another direction the episode was repeated. This time the little fish was still struggling feebly in the spider's chelicerae."

A female nursery-web spider spins a silken ball nearly as big as her body to contain her eggs. To protect them, she carries this ball around by holding it with her large chelicerae (mouthparts tipped with fangs). "No more striking instance of maternal devotion is to be found among spiders" (Comstock 1948). Willis Gertsch, an authority on spiders, further commented (1979): "From the time it is made until the spiderlings are ready to emerge, the mother carries the treasure around with her where ever she may go, holding it between her legs and underneath her body. It's often so large that the mother must run on the tips of her tarsi in order to hold it clear of the ground."

Shortly before the young hatch, the female secures her egg ball within a tentlike nursery web suspended between leaves. After hatching, the spiderlings remain in the nursery for about a week, during which the female often stands guard. In Highlands Hammock, Kathy

Figure 33. A four-inch-long Okefenokee Dolomedes spider (*Dolomedes okefenokensis*) sits on a pop ash trunk waiting for insect prey to pass by.

and I once found a female Pisaurina nursery-web spider. She was dark brown with a prominent cream-colored line running down each side of her body. For the protection of her marble-sized brood she had constructed a silken nursery by pulling together the leaves of a primrose willow. This behavior may prevent certain wasps from laying their eggs on the spider egg masses. The maternal care shown by these spiders is unusual among invertebrates.

Before leaving the spiders, I want to mention one of their close relatives, the harvestmen or daddy-long-legs. Harvestmen can be numerous in swamps, especially alluvial swamps. One May, Kathy and I saw hundreds of them resting on low plants along the river at Torreya State Park. They were relatively large, some four to five inches from leg tip to leg tip. Harvestmen are usually inactive during the day, but at night they search for insect prey or feed on other small invertebrates, dead animals, or suck fluids from plants.

Insects

Moths

Lepidoptera (moths and butterflies) are among the most striking swamp animals. Who has not marveled at the colorful swallowtail butterflies flying through our wetlands in spring and summer? Although moths are seen less often than butterflies, they are vastly more numerous. Their caterpillar larvae eat the leaves of swamp plants and can sometimes defoliate trees over sizable areas. Both larvae and adult moths are important prey for spiders, treefrogs, lizards, birds, and bats and thus play a crucial role in wetland ecosystems.

Although most moths are small and drab, some, such as the silkmoths, are among the largest and most beautiful insects. One of the most spectacular of these is the Luna moth. Finding a satin-sheened Luna "asleep" on a gnarled cypress knee in a dark swamp is a memorable experience. The lime-green wings are ornamented with long graceful tails, and a deep maroon arch frames the thickened edge of the forewing. Each wing contains a single small but prominent eye-spot. The Luna's plump body is hairy, like that of a small mammal. Golden antennae adorn the head. The paired antennae of the male are large and delicately branched like miniature radar antennas.

Adult silkmoths, including the Luna, do not feed, and therefore they are short-lived. Their brief life is devoted solely to reproduction. Silkmoths are so widely dispersed that they must have a highly evolved mechanism for locating one another. By day these moths are torpid; but at dusk they begin twitching their strong flight muscles, warming them up. After a few minutes, they flutter off for a night of sex. Females lure mates by releasing a pheromone, a chemical sex attractant so enticing that it draws males from distances of a mile or more (the perfume industry has been diligently trying to do this for humans, but with less success). The large antennae of males have more than a thousand sensory hairs, which literally sieve the air to capture the scarce pheromone molecules, enabling males to detect females from just a few molecules of scent.

After mating, the female lays many eggs on the appropriate food plant, and then dies within a week. The finger-sized caterpillars, translucent green with rows of black dots, feed on the leaves of various trees, including pecan, red maple, hickories, sweetgum, willows, and others (Holland [1903] 1968; Brown 1972; Covell 1984).

Because there is so little protein in leaves, the larvae must eat vast quantities to grow to maturity. Once a larva reaches its maximum size, it spins a silken, paper-thin cocoon about one inch long by three-quarters of an inch in diameter. The cocoon is spun among leaves on a twig; or the caterpillar crawls to the ground and spins its cocoon among fallen leaves (Brown 1972). When the cocoon is touched, the pupa inside wiggles, attempting to frighten off the curious.

Another superb silkmoth that frequents our swamps and hammocks is the Polyphemus, which is perhaps our most common large moth. The five- to six-inch-broad forewings and body are a rich chestnut brown that blends with the bark of trees. The moth looks furry because of its hairlike scales. When the hindwings flash open, two yellow "eyes" rimmed with black stare from a furry face, making the moth look convincingly like a mammal or owl (plate 18). The effect must be startling to small predators, perhaps allowing the moth to escape. Experiments, in fact, have shown that insects with eyespots are avoided by some birds (Blest 1957).

The Polyphemus larvae are no less attractive than the adults: they are two inches long, translucent, and lime green with rows of orange or pink papillae (each with a protruding stiff bristle). They feed chiefly on oak leaves but also eat those of hickory, elm, maple, pine, birch, wax myrtle, and others (Holland [1903] 1968; Brown 1972; Covell 1984). Like most moth larvae, Polyphemus caterpillars are camouflaged and thus are difficult to see amid the foliage on which they feed.

The large Polyphemus cocoon, which hangs from the food plant, is about the size and shape of a small hen's egg with bluntly rounded ends. It is made of silk like that of the Luna moth, but instead of being papery, it is thick and extremely tough, like felt. To discourage vertebrate predators from eating the pupa, the larva secretes calcium oxalate crystals into the cocoon, which when tasted produce an intense burning sensation. The cocoons are commonly seen on wax myrtle where they may remain for some time attached to the leaves. If the moth has emerged, the cocoon will have a pencil-sized hole at the upper end. This opening is produced by an enzyme called cocoonase that is secreted by the emerging moth.

Yet another attractive silkmoth in our swamps is the sweetbay silkmoth (fig. 34). Its white larvae eat sweetbay leaves, hiding on the undersides where they are rarely seen. The cocoon is spun among the leaves. The wings of the moths are delicately pigmented in brownish hues above, rusty below.

Figure 34. A newly emerged sweetbay silkmoth (*Callosamia securifera*) rests beside its silken, leaf-shrouded cocoon. The caterpillars eat only the leaves of sweetbay.

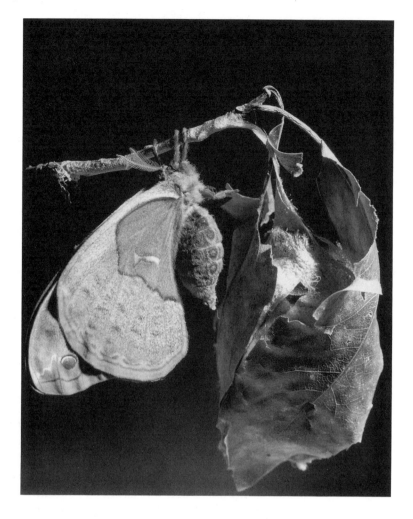

Most silkmoths are uncommon, and unfortunately they are becoming imperiled. Habitat destruction and pesticides are among the possible causes of their losses. But researcher Douglas Ferguson, who specializes in silkmoths, feels that outdoor mercury-vapor lighting is the major culprit (Ferguson 1971). The largely nocturnal moths are strongly attracted to outdoor lamps that give off UV light. Endlessly circling the lights, they ignore potential mates. A further barrier to their reproduction occurs when they collide with the lamps and become trapped in the fixtures.

Among the most abundant medium-sized moths in our swamps are the underwings. They are smaller than the silkmoths, about two inches long. These members of the Noctuid family flash their colorful, often red, underwings when flying, but they magically disappear when they land on tree trunks, covering their underwings with camouflaged forewings. Besides startling or confusing predators, the prominent coloration of the hindwings serves to direct the attention of avian predators away from the more vulnerable body (Sargent 1976). Thus, bite marks from birds tend to be concentrated on the hindwings. This is similar to the function of small eyespots on the margins of butterflies' wings (Blest 1957). Underwing moths are cryptic, having wing patterns that mimic the bark on which they spend the day. The variable patterns make it difficult for birds to learn specific search images; also, the moths may instinctively seek bark with colors that closely resemble their own markings.

W. J. Holland ([1903] 1968), in his enjoyable moth book, described the baiting of underwings at night by "sugaring": "What is there? Oho! My beauty! Just above the moistened patch upon the bark is a great catocala. The gray upperwings are spread, revealing the lower wings gloriously banded with black and crimson. In the yellow light of the lantern the wings appear even more brilliant than they do in sunlight. How the eyes glow like spots of fire!"

Butterflies

Butterflies add brilliant and varied colors to our emerald swamps. Unlike most moths, which are cryptic and nocturnal, butterflies are frequently gaudy and are strictly diurnal, and thus we take more notice of them. In fact, butterflies want to be seen. They flaunt bright hues to attract mates. Or they may advertise to predators that they are defended by noxious chemicals. Yet most of them are palatable, and they can only avoid being eaten by being superb fliers—bold aerialists.

Florida has more than 160 species of butterflies, many of which are large and showy (Gerberg and Arnett 1989), and it is one of the few states where butterflies are active in winter. While much of the United States is blanketed under snow, butterflies sip nectar at Florida's wildflowers.

Some butterflies are fast and strong fliers that cover great distances searching for mates or for such foods as nectar, rotten fruit, tree sap, and even dung and carrion. Others are intrepid migrators. Eastern populations of monarchs may fly hundreds of miles toward the Gulf Coast and through Florida as they head to their wintering colonies, possibly as far south as Guatemala. Less well known are the gulf fritillaries, which fly south each fall through Georgia and Alabama and into Florida (Arbogast 1966). These brightly colored butterflies, related to zebra longwings, are orange-winged above with silvery spots below. Various other butterflies, including cloudless sulfurs and long-tailed skippers, fly to Florida by the millions each fall from Georgia and perhaps farther north. No reverse flights in spring are evident, so these are not true migrations. The reasons for these movements are poorly understood, but they may be related to availability of larval food plants.

Because nectar-producing flowers and larval food plants are patchy, many butterflies must spend much time searching for them. Swallowtails are seemingly nonstop fliers, while sedentary species like pearly-eyes may remain in one area for their entire, albeit short, lives.

Despite the year-round availability of nectar in Florida, flower abundance and diversity change with the seasons. The white flowers of the Virginia willow are vernal favorites. Later, globelike button-bush flowers are much sought after, especially by swallowtails, which seem to have a pecking order at the choice feeding sites, with the larger swallowtails dominating. In summer, the white racemes of titi (in June) and sweet pepperbush (July and August) entice swallow-tails, skippers, and other butterflies (plate 23). The blue-flowered pickerelweed is also very attractive throughout the summer. In autumn, hungry butterflies seek the tall white-flowered frostweed. One October, Kathy and I marveled at the variety of species, including gulf fritillaries, monarchs, queens, swallowtails, skippers, zebra long-wings, and viceroys, that nectared on the eight-foot-high frostweeds on Hontoon Island in the St. Johns River. In winter, weedy beggar's-ticks are a critical source of nectar for overwintering butterflies, especially farther north where there are few winter flowers.

Our largest and most colorful butterflies are the swallowtails. Four species are common in Florida's swamps. One of the most engaging is the spicebush swallowtail, which has velvety black wings with creamy-colored lunules (markings that look like a crescent moon), and a luminous bluish-green frost across the hindwings. The under-sides of the hindwings have conspicuous sunset-orange spots.

Spicebush swallowtail larvae feed on the leaves of spicebush, swampbay, and sweetbay. The young larvae look like bird droppings, but as they grow and molt, they become green and have two pairs of eyespots atop a false head. One eyespot pair is prominent—each eye with a large black pupil surrounded by orange—and the other pair is smaller, tinted orange and without a pupil (plate 19).

Spicebush swallowtail larvae make nests by forming on a leaf a silken pad that contracts when it dries, causing the leaf margin to curl inward. From this refuge, the caterpillar makes feeding forays several times a day and then returns to the safety of its leafy shelter to slowly digest its meal. It apparently finds its way back to its nest by leaving a trail of silk. When disturbed, the larva arches its head back and protrudes a fleshy, bifurcated projection (osmeterium), which emits a pungent odor of the larva's food plant. All swallowtail caterpillars can extend these protrusions, which are just as quickly retracted.

One of our most common swallowtail butterflies is the tiger. Males and most females (there are two color phases for females) both have bright yellow wings with contrasting black tiger stripes and a black, yellow-spotted border. Tiger caterpillars also resemble bird droppings when young, but later turn green or brown and have small eyespots with a robin's-egg-blue iris outlined by black and gold; a yellow or brown collar is behind the eyespots. Tiger swallowtail larvae can feed on a wide variety of plants, but in south Florida may eat only sweetbay leaves (Scriber 1986). The finger-sized larva rests exposed on the upper side of a leaf, but its dark green coloration makes it inconspicuous.

The large brownish Palamedes swallowtail abounds in our swamps, especially where there are bay trees on which the larvae feed. In April, it is one of the most common butterflies in areas near north Florida wetlands, and is especially plentiful at Okefenokee.

Kathy and I found our first Palamedes larva living on a swampbay in Ocala National Forest. The inch-long caterpillar was the shape and color of a bird dropping—gray and white and even appearing moist. To make the bluff even more realistic, it was situated just where a dropping should occur—on the upper surface of a leaf. If that disguise failed, it had another costume. When seen from the front or side, the caterpillar became a small snake, with large and conspicuous eyespots that were inky black with yellow rims, and a large "mouth" edged with black lips.

Feeding the Palamedes caterpillar at home on a diet of swampbay and redbay leaves, we watched it grow quickly, doubling its size several times in a few weeks. It ate only two or possibly three times each day. Most of the time, day or night, it remained motionless on the top of the leaf. Using silk, it made a small sleeping pad to which it returned after feeding. During the time we had it, it made several of these beds; after using each for several days, it ate both pad and leaf.

When searching for food, it moved slowly, inching forward in spurts. After finally finding a suitable leaf, it ate quickly. When satiated, it often would bite through the petiole, allowing the uneaten portion of the leaf to fall.

After a few days, the Palamedes larva molted and became bright forest-green over the upper half of its body, and a darker cinnamon below. Now it looked like a short-tailed, green snake with brown counter-shading. The eyespots were amazingly realistic because they appeared to glisten from the moist, fake cornea. In fact, it was difficult to accept that its real head was hidden below the false head. Two weeks later, it turned yellow, signaling that it was getting ready to pupate. The green chrysalis, about an inch long, was suspended midway between two thin threads attached to the middle of a leaf, with the posterior point glued to the leaf.

Probably the most abundant, but little noticed, butterfly in our swamps and hammocks is the Carolina satyr. This postage-stamp-sized forest sprite seems to spend much of its time fluttering through the undergrowth. Its wings are ashy brown with several darker thin vertical lines. Near the outer margins of the hindwings are small dark eyespots outlined by lighter brown. The Carolina satyr nectars on short flowers that larger butterflies ignore; its larvae feed on grasses.

A larger, related satyr, the common wood nymph, is sometimes numerous in north and central Florida swamps and other woodlands. The undersides of its wings are light brown, with many short, darker olive-brown lines; the forewings have bright yellow patches (fig. 35). Also on the underwings are a series of coal-black eyespots rimmed with chocolate brown; sky blue and white scales form the pupil. These butterflies are nearly invisible when they land on leaf-covered soil; but in the sun, their bright-blue pupil spots and yellow forewings make them obvious.

Another satyr found in our hammocks and swamps is the two-inch-long pearly eye, which often perches upside down with its wings together. These butterflies are sometimes curious and will investigate intruders. Although rather drab, this satyr is notable for its many black eyespots rimmed with pumpkin orange—all bordered by white streaks. Furthermore, the spots on the hindwings bear a silver gleam, giving the pearly eye its name.

One place where I have regularly seen the pearly eye is along the Alexander Springs nature trail in Ocala National Forest. What surprised me was that these butterflies are always in one area of the hy-

Figure 35. Some woodland butterflies have color patterns and eyespots that make them both camoflaged and conspicuous. Here a common wood nymph (*Cercyonis pegala*) basks amid sunlit leaves.

dric hammock. Nearby is switch cane, on which the larvae may feed. Pearly eyes are known to sip at sap, scat, and rotting fruit, but not at nectar (Scott 1986).

Another butterfly that is easily overlooked when at rest is the ruddy daggerwing of south Florida swamps and hammocks. In Fakahatchee Strand, this species is abundant in summer. The upperwings are bright orange, making the daggerwing showy when it flies through a sunlit area or when basking with wings spread. When it lands on the underside of a leaf and closes its wings, however, it almost disappears because the mottled, fawn-brown underwings and irregular margins make it resemble a dead leaf (plate 20). It also sits still until closely approached, when it suddenly flits away.

Daggerwing larvae, sporting spectacular Halloween colors of yellow, orange, and black, are among our most embellished caterpillars (plate 21). Besides their gaudy dress, they have a pair of long, curving black antennae as well as four dorsal spines projecting from the abdominal segments. Most likely this harlequin costume warns birds that the larvae are distasteful. Daggerwing larvae feed only on the leaves of fig trees. When the larvae pupate, they form a translucent chrysalis the color of lemon pudding. Several black filaments of unknown function extend from it. The chrysalis, attached to a fig leaf, becomes lime-green within a few days and is hidden among the foliage. Prior to emergence, the cinnamon-tinted underwings are visible through the transparent case.

The zebra longwing—a convict dressed in stripes—is unmistakable. Its long and narrow jet-black wings with rounded tips are boldly banded with neon-yellow streaks. This gaudy garb is no doubt related to its unpalatability, gained by its larvae, which store noxious alkaloids and cyanide-releasing chemicals produced by passion vines, their only food (Gilbert 1972).

Besides their audacious wing pattern, zebra longwings are identifiable by their flight. Often they fly with just the barest flap of the wing, as if weightless. By flying slowly, longwings skillfully navigate through thick vegetation. One writer says that longwings can fly backward and even "flit upside down," and, remarkably, can avoid the larger strands of spider webs (Douglas 1986). I haven't observed this particular feat, but the zebra longwing is certainly unique.

Zebra longwings have unusual sleeping habits. They may roost communally at night, and may even return repeatedly to the same roost (Jones 1930; Mallet 1986). One day near the end of June, Charles DuToit, former biologist for Fakahatchee Strand State Preserve, and I were searching for the elusive ghost orchid in the Preserve. The morning sky was filled with foreboding gray clouds, and rain was imminent. Sure enough, it soon came. Wet and disappointed, we were heading back to the car when we disturbed a group of late-sleeping longwings. Five longwings fluttered slowly around us, displaying their prominent yellow-striped wings. After being satisfied we meant no harm, they settled down again, each one at the tip of a nearby branch. Gregarious roosting may have arisen as younger butterflies followed older ones on their pollen-collecting routes (Gilbert 1972). Another advantage of this behavior might be that since zebras are nasty tasting, predators would quickly learn to avoid them if several longwings lived in the same area. Readers interested in learning more about longwing behavior should read Allen Young's *Sarapiquí*

Chronicle, an engaging account of Costa Rican entomology, especially butterflies (Young 1991).

The ability of female zebra longwings to find the scarce passion vines among the multitude of plants, including many other vines, is amazing. Apparently longwings use smell, taste, and vision to locate the vines. I once watched a female zebra longwing fly back and forth above a leafless passion vine; she finally laid eggs on the tendrils. Apparently she recognized the vine by its odor. In south Florida, zebra longwings lay eggs mostly on the corky-stemmed passion vine. In north Florida, the maypop is the larval food plant of both zebra longwings and the related gulf fritillary. But the maypop may deter these voracious larvae by attracting ants to pairs of swollen glands near its leaf bases. Ants will attack herbivorous insects and carry away their eggs and larvae.

The zebra longwing caterpillar is easily recognized. It is white, flecked with small black dots, and bristling with long black spines. The brown-shrouded chrysalis, which hangs upside down, is best described as *fantastic* (fig. 36). In fact, it is so bizarre that if dragons

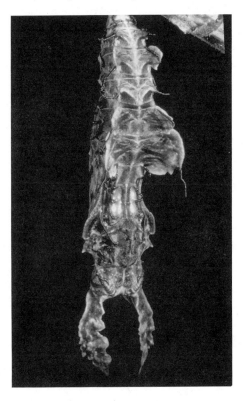

Figure 36. The grotesque chrysalis of a zebra longwing butterfly (*Heliconius charitonius*) reveals reflective crystals that shine like luminous eyes.

hatched from a chrysalis, this is what it might resemble. Its humped form is grotesquely armored and prickled with thorns. Two long pincers, scalloped along one edge like crab claws, jut downward from the head. Winglike projections reminiscent of the large bony plates of Stegosaurus dinosaurs protrude in rows from the abdomen. And when viewed askance, three pairs of silvery scales shine like sunlit mirrors. Why is the chrysalis so odd and fanciful? Perhaps the guise makes the pupa frightful, or at least makes it appear to be something other than what it is—a potential meal.

Around the sunny margins of Florida's swamps can be found the viceroy butterfly, which is often confused with the monarch, although the latter is somewhat paler and lacks the viceroy's noticeable black bar across each hindwing. The wings of viceroys in the Southeast are brick-red with distinct black veins; and crescent spots occur along the wing margins (plate 22). In Florida, viceroys also resemble the distasteful queen butterfly, a southern sister of the monarch (Scott 1986). Farther north and outside of the queen's normal range, viceroys are orange-colored to more closely match monarchs.

Monarchs and queens are milkweed butterflies whose larvae store noxious plant compounds obtained from their food plants, making both the larvae and the butterflies unpalatable. Viceroys are also known to be distasteful to birds because they feed on willows (Ritland 1994). Thus, monarchs and queens and viceroys—by appearing similar and being distasteful—may benefit from their combined advertising. This kind of mimicry (called Müllerian mimicry) is common in the tropics where many unrelated distasteful butterflies look alike.

Mosquitos

For most of us, butterflies are acceptable insects; but who likes a mosquito? We might not, but larval mosquitos are eaten by many aquatic predators, such as mosquitofish; and adult mosquitos are consumed by dragonflies, swifts, swallows, bats, and many other predators.

Mosquitos in Florida are not only plentiful, they are also surprisingly diverse. More than seventy species have been described. Fortunately, only a few regularly bite people. The largest biting species, colorfully named the gallon-nipper, resembles a small cranefly (fig. 37).

The abundance of adult mosquitos depends on the successful development of aquatic larvae. Thus, most species are prevalent in the rainy summer season. Although the larvae live in sundry aquatic habitats, they are most numerous where fish and other predators are

Figure 37. The gallon-nipper mosquito (*Psorophora* sp.), at about half an inch long, is one of Florida's largest. Photo courtesy of Charissa Baker.

absent (Laird 1988). Some female mosquitos lay eggs in tree holes, bromeliads, discarded tires, and other places that are temporarily filled with water—often where predators are scarce. Other mosquitos lay their eggs in depressions that later become flooded. Once covered by water, the drought-resistant eggs hatch. This strategy ensures that water will be present long enough (one or more weeks) for the larvae to grow into adults before the pool dries up.

Most mosquito larvae feed by filtering bacteria, fungi, algae, protozoa, and other microscopic organisms from water. Some are predatory, and feed on other mosquito larvae. Wrigglers, as the larvae are commonly called, usually swim to the surface to breathe through a snorkel at the tip of their abdomen. Larvae of Mansonia mosquitos, however, avoid coming to the surface to breathe, where they could be detected by mosquitofish and other predators. Instead, they attach to roots of floating plants, like water lettuce, which they pierce with their abdomen to obtain oxygen through specialized siphons (Louni-bos and Dewald 1989).

Mosquito larvae grow quickly, then metamorphose into a brief pupa stage. Within several days to a week, the pupae transform into adults. Adult mosquitos are short-lived, surviving only two to three weeks (under optimum conditions). For species that are dependent on high water-levels for their eggs to hatch, their abundance is correlated to peaks in rainfall. Thus, adults are most numerous a week or so after a heavy shower.

All adult mosquitos feed on nectar. Males feed exclusively on it, but most females also feed on blood. A blood meal is not essential for egg-laying in some species, but the protein in blood enables a female to lay more eggs. Male mosquitos are attracted to the buzzing wingbeats of females—a familiar sound. The buzz, which varies from about three hundred to eight hundred cycles per second, is heard by the males at short distances only. Is this why females buzz in one's ear?

Different mosquito species are active at different times of the day, although most adults forage in dim light. Some are most active at dusk, becoming less active through the night. At daybreak, they seek a dark and humid hiding place, such as a hollow tree. In swamps, nocturnal mosquitos will bite whenever prey are present, especially if it is raining.

The bromeliad mosquito, whose larvae live in bromeliads in south Florida (in north Florida, related species live in pitcher plants), is active only during the day (Edman and Haeger 1977). This corresponds to the activity periods of rabbits and other small mammals—not to mention humans—that it bites. Raccoons are mostly active later in the night, and thus they may avoid the period at dusk when mosquitos are most active. By retiring to burrows or tree holes before mosquitos become active, rodents and woodpeckers may be bitten less often.

Fortunately, those female mosquitos that feed on blood generally attack a limited number of hosts. Some species feed mainly on the blood of mammals, others on birds, and some even on reptiles and amphibians. The crab-hole mosquito, which lives in the holes of blue land crabs, feeds on wading birds, which are abundant in its coastal swamp habitat (Edman 1974).

Because a number of diseases are blood-borne, mosquitos serve as vectors. Formerly, malaria and yellow fever were spread by mosquitos in Florida. Although yellow fever in Florida was wiped out long ago, malaria was still prevalent there in the 1940s, when hundreds and even thousands of people died in epidemics. Several kinds of viruses (St. Louis encephalitis, eastern equine encephalomyelitis, and others) are still carried by mosquitos in Florida (Davis 1984). Fortunately, these viruses are rarely transmitted. In order for mosquitos to carry a virus from one host to another, the females must first bite an animal infected with the virus. Then ten to twelve days later, when the virus reaches the infective stage, the mosquito must bite another victim (Nayar 1982). The odds of a mosquito living long enough to bite two animals ten days apart, and thus transmit the virus, are extremely small. Nevertheless, occasional outbreaks occur. For example, in 1990 there was an outbreak of the sometimes deadly St. Louis encephalitis in Florida, the primary vector being *Culex nigripalpus*, a woodland mosquito. Conditions necessary for such outbreaks include a large mosquito population and sufficient hosts infected with the virus. Recent studies at the Florida Medical Entomology Laboratory in Vero Beach indicate that rainfall patterns regulate mosquito populations, and thus could trigger the outbreaks (Nayar 1982; Phil Lounibos, Florida Medical Entomology Lab., pers. comm., 1990).

Other Insects

The most obvious nonflying insect in our swamps and other woodlands is the lubber grasshopper. This large (three inches long) grasshopper has big glassy eyes and can be black or orange, yellow and black (plate 24). Juveniles (which appear in the spring) are smaller and shiny black, with a bold longitudinal yellow line down the back and head. After emerging from eggs laid in the ground in late summer, the juveniles remain in groups until they are larger. Before dispersing, they sometimes form herds—long lines comprising up to a thousand small, crawling and jumping black grasshoppers.

Lubbers are atypical grasshoppers. They are usually lethargic and make only feeble attempts to escape when picked up. Lubbers cannot fly because their wings are too short. Their main defense is a foul-smelling, and probably distasteful, black secretion. During the summer, lubbers are crushed by the hundreds when large numbers of them cross roads in search of mates and places to lay eggs. Amorous males may fight over a female by kicking each other with their hind legs. This may be the only time that they are truly active.

Other conspicuous insects are the dragonflies, which are frequently seen patrolling sunny marshes and the borders of swamps. Few of these inhabit the dark interiors of swamps where smaller damselflies—my favorite—dominate. One damselfly species in particular is common here—the ebony darkwing or ebony jewelwing. This insect is abundant in woods bordering creeks throughout most of north and central Florida (Dunkle 1990). Adults sit on creekside vegetation with their wings folded. When disturbed, they slowly flutter up. The two-inch-long inky black wings seem to rotate like the blades of a helicopter rather than flapping up and down. Male ebony darkwings have jet-black wings and a long, thin, metallic-green body. Females, which lack the metallic body coloration of their mates, advertise their presence by the prominent white spot near the tip of each dark wing. The closely related sparkling jewelwing has iridescent wings with tips blackened as if dipped in ink.

Damselflies, like dragonflies, are predators both as larvae and as adults. The larvae are aquatic. Adult damselflies intercept prey in the air using a prey-catching basket formed by comb-like rows of long sharp spines on their legs.

Darkwing damselflies have a complex reproductive behavior (Johnson 1962; Waage 1973). Because suitable aquatic egg-laying sites are few, males defend them. A male with such a site is much more likely to secure a mate and produce offspring than a male without a territory. Males defend areas several yards in extent. These territories comprise water and emergent vegetation where the female can lay eggs, as well as a nearby perching area where males watch for females and encroaching males. Males who enter another's territory are evicted by intimidating, rapid, spiraling flights. Most of these encounters are brief, but some may continue intermittently for more than an hour. Only very rarely is the owner of a territory displaced by a newcomer.

A female darkwing damselfly, searching for a site to deposit eggs, first flies into a male's streamside territory. The male, flying toward the female, performs a courtship flight by beating his wings rapidly and asynchronously, like a lopsided rotor. He may then fly down to the egg-laying site where he exposes a white patch on the underside of his abdomen that may entice the female to the site. If she lands near the site, he may perform another courting behavior—the cross display—by tilting his dark green abdomen up and folding one pair of wings up while the other pair is held parallel to the ground. After the female lands, she may signal that she is not receptive by doing a wing-spreading display. If she is receptive, her wings remain folded.

During mating, the male uses special claspers on the tip of his abdomen to grasp the female behind her head. She then arches her abdomen forward to contact his second abdominal segment where sperm are transferred. After mating, the female flies to the egg-laying site and probes submerged vegetation with the tip of her abdomen. She may even become submerged searching for a place to deposit her eggs. As the female attaches her eggs to the vegetation, her mate guards, preventing other males from disturbing her.

Although insects and other invertebrates demonstrate much elaboration of physical characteristics and many intriguing rituals, they lack the behavioral complexity and intelligence shown by the vertebrates, our next group of swamp dwellers.

 *8*

Air-Gulping Fish, Barking Frogs, and Slinking Skinks

Fish

The dark waters of Florida's swamps harbor a rich and varied fish fauna. It is difficult to think of a more inhospitable place for fish than the highly fluctuating, often oxygen starved, frequently acidic waters of cypress domes, gum ponds, and other aquatic habitats in Florida's swamps. Yet this is exactly where more than seventy-five species of fish live. None of the fish that use Florida's swamps live solely in that habitat, however. They, like most other vertebrates, are opportunistic and live wherever they can find food, cover, and a place to rear young successfully.

When flooding occurs, fish move from rivers and other permanent water bodies into swamps where they feed and reproduce (Wharton et al. 1981, 1982). As an example, during winter flooding nearly fifty species—three-quarters of the fish species in north Florida's Och-lockonee River—move into the adjacent swamp to feed (Leitman, Darst, and Nordhaus 1991).

Fish use swamps because they can be rich in such foods as small clams, crayfish, freshwater shrimp, isopod crustaceans, and insects. Young fish feed on the abundant plankton such as copepods. Some fish are so dependent on bottomland hardwood swamps that their eggs are adapted to conditions there. For example, some gars have eggs that can resist drying and resume development when reflooded

(Wharton et al. 1981). In the Lower Mississippi, about half of the fish species are dependent on floodplain swamps as nursery areas.

Where flooding is unpredictable or depths are shallow, many of the fish found in swamps are small. Some, like the mosquitofish, as well as the least, bluefin, and pygmy killifish; flagfish; and pygmy sunfishes, are only an inch or two in length; and most others are less than eight inches long (fig. 38). These bantam-sized fish can easily swim into shallow and temporary ponds and can grow quickly and reproduce before retreating when the pond dries. The mosquitofish and least killifish are live-bearers and release their young into ephemeral wetlands where they will grow rapidly. Because these fish are small, they are often ignored by wading birds and mammals who prefer a bigger meal. In deeper backwater sloughs, lettuce lakes, and other permanently flooded habitats, however, larger predatory fish like largemouth bass, bowfin, and Florida gar can be abundant; and they also move into swamps during flooding, and eat smaller fish.

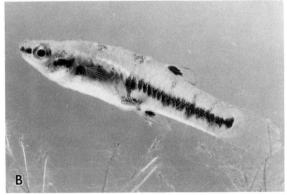

Figure 38. Small fish move into wetlands that are seasonally flooded. The most common are the mosquitofish (*Gambusia affinis*) (A) and the least killifish (*Heterandria formosa*) (B).

The mosquitofish, least killifish, and mangrove Rivulus are highly tolerant of low oxygen levels, and thus can survive in drying pools where oxygen is depleted. They tend to swim near the surface where oxygen is concentrated and can even gulp air if necessary. These adaptations were probably present in ancient fishes as well, and perhaps drying swamp ponds were the environments that fostered the evolution of our next group of wetland denizens—the amphibians.

Amphibians

Frogs and Toads

Swamps abound with amphibians. An abundance of insects, plentiful cover, high humidity, mild temperatures, and ample water provide optimum conditions for them. Of the more than fifty species of amphibians in Florida, more than half occur in swamps and hydric hammocks (Ashton and Ashton 1988). Many others that live as adults in other habitats are dependent on swamp ponds and sloughs as sites for egg laying and development of young.

Frogs are perhaps the most numerous vertebrates in our swamps, especially in south Florida. Just how abundant frogs are is indicated by the calls of hundreds or even thousands of frogs heard at night, or even during the day in spring or summer when it is raining. Astonishingly, these choruses represent less than half of the frog population: females and immature males do not sing, and not all of the males are vocal at any given time.

I had no idea how numerous treefrogs could be until one day in July when I was in Fakahatchee Strand. The morning was clear and fresh under the canopy of cypress and pop ash, which had retained the coolness of the night long into the late morning. However, by 11 A.M., the humidity was high. Overhead, lead-tinted clouds were forming, and before long big drops of rain were plopping on the leaves. Within minutes I was enveloped by the "quonk-quonk-quonk" of innumerable green treefrogs. Judging by their calls, I must have been within earshot of hundreds of small treefrogs with big voices.

Unlike most birds and fish, which attract mates with vibrant colors, frogs, less able to avoid predators, must rely on their singing ability to advertise their attractiveness. But vocalization can also attract predators, so frogs reduce their chances of being eaten by singing in chorus, as part of a crowd. The loud calling of many males also attracts distant females, thus increasing the number of potential mates.

A chorus may be composed of males of a single species or may include representatives of several species. The resulting din is reminiscent of a large party in a small room. With everyone singing, it may be hard for predators to single out one frog. So how do females recognize potential mates? Female frogs have acute hearing and can identify the calls of males of their own species by differences in sound quality. Also, frogs sing at different seasons, from different habitats, and from different sites.

Treefrogs are among our most common and widespread frogs. Approximately twenty species live in the United States, and half of these are native to Florida. Treefrogs were formerly referred to as treetoads because they are more closely related to toads than to true frogs, or ranids.

Adult treefrogs live on vegetation near the ground or high in the canopy. In swamps dominated by hardwoods, the bulk of the insects occur in the canopy where they can feed on the leaves. Thus it is not surprising that treefrogs find the hardwood canopy to their liking. Except during the breeding season, when treefrogs are near water, we seldom see them because of their cryptic markings and arboreal habits. During the winter, some species bury themselves or hide under bark. Archie Carr once found more than thirty squirrel treefrogs hibernating together under a piece of bark (Carr 1940).

To travel in their treetop homes, treefrogs have large toe pads that firmly grip slippery vegetation, and their limbs are long and muscular, enabling them to leap long distances. Some tropical species from Asia even glide between trees like flying squirrels.

Although most treefrogs are infrequently seen, their calls may be more familiar. Yet those in Florida have a bewildering variety of songs, and many may be confused with insects or even birds. Treefrog calls include barks, buzzes, keks, peeps, quacks, quonks, trills, and other sounds that can't really be described. The pitch of the call is related to the size of the frog, with small frogs having a high pitch and large frogs a low pitch.

One treefrog found in the Panhandle and in south Georgia is named the bird-voiced treefrog because of its high-pitched, birdlike whistle. The small squirrel treefrog has a coarse, raspy call sounding something like that of a squirrel. The large, barking treefrog barks loudly from the treetops during rains. The ornate chorus frog has a call that has been described as a squeaky pulley. For such small frogs, their voices are disproportionately loud, and several writers have noted that treefrog songs can be deafening when many are calling nearby. In some species, the male's call is actually amplified by specialized resonating sacs. Female treefrogs lack these sacs and are nearly mute.

Trying to recognize the calls of our frogs can be frustrating. For example, even though the green treefrog's call is one of the most characteristic anuran voices of the South, it has been described as sounding like a cow bell, as "quonk, quonk, quonk, quank," as "grab, grab, grabit, grabit," and even as "fried bacon, fried bacon"!

The easiest way to learn the varied frog songs, besides going out with someone who knows them, is to buy a recording. One entitled *Florida Frog Calls,* by Richard Bradley, is available from the Florida Museum of Natural History in Gainesville. Herpetologist Ray Ashton has taught many people to recognize frog vocalizations with his field guide and recordings of calling frogs. Or you can use a portable cassette recorder to make your own tapes. One January, when Kathy and I were camping at Paynes Prairie State Preserve near Gainesville, we had fun recording southern spring peepers and then playing the tape back. Not to be outdone by high-tech competitors (which must have sounded a lot like themselves), the peepers were promptly stimulated to sing again.

Each treefrog species may produce several kinds of calls, depending on the circumstances. For example, throughout the summer, male green treefrogs produce territorial calls, which are the same as rain calls. When actually breeding, the frogs move to the water's edge, where they give aggressive calls to warn off competitors. These males may even joust, by pushing one another with their forelegs. Once the males have selected calling sites, they begin to attract females with courtship calls. Some males do not call but instead intercept females attracted to another calling male.

Treefrogs, like other frogs, are visual predators. They feed on relatively large and active insects and are especially fond of caterpillars and beetle larvae. Normally treefrogs search for insects at night; however, the little grass frog, the smallest land vertebrate in North America, feeds during the day.

Treefrogs are usually cryptically colored, either brownish or greenish, to resemble the bark or leaves on which they live. Some treefrogs vary their color seasonally, being green in the summer and gray in winter; however, color is generally more dependent on temperature than on season. Others have incredible abilities to alter their color. For example, the green treefrog can range in tone from yellow to dark olive, although it is usually green (Wright and Wright 1949). Deckert (1915) called this frog "an aristocratic looking treetoad, with its long, slender figure of the brightest green, edged on each side with a band of pale gold or silvery white." Usually, no single green treefrog shows the entire range of colors (plate 27).

Although our treefrogs are inconspicuous, some, strangely, are more obvious when escaping. The gray treefrog, for example, has a roughened gray, white, and black skin to match lichen-mottled tree limbs; but when it jumps, its bright yellow or orange inner thighs are displayed. Why would this frog be camouflaged when sitting still, and then suddenly become prominent when fleeing? Perhaps this is the same kind of signal that underwing moths present as they flee, flashing their brightly colored hindwings. If animals using such flash colors appear to be something else, they might startle a predator or at least confuse it, and thus escape. Other treefrogs, including the pine woods and the bird-voiced, also have flash colors.

Although life in the canopy can be hazardous because of lack of water and exposure to predators, treefrogs have partially overcome these problems. During the day, or even at night when it is cold or too dry, they crouch on leaves or bark; or they may hide in leaf bracts, under bark, or in knotholes. In this crouched position—with their eyes partly closed, their front legs drawn below the chin, and their hind legs drawn close to the body—they appear to be sleeping. Sleeping behavior serves two key functions: it makes the frogs less visible, and it reduces the amount of skin exposed to drying air. At night, when the humidity rises, treefrogs can assume the alert posture necessary for catching prey; they are, however, most active during or following rainfall.

Treefrogs can replace water lost to evaporation from their skin by absorbing water from their urine. In addition, when it rains, or at night when dew forms, treefrogs absorb moisture through their thin belly skin, which is always in contact with the surface of their perch.

One of our most distinctive treefrogs is the southern spring peeper. This frog, three-quarters of an inch long, has a gray X on its brown and gray back (plate 25). Peepers are more often heard than seen. In winter and early spring, when they breed, their call is a high-pitched "peep-peep-peep"; however, they also trill. Herpetologists Rosen and

Lemon (1974) observed that the "peep" call of one male may be followed in succession by a similar call from other males. When several do this, the peepers form duets, trios, and so on. Apparently the male with the fastest calling rate is the leader of each group. The trill occurs when one male peeper is intimidated by another. Thus the trill appears to be an aggressive call used to maintain territories. It may even lead to aggressive encounters whereby one male is physically displaced by another.

True frogs, ranids, are the large frogs seen on the ground or in the water. There are eight species in Florida. The most common large ranid is the six-inch-long pig frog, named for its rapid-fire gruntlike calls, given while the male is floating. Pig frogs commonly call during the day, beginning in early spring, but they are more vocal in summer. When one frog begins grunting, it stimulates others. Pig frogs are our second-largest frog, after the bullfrog, and they are much sought after for their savory legs.

Slightly smaller than the pig frog is the bronze frog, which has a call like a plucked string—"blonk, blonk, blonk." It is yellowish brown in color, and is primarily found along streams. The southern leopard frog is our most common medium-sized frog; it is found throughout Florida. It usually lives near water but may be found elsewhere, especially following heavy rains. It is recognized by the rows of dark spots down its back and on its legs.

True toads live primarily in dry habitats. Three species are found in Florida. The most common is the southern toad, which is gray, reddish, or brown and about three inches long (fig. 39). It is readily recognized by the prominent crests on its head that end in knobs behind the eyes. The less common Fowler's toad, which lives in bottomland hardwood habitats in northwestern Florida, lacks the knobs on its crests. The one-inch-long oak toad dwells in longleaf pine habitats.

Another group of amphibians that is primarily nonaquatic includes the narrowmouth toads. Although called toads, they are not closely related and lack the warts obvious on true toads. Of the three species found in the United States, only the eastern narrowmouthed toad occurs in Florida. This small, nocturnal toad, which inhabits pond-edge habitats, is about one inch in length and has a small head and pointed snout. It often burrows under rotten logs to feed on ants and termites.

A toadlike frog found in hydric hammocks is the eastern spadefoot toad. The spadefoot is unmistakable because of its bulging golden

Figure 39. The southern toad (*Bufo terrestris*) is our most common toad. Nocturnal, it usually buries itself under leaf litter during the day.

eyes with vertical pupils. One rainy January night in Paynes Prairie State Preserve, Kathy and I found several of these flabby frogs sitting on a wet trail that meandered through a hammock. Spadefoots are good burrowers and quickly disappear into holes dug with the hind feet, which are equipped with hard black "spades" for digging.

Salamanders

Salamanders are among the most numerous vertebrates in bottom-land hardwoods over most of the Southeast. In Florida, they are represented by twenty-six species. In north Florida, where salamander species are most diverse, they can be relatively abundant but rarely seen: some hide under logs and in leaf litter, some burrow into the ground, and some are aquatic. Ten species of salamander are found in central Florida, but only six occur as far south as Lake Okeechobee.

As with frogs, rain may signal to salamanders that the breeding season has arrived. Unlike most of our frogs, which breed during the warmer months, salamanders in Florida are primarily winter breeders. Males reach the ponds first; when the females arrive, pairs perform an aquatic courtship dance. During mating, males secrete a pheromone that stimulates females to pick up sperm packets that fertilize the eggs as they are released. The eggs are deposited in water or laid in depressions where they hatch after being covered by rainwater. When fish are present, large numbers of salamander eggs and larvae may be eaten.

Mole salamanders are represented by four species in Florida. They are four to eight inches long and are usually nocturnal. During the day, they hide under debris on the forest floor or in rotten logs, or burrow into the soil—hence their name. If it rains they may come out and hunt for insects, worms, and other invertebrate prey. In the winter breeding season, mole salamanders make relatively long migrations to ponds. The Ashtons once tracked a flatwoods salamander for two-thirds of a mile to a breeding pond (Ashton and Ashton 1988).

One common mole salamander is the marbled salamander, which is dark gray or black, with conspicuous white markings on its back. In Florida, it dwells primarily in hydric hammocks and floodplains west of the Suwannee River. It frequently hides in rotting logs inhabited by the glossy black patent-leather beetle (Ashton and Ashton 1988). In Georgia, the marbled salamander is mostly confined to floodplains (Wharton et al. 1981).

Lungless salamanders (family Plethodontidae) are the only vertebrates without lungs or gills. They are a diverse group in Florida, comprising fourteen species. One of these is the southern dusky salamander, which occurs in swamps in north and central Florida, where it spends much time in the water. It is brownish, with small white spots along the lower sides and tail. Two closely related species, the southern two-lined salamander and the three-lined salamander, have slender bodies with either two or three lines running along the back. They live mostly in streams in the Panhandle. The related dwarf salamander, only about two inches in length, is mostly tail. It is one of the few salamanders whose range extends into southern Florida.

A number of primarily aquatic salamanders also frequent our swamps. One group is the newts, which have large eyes and vertically compressed tails that they use for swimming. They can be found in virtually all freshwater habitats in Florida.

The Sirens are one of two peculiar groups of aquatic, eel-like salamanders inhabiting our swamps. Only four species of Sirens exist, and all of them occur in Florida. They resemble eels because their hind legs and entire pelvis have disappeared; and their forelegs have been reduced to stunted arms. Underwater, Sirens move by undulating their long tail. Although they have external gills like those of larval salamanders, they mostly breathe through lungs and skin.

Sirens feed on aquatic invertebrates like insects, snails, shrimp, and worms. If its pond dries up, a Siren can live for months, burrowed in the mud. Sirens only rarely leave the water for short excursions. Although not uncommon in our swamps, they are infrequently seen because they remain hidden in dense aquatic vegetation.

The other odd group of eel-like salamanders are the Amphiumas. Like the Sirens, they have no distinct separation between body and tail. Amphiumas differ from Sirens in having two pairs of tiny legs and no external gills. Like the Sirens, Amphiumas are a small group. Of the three known species, two live in Florida. One of these, the two-toed Amphiuma, or Congo eel, is found in cypress ponds, in roadside ditches, and elsewhere (Ashton and Ashton 1988). It is our longest amphibian, reaching more than three feet in length. The Congo eel is gray or brownish in color and is round in cross section. The small eyes are flush with the surface of the head. Amphiumas are active predators with sizable teeth, and they can bite when handled. During heavy rains, Amphiumas can slither overland, which accounts for their presence in isolated ponds and ditches. They burrow into mud if their pond dries up.

Reptiles

Snakes

Snakes are a sometimes conspicuous and important vertebrate group in our wetlands. Some forty-four species occur in Florida (Ashton and Ashton 1988). Of these, about fifteen are common in swamps and hydric hammocks.

One of the best known but not necessarily the most abundant swamp snake is the cottonmouth. Fortunately, cottonmouths are usually nonaggressive and lethargic, and they generally don't bite unless provoked. The most likely way to get bitten by a cottonmouth would be to step on one. Their coloration of dark brown with faint darker bands makes them blend perfectly with their swamp-floor habitat. This dusky pigmentation not only serves as camouflage, but also aids in heat absorption during sun bathing.

Sun bathing is important to cottonmouths and other reptiles that spend much time in the water, which can lower their body temperature. When seen basking, the cottonmouth tends to remain motionless unless closely approached. When threatened, it bends its head back and opens its white mouth wide, making itself obvious. Its large triangular head is readily recognized. The top of the head is dusky brown. A lighter brown stripe passes through the vertically slitted eye, making the eyes difficult to see. White markings around the mouth and under the jaw further enhance its camouflage. Cottonmouths have a musk gland that produces a noticeably strong odor, especially during the breeding season.

Cottonmouths eat mostly frogs, fish, and aquatic invertebrates. They will also feed on baby alligators, young turtles, and small rodents (Ashton and Ashton 1988; Dundee and Rossman 1989). Juvenile cottonmouths have an unusual way of getting food. They attract small prey, such as frogs and lizards, within striking range by using their bright yellowish tail as a lure, wiggling the colorful tip like a worm. Tom Stubbs reported that a small cottonmouth "will lie in a tight coil for hours, his conspicuous tail protruding from the center, twitching regularly like some small grub" (Stubbs 1974).

Although the eastern diamondback rattlesnake is occasionally seen in swamps, it lives primarily in drier habitats like pine flatwoods. It has distinctive dark brown diamonds outlined by tan. Like cottonmouths, rattlesnakes are difficult to see because of their disruptive color pattern, which makes the snakes blend almost perfectly with their background. The bold diamond pattern is unmistakable, however, and, from my own experience, alerts large vertebrates to the presence of the snake.

Another rattlesnake, the canebrake or timber rattler, is found primarily in swamps in north Florida between Alachua and Hamilton Counties but is relatively common elsewhere in the Southeast (Ashton and Ashton 1988). It is a large, heavy-bodied rattler with a series of distinctive dark chevrons along its back.

Most of our swamp snakes are nonvenomous. One of these is the ribbon snake, a slim, long-tailed snake with several longitudinal stripes that make it resemble the closely related garter snakes. Ribbon snakes are thinner, being only about as big around as a pencil. Although primarily terrestrial, they are agile climbers of shrubs and trees, where they hunt insects and treefrogs. Another climber that feeds on insects is the attractive rough green snake. Lime-green above and creamy to pale yellow below, it is easily overlooked amid the foliage.

A number of medium-sized, dark-colored snakes are common near streams and ponds in swamps, where they are often seen basking. Although somewhat resembling the cottonmouth in size and color, these are harmless water snakes. Because they grow to four feet in length and possess relatively large heads and thick bodies, they can easily be confused with cottonmouths; but they lack the triangular head of the cottonmouth, and their bodies are slimmer. Water snakes feed on aquatic invertebrates and amphibians. We once watched a large water snake probing deeply into crayfish holes along the margin of Charlie Bowlegs Creek, just below the boardwalk in Highlands Hammock State Park; another water snake was sunning nearby at the base of a cypress. Although these snakes can be pugnacious if provoked, they are nonvenomous.

The rat snake is one of our most abundant snakes, and is found in many habitats. It is also one of our most beautiful snakes, appearing in a range of attractive patterns and colors (plate 28). Rat snakes can reach six feet in length, and are constrictors: they suffocate their prey by coiling tightly around it. Rat snakes are noted climbers, a feat facilitated by the squared-off edges of their belly plates. A yellow rat snake shooting up the trunk of a cabbage palm is an amazing sight.

Although all snakes are predators, they too are preyed upon by a variety of larger animals. Several times Kathy and I have seen a red-shouldered hawk suddenly swoop down and pick up a snake. Bobcats occasionally prey on snakes, too (Maehr and Brady 1986). Rat snakes can deter bobcats by releasing a strong-smelling musk that acts like catnip, causing the cat to ignore the snake (Ashton and Ashton 1988).

American Alligator

"The alligator is the enemy of all living creatures, the tyrant of the water, and the death of one saves the lives of hundreds of other animals. So blast away at the 'gators,' O ye Florida tourists!—you will not kill many of them, anyway: their skulls are too thick." So wrote a journalist visiting Florida in the 1870s (Clarke 1874).

The American Alligator, or gator, is the quintessential Florida animal; few other native species fascinate people as much. The very idea of a large and potentially dangerous reptilian predator living so close to people is, no doubt, one reason for the attraction. When naturalist William Bartram visited Florida in the 1700s, he described alligators that would dwarf most seen today (Bartram [1791] 1955). In the 1870s, tourists traveling by steamboat down the St. Johns River made sport of shooting gators, and almost anything else that moved. It was estimated that some ten million alligators were killed for sport, skins, and meat between 1870 and 1970 (Fogarty 1978).

Although gators occur in the interior of cypress and hardwood swamps, they are more common in marshes, lakes, and rivers where invertebrates, fish, and other prey are more abundant and where they can more readily sun bathe.

Alligators have peglike teeth that they use for holding prey. They feed both day and night and consume a variety of prey that changes as they grow. Juveniles eat mostly aquatic insects and small fish (Delany 1990). In terms of volume of food eaten, larger gators eat mostly fish; but, surprisingly, apple snails often predominate in their diet in terms of numbers of prey consumed (Delany, Woodward, and Kochel 1988). Other gator prey include insects, crayfish, amphibians, snakes, turtles, other alligators, wading birds, and small mammals. Large gators feed extensively on turtles and gar (Delany and Abercrombie 1986), but terrestrial mammals can be important, too. In one study in southeastern Georgia, raccoon hair was found in seventy percent of the Alligator fecal samples examined; other mammal prey included feral hog, marsh rabbit, and white-tailed deer (Shoop and Ruckdeschel 1990).

The abundance of mammals in the diet of large alligators suggests that gators once played a pivotal ecological role—one that cannot be fully appreciated today. The numerous big alligators found in Florida more than a century ago by Audubon, Bartram, and other naturalists could have regulated the numbers of raccoons, which are now unnaturally high. Raccoons spread rabies and other diseases and are serious predators of birds' eggs and nestlings. A reduction in raccoon numbers could aid in the recovery of several increasingly threatened wading birds, including endangered wood storks (Shoop and Ruckdeschel 1990).

In summer, female alligators are often aggressive in guarding their nests—three-foot-high piles of aquatic vegetation in swamps or marshes. In the Everglades, nesting female gators have attacked passing trams at Shark Valley; they have also hissed and charged at people on the boardwalks in Corkscrew Swamp Sanctuary and at Okefenokee National Wildlife Refuge (Duever et al. 1986). This pugnacious behavior is, no doubt, due to the prevalence of egg predators. In one study in Okefenokee, such predators as black bears, otters, and raccoons destroyed more than 90 percent of the nests; those nests that remained intact were defended by highly aggressive females (Duever et al. 1986). Upon hatching, the young gators vocalize so the female can dig them out of the nest pile. These calls actually begin before hatching, and may synchronize their development and initiate hatching. The young stay together for at least a year, and females continue to respond to distress calls from their young for some time.

Turtles are known to take advantage of the nest-building activities and vigilance of female alligators. A number of turtles, including the red-bellied, lay eggs in these mounds (Goodwin and Marion 1977). The eggs probably receive some protection from egg predators, and the elevated temperatures in the nest may speed their development. Gator biologist Greg Masson, who studied the reproductive biology of alligators in Lake Apopka, told me that alligator nests are also frequently used by fire ants. Apparently the ants do not disturb the gator eggs, and perhaps even repel some nest predators.

Alligators are territorial, but territory size varies seasonally and is sex dependent (Goodwin and Marion 1979; Fogarty 1984; Van Meter 1987). During cold weather, male and female gators are generally quiescent, often holed up in dens beneath a riverbank or under tree roots (Goodwin and Marion 1979). By spring, warmer temperatures and the onset of the breeding season stimulate both sexes to dramatically increase their activity, expanding their home ranges and extending their foraging forays. In summer, however, when females are tending their nests, they may move less than one hundred feet in a one-day period, even though their territories are about fifty acres in extent. Males, on the other hand, range much farther and can occupy areas of several thousand acres. One male was tracked over a five-mile distance in one day, and another moved thirty-three miles during a five-month period (Fogarty 1984). During removal of nuisance alligators, biologists discovered that gators would return if they were moved less than five miles. Some experts believe that homing from up to forty miles away is possible.

During the dry season, gators move to ponds known as gator holes, which retain water; the biggest gators occupy the biggest holes. Their well-developed homing instinct enables them to return to their dry-season ponds. In Fakahatchee Strand during the spring "drawdown," it is common to find gator tracks in the drying ditches paralleling the trams. These tracks often lead to lettuce ponds, which remain filled with water through the dry season. Besides being ecologically significant predators, gators are important because they keep gator holes free of mud, vegetation, and debris, providing a refuge for fish and other aquatic species during droughts.

In many ways, the alligator is unique among our native wildlife: it is both attractive and repulsive. In their interesting and amusing book, Gillespie and Mechling (1987) describe how the alligator has been an important animal in American folklore. The origin of alligator encounter stories no doubt stems from the colorful accounts of early naturalists. Among the most picturesque is this vignette by William Bartram ([1791] 1955): "Behold him rushing forth from the flags and reeds. His enormous body swells. His plaited tail brandished high, floats upon the lake. The waters like a cataract descend from his open jaws. Clouds of smoke issue from his dilated nostrils. The earth trembles with his thunder."

Although alligator populations were once quite low because of overhunting, they have rebounded since receiving federal and state protection. Now wildlife biologists must decide how to best manage alligators in habitats that are increasingly overrun by humans.

Green Anole

Few lizards occur in swamps; most live in drier habitats where they obtain water from insect prey. The most common lizard seen in southeastern swamps and other forested habitats is the green anole. Although commonly called a chameleon, it is not closely related to true chameleons. Nonetheless, green anoles do change color as chameleons do, to green, brown, or tan. Also, their eyes can move independently, like those of true chameleons. Like octopuses, green anoles vary their color according to their psychological state. During aggressive encounters, their colors change rapidly. Dominant males can shift from green to brown in only three seconds (Greenberg 1977). Temperature also affects their color; in winter they are dark brown to absorb heat.

In May, male green anoles are easily recognized by their reddish (or, rarely, green) dewlap—an extendible throat-fan that they use to attract females for mating (females have a small dewlap). The reddish fan contrasts with the surrounding green vegetation, thus luring females from a distance (plate 29). At closer range, the male uses head nodding as a courting stimulus (Sigmund 1983). Nodding can also be done by females to entice males (Greenberg 1977). Along with dewlap extension and head nodding, male anoles can also raise a crest on their neck and back and do "push-ups." These courting behaviors also serve as territorial displays.

Green anoles are at home in shrubs and trees, where they hunt insects during the day. They are highly skilled predators with keen eyesight, and they stalk insects by slowly inching forward, lifting one leg and then another. Rough pads on the feet aid in climbing smooth branches and leaves. If approached slowly, green anoles are sometimes unafraid, especially when it is cool and they are basking. They readily invade gardens, where they become effective bug catchers and patioside entertainers.

Other anoles also occur in Florida: in urban areas, the introduced brown (Cuban) anole can frequently be seen hunting, displaying, and courting on the ground. Other introduced species occur around Miami.

Skinks

Skinks are small- to medium-sized lizards that are common in hammocks. They can sometimes be seen searching for insects in leaf litter or among the bootjacks of cabbage palms, or basking on sunny logs. Skinks have a smooth but scaly skin and look like short snakes because they have no obvious neck and their legs are short. When foraging, skinks are highly active. This is in contrast to anoles, which either wait for prey to approach or slowly stalk it.

One of the most common skinks, and perhaps our most abundant reptile, is the three- to five-inch-long ground skink. This species has tiny legs and is brown with lateral black stripes. It frequents hammocks, where it busily searches under leaf litter for insects. When disturbed, the ground skink rapidly disappears by scurrying through the leaves.

Our largest skink is the broadhead, which reaches just over a foot in length. As its name implies, the head of the male is wide; during the breeding season, it is also rusty red. These skinks can be approached closely, but they should not be handled because they will bite. Also, the tails readily break off if held, as is true for other skinks. Broadheads can be fairly numerous in hammocks, where their leathery eggs are laid in rotting wood. The female attends the nest—unusual behavior for a lizard.

The closely related, but smaller, southeastern five-lined skink is also found in hammocks, where it forages for invertebrates under logs, in leaf litter, and in trees. When searching for prey among dead cabbage palm fronds, it can be quite noisy. It has two pairs of longitudinal white lines, and one dorsal white stripe along most of the body. Striped juveniles of both the broadhead and the southeastern five-lined skink are similar and have electric-blue tails that often twitch nervously, perhaps acting as a lure to divert the attention of predators toward the replaceable tail. The stripes may also confuse predators by making it difficult for them to judge the speed of an escaping skink.

Turtles

Florida has some seventeen species of freshwater turtles (Carr 1940; Ernst and Barbour 1972; Ashton and Ashton 1988), but few occur in swamps. Instead, most turtles prefer rivers, lakes, or ponds where the rank growth of aquatic vegetation serves as both food and cover. You will frequently see turtles basking on logs; or showing only the tips of their noses while they are at the water's surface, breathing or sunning.

Our most visible aquatic turtles belong to the genus *Pseudemys*. This is a widely distributed group, found from Canada to Brazil (Ernst and Barbour 1972). Four forms occur in Florida: the Suwannee river cooter, the Florida and peninsula cooters, and the Florida redbelly. The less common yellowbelly slider (or pond slider) is closely related.

Cooters and sliders are large turtles (about a foot in length), seen along sluggish rivers and in spring runs, lakes, ponds, and sloughs; occasionally they live in cypress dome ponds or in lettuce lakes. They spend much of the day basking. The head and legs of both are boldly patterned with thin lemon-yellow stripes over the inky-black skin; the carapace is dark with yellow or red markings, depending on the species (plate 30). Conspicuous dark spots also occur on the sides of the plastron (belly). Cooters and the Florida redbelly have thin yellow stripes on the front legs, whereas the chicken turtle (of similar size but without marks on the plastron) has a single, broad, yellow stripe. These turtles are difficult to identify without close examination; field guides like Ashton and Ashton (1988) and Conant and Collins (1991) are helpful.

Because juvenile cooters and sliders are attractively pigmented with yellow markings on the head and carapace, they were formerly heavily exploited for pets. Most of these pet turtles were red-eared sliders, which have a prominent and distinctive red spot behind the eyes. When it was discovered that young pet turtles sometimes carried Salmonella bacteria, they were taken off the market. Now, sale of turtles under four inches long is illegal in Florida.

As adults, cooters and sliders are vegetarians, but young turtles feed on aquatic insects. In ponds, lakes, and sluggish rivers with an abundance of aquatic vegetation, cooters generally feed in the morning and evening; at night, they sleep on the bottom or float amid aquatic vegetation. Underwater, turtles move with ease, and they can reduce their oxygen consumption when submerged. In some species, dissolved oxygen from the water is absorbed by the lining of the mouth, thus extending their diving time. Submergence time varies according to water temperature, activity level, species, and size, but is generally less than one hour.

Cooters and sliders are mostly homebodies, staying in the same pond or moving short distances between ponds. They can, however, cover considerable distances over land, especially when searching for a place to lay eggs, or to find water if their pond dries up. They navigate by the sun (Ernst and Barbour 1972), and most also have some homing ability if the distance is not too great. Once a year, or more frequently, females dig shallow nests in sandy soil and lay from ten to thirty leathery eggs that are smaller than ping-pong balls. They may even lay their eggs in gator nests. Hatching occurs after about a hundred days of incubation, depending on the temperature. Most eggs are consumed by raccoons and other predators, and the rubbery eggshells are often seen discarded near excavated nests.

A variety of other semiaquatic turtles also live in swamps. These include the large and powerful snapping turtles, as well as the peculiar softshell turtles that have pancakelike bodies and long tubular noses. Several smaller aquatic turtles may also be seen in swamps. One of these is the stinkpot, which emits a pungent odor from its musk gland. It has a high domed shell and a large head with two light-colored, longitudinal lines. Stinkpots feed on aquatic plants and invertebrates. Other small turtles include the mud turtles, which have dome-shaped shells and a hinged plastron (belly plate). They spend much of their time foraging on the bottom for aquatic vegetation and invertebrates but are sometimes seen traveling overland. When held, they retract their head and legs and bend their tail close under the shell.

Terrestrial turtles can also be found in swamps and hammocks. Occasionally a box turtle is seen sauntering along the floor of a dry cypress dome or hammock. Their high, domed shells are ornamented with yellow or orange markings that are highly variable from one individual to the next (fig. 40). Box turtles also have a hinge on the plastron. They are omnivorous, eating snails, slugs, worms, insects, mushrooms, leaves, roots, and berries. When inactive, such as during dry periods, they retreat into shallow depressions. Captive box turtles are known to outlive their owners; one lived more than 125 years!

Humans are probably the major predator of adult turtles because of accidental roadkills and deliberate hunting. "Crackers" formerly ate many turtles, and many others were shipped north to markets in the Northeast. The highly esteemed river cooter of the South was called the "Suwannee chicken." Another Florida turtle, the chicken turtle, was named for its poultrylike flavor. Other consumers of turtles include alligators and feral hogs, which eat small turtles; eggs and juveniles are preyed upon by a wide variety of animals, including other reptiles, birds, and mammals.

These latter two groups are the subjects of the next chapter.

Figure 40. The box turtle (*Terrapene carolina*) is a common terrestrial turtle found in wooded habitats throughout the Southeast.

 *9*

Feathered and Furred

A Beleaguered Fauna?

The "higher" vertebrates are animals whose complexity rivals our own. Most ancient cultures revered and respected the birds and the mammals, including them in their ceremonies and apologizing to their spirits when it was necessary to kill one for food or other use. I have already mentioned many of the birds and mammals found in our wetlands in the course of discussing other aspects of Florida's swamps. In this chapter, besides the general descriptions of these animals in wetland habitats, I want to tell you about some that are particularly beautiful, or of special interest. Some of these we latecomers have already managed to do away with; others are barely hanging on to existence—often in the depths of a swamp or other wild place.

Birds

What makes a wetland scene memorable? Perhaps the orange glow of a sunset through palm trees lining a pond where egrets cast white reflections across dark waters. Or the flashy yellow images of prothonotary warblers foraging amid the pastel green foliage of bald cypress and water tupelo. Whatever your favorite wetland scene is, it probably includes birds.

Birds are our most diverse and visible vertebrates. Nearly 180 bird species nest in Florida, and about three hundred are winter residents or pass through as migrants (Kale and Maehr 1990). Many of these birds use forested wetlands to varying degrees, and at times may be more abundant in swamps than in upland habitats (Harris and Mulholland 1983). Because of Florida's mild climate, insects and fruit are present throughout the year, enticing migratory birds to winter in Florida instead of flying farther south to the tropics. From fall to spring, the diversity of birds in Florida's swamps more than doubles, and their numbers also greatly increase.

Ecologists have found that bird diversity is often correlated to structural complexity of the habitat (Maehr, Conner, and Stenberg 1982). Thus, swamps and hammocks attract arboreal birds because of the variety of trees, shrubs, and vines of varying heights. These plants provide a three-dimensional environment that is rich in food and cover. This contrasts with managed plantation forests or "fiber farms," which are dominated by a single tree species of one age and which support far fewer birds.

Forest size also affects birds (Burdick et al. 1989; Harris and Gosselink 1990; Robbins, Dawson, and Dowell 1990). State nongame biologist James Cox found that large maritime hammocks were richest in resident and migratory birds (Cox 1988). Species like the black-and-white warbler, ovenbird, northern Parula, and summer tanager were more numerous in large hammocks than in small ones. Some "interior" or "area-sensitive" birds such as Swainson's warbler may nest only in forest tracts exceeding several square miles in area. Swamp raptors like barred owls, red-shouldered hawks, and swallow-tailed kites are also sensitive to forest size. By nesting deep in forests, these birds may avoid competition with the more numerous forest-edge nesters. In addition, forest-interior species may suffer less from egg and nestling predation, which is high along forest edges where snakes, crows, jays, grackles, and raccoons are often plentiful. Parasitic cowbirds are also more frequent near clearings.

Forests not only furnish nesting sites, they also provide birds with food. Small birds, because of their high activity, spend much of their time searching for food. Rarely do warblers, kinglets, gnatcatchers, and other small birds sit still for more than a few minutes. Insects, rich in proteins and fats, are vital nourishment and form the bulk of the diet for most forest-dwelling birds.

Insects are abundant in forests of all types, but most are cryptic and thus difficult to find. The inchworm larvae of geometrid moths, for example, can be very numerous; yet most go unseen because they appear to be twigs. Other caterpillars hide by rolling a leaf around themselves. Still others take cover in cracks or holes, only coming out at night to feed. Insectivorous birds must be expert at finding them.

Indeed, bug-eating birds find and pursue their prey in many amazing ways. They not only search particular parts of their environment but also use specific feeding behaviors. This strategy probably makes them more effective hunters and could reduce competition among birds. Although birds use stereotyped behaviors, individuals may change their foraging techniques depending on what food is available.

Many small songbirds, such as warblers and kinglets, forage by moving rapidly through the canopy, actively hopping from perch to perch or making quick flights between branches. Such activity is especially evident when there is an outbreak of insects. This was amply demonstrated one April when Kathy and I were exploring a gum swamp in southeast Georgia. An amazing abundance and variety of birds had gathered to feast on eastern tent caterpillars. The half-grown caterpillars were so numerous that they were rapidly defoliating the tupelos. As we stared up at the leafless branches, a rain of frass (caterpillar excrement) pattered into the water near us. And all around, we watched the frenzied searching by gnatcatchers, kinglets, warblers, and vireos as they chased through the canopy, eating the caterpillars. Many of the larvae tried to escape the avian onslaught by bailing out—hanging from the trees on long silk threads.

Not all birds are this active. Some, such as the solitary Vireo, are slow searchers, spending more time sitting, on the lookout for prey, than they spend moving. This behavior probably prevents slow searchers from finding as many prey as rapid searchers, but the prey may be more substantial. One large meal could be worth ten smaller ones and require less energy to secure. Indeed, swamp raptors like the red-shouldered hawk and barred owl conserve energy by sitting and watching for large prey—often from a favorite perch.

Insectivorous birds learn to search for food in particular places. For example, small birds like gnatcatchers and the northern Parula warbler, because they weigh so little, can feed at the tips of branches. Chickadees quickly learn to find those caterpillars that are hiding in curled leaves. Once these birds have developed a search image, they will consistently look for a particular clue, such as those curled leaves. This could be the reason that swallowtail butterfly larvae sit on top of leaves where they are highly visible: birds may not search for prey in such obvious places.

Black-and-white warblers, brown creepers, red-bellied woodpeckers, and nuthatches meticulously explore trunks and limbs for hidden prey. This is called gleaning (Robinson and Holmes 1982). Other birds, such as warblers and flycatchers, snap up prey from hard-to-reach areas where they must hover. Chickadees also do what has been called hanging, where they pluck insects from the undersides of twigs or leaves while hanging by their toes and fluttering their wings for added stability. Flying insects like bees and flies are often caught in midair by "hawking" or "flycatching" behavior. Scarlet tanagers and many flycatchers, such as the great crested flycatcher and eastern kingbird, hawk: they catch flying insects by darting after them. The eastern phoebe is a common winter resident often seen flycatching in swamps and hammocks, making short flights from an exposed perch to snatch insects out of the air.

A different type of hawking behavior is shown by the much larger American swallow-tailed kite, which inhabits Florida's wetlands in spring and summer. Rather than perching and darting out for aerial prey as do most forest hawkers, this soaring kite pursues and catches dragonflies in midair. It also swoops down to grab large insects, frogs, green anoles, and snakes from trees (Bent [1937] 1961).

In another foraging maneuver, called flush-chase, forest-dwelling birds fly after escaping prey. Blue-gray gnatcatchers use this method to feed on leafhoppers; and many warblers, such as American redstarts, often flush small moths from foliage, actively pursuing them in the air with amazing aerobatics. Anhingas may use a similar method to capture prey, first flushing fish from hiding places among aquatic weeds and then chasing them through the water.

Insects are eaten by many fall and spring migrants because they provide essential fat to fuel the birds during their long flights. Other migrants feed on fruits, which are easier to "catch" but which provide less energy. These frugivorous birds are mainly the thrushes (the American robin and hermit thrush, for example), but also include flycatchers, vireos, yellow-rumped warblers, and woodpeckers. Most such birds arrive in Florida in late autumn and early winter. These species, together with such residents as the gray catbird, red-bellied woodpecker, northern flicker, and others, make for a considerable number of fruit-loving birds at that time of year.

The sudden influx of robins and other fruit-eating birds in November and December is a familiar sight, but it is no coincidence in timing. Ornithologist Stewart Skeate found that winter was the peak fruit season in Florida (with nearly thirty species of plants bearing fruit in December), and that migrant birds were responsible for 98 percent of the fruit eaten in a northern Florida hammock (Skeate 1987). Birds can disperse seeds widely, so it benefits plants to entice them with an edible seed covering.

But not all avian fruit-eaters disperse seeds by eating the fruit in one place and depositing the seeds in another. Some, like the northern cardinal, rose-breasted grosbeak, and summer tanager, eat the pulp and discard the seeds beneath the parent plant. Skeate (1987) called these birds "fruit thieves" because they do not disperse seeds. Luckily for the plants, such cheating is rare; otherwise, they would have to evolve other means of dispersal.

Unfortunately, native plants are not the only ones that benefit from seed dispersal by birds. One of Florida's most troublesome exotic plants, the peppertree (Brazilian pepper), is successful in part because its numerous red fruits ripen when migrants arrive in south Florida. In December, large flocks of robins congregate in the peppertrees, where they become drunk on the toxic berries, later dropping the seeds in their excrement. If fruiting occurred at any other season, peppertrees probably would not be such a widespread pest.

Wading Birds

Arboreal birds may be the most diverse group of birds using forested wetlands, but wading birds are certainly the most conspicuous. Florida has more large wading birds than any other state—nearly twenty species. Herons, egrets, spoonbills, and wood storks dot the shorelines of estuaries and lakes; bitterns hide amid cattails; white ibis and night-herons forage and fish deep in swamps; and, along streams, limpkins search for snails amid water lilies and pickerelweed.

The limpkin is one of my favorite wading birds because of its tameness and entertaining habits. It is a medium-sized dark brown bird, spattered with white spots. It rarely occurs outside of Florida, but does live in the Neotropics. Frequently seen along the weed-lined shores of blackwater rivers and spring runs, the limpkin uses its long decurved bill to probe among aquatic vegetation for invertebrates, especially apple snails. Limpkins are unrelated to typical wading birds like egrets and herons, or even ibis, which they somewhat resemble; rather, they are more closely related to rails and cranes.

Where they are not persecuted, limpkins are tame and engaging. At Wekiwa Springs, Kathy and I once sat in a canoe for over an hour, watching a male limpkin feeding its mate a seemingly endless supply of golf-ball-sized apple snails. Another time, along Alexander Springs Run, we watched a family of five limpkins foraging in single file among water-hemlock and pennywort (plate 31). Four "youngsters," almost full-grown, were apparently following an adult, which we dubbed Mother. One juvenile always lagged behind and would shriek for the others when they were out of sight. Empty snail shells littered the area behind the perambulating clan. Eventually they stopped at what appeared to be their nest site, where they preened and basked in the afternoon sun. Later, when Mother flew across the stream, the young hesitated, piling up at the closest end of a nearby log. Then, one by one, they awkwardly swam across.

Limpkins have a distinctive call, or cry, which the noted ornithologist Alexander Sprunt, Jr. (1954), describes as "a loud mournful wail suggesting the cry of a child." He goes on to say, "A chorus of these birds, wailing and yelling through the marshes either by day or night, produces one of the weirdest cacophonies of nature."

More abundant and widespread than limpkins are the white ibis. Small flocks of ibis are common in swamps, where they probe for crayfish and earthworms or search in shallow water among submerged plants for apple snails, dragonfly larvae, waterbugs, waterbeetles, and small fishes (Kushlan and Kushlan 1975). White ibis are picturesque in flight, with carmine-red bills arched downward and outstretched white wings tipped with black. From my office window in Fort Pierce, I often watched their v-shaped flocks flying back to mangrove islands in the Indian River to roost for the night. As the sun set, a blushing glow reflected from their cloud-white plumage. Ibis were once shot in Florida by the thousands for food, but they are highly adaptable, and today they are one of our most plentiful wading birds.

Several larger wading birds also use forested wetlands. Lettuce lakes make good feeding areas for great egrets and great blue herons. Drying ponds in cypress domes attract herons, egrets, and sometimes endangered wood storks to feed on the concentrated fish. Storks are adapted for thermal soaring, and, once aloft, they may cover great areas, looking for groups of other waders that indicate the presence of food (fig. 41). Because wood storks and egrets are white, these feeding congregations are visible from long distances.

But why would these birds show their competitors where to find dinner? Actually, feeding in groups can benefit wading birds because

Figure 41. The en-
dangered wood stork
(*Mycteria americana*)
was once abundant
throughout south
Florida. Extensive loss
of wetlands has
greatly reduced its
numbers. Photo
courtesy of Joan
Hesterberg.

their prey may panic, thus being more readily caught by all the birds
(Kushlan 1990). Herons and egrets feed by sight and dart at prey,
whereas wood storks feed by touch, sweeping their sensitive bills
through shallow water to locate and trap food. This latter method
gives the storks an advantage in murky water where prey are difficult
to see; however, the prey must be concentrated in order for the storks
to feed successfully.

Florida populations of most of the large waders are decreasing.
Plume hunting in the last century and the dewatering of south
Florida (the result of widespread drainage) have taken their toll. John
Ogden, of Everglades National Park, notes that there has been a recent
trend of northward movement of wood storks, and a reduction in
rookery size. Restoration of the Everglades will be beneficial to wading birds and many other species that depend on these valuable wetlands.

Warblers

Perhaps no group of North American birds is as colorful as the several
genera collectively called warblers. Their plumage is marvelously varied—from gray, brown, black and white to reds, yellows, and blues.
Although only about ten of the forty warbler species that breed in
North America nest in Florida, we are fortunate to have many wintering birds. It is amazing how sudden the influx of palm and yellow-
rumped warblers can be, following the passage of a winter cold front.

The prothonotary warbler has been called "the essence of the cypress country" (Sprunt 1954) because it is restricted to swamps during its breeding season. It is sometimes called the "golden swamp warbler" because of the male's bright yellow head and underparts. Breeding occurs as far south as central Florida, where the birds use cavities in cypress and other trees, even nesting in cypress knees. Nests are usually located only a few feet above the water, and are lined with a variety of plant materials including cypress bark. Not surprisingly, nestlings can swim if they have to.

The prothonotary often forages on the lower parts of tree trunks (like a nuthatch), or at the water's edge (like a waterthrush), but can also feed in the upper canopy. Kathy and I once watched a male prothonotary dismember and eat a four-inch-long dragonfly. Unfortunately we did not see how it was captured. The prothonotary's call is a loud and penetrating "sweet-sweet-sweet-sweet." Like many warblers, it winters in Central and South America.

With its bold pattern of black and white streaking, the black-and-white warbler is unmistakable (fig. 42). Rather than gleaning prey from foliage as do many warblers, the black-and-white typically forages for insects that hide in cracks in the bark of tree trunks and limbs. Its mode of feeding is less hurried compared to its gleaning relatives that rush around in the canopy. Although the black-and-white warbler does not breed in Florida, and its main migration route is farther west over the Gulf of Mexico, many black-and-whites spend their winters in Florida swamps and hammocks.

Figure 42. The black-and-white warbler
(*Mniotilta varia*) is an atypical warbler because
it gleans insects from tree trunks. It is common
in Florida's swamps in winter.

No less distinctive than the warblers already mentioned is the common yellowthroat, a familiar black-masked bird. True to its name, the male has a rich, butter-yellow throat; the color is less obvious in the female. The male wears a prominent black mask. This warbler is widely distributed and includes no fewer than twelve subspecies (Griscom and Sprunt 1957). The common yellowthroat inhabits brushy areas, such as the edges of cypress swamps where titi and tangles of greenbrier and wild grape provide cover. In habits, it has been described as wrenlike because it lives mostly in the shrub layer of the forest. It is often seen close up when it suddenly appears beside a trail. The yellowthroat is represented in Florida by both residents and migrants. Its song is a distinctive, repeated "wichy" or "wichity."

The northern Parula is a small warbler with white wing bars, a bluish back and a yellow-green "saddle" patch; the throat is a brighter yellow and, in the male, is bordered by a distinctive dark band. The Parula breeds as far south as Collier County, and supposedly the distribution of the southern race is governed by that of the Spanish moss, which is its primary nesting material. The Parula is highly versatile in its feeding methods. One way it forages is "creeper-fashion" on tree trunks. In fact, the early American naturalist Gatesby called it a "finch creeper." It also searches for insects by fluttering like a chickadee among smaller branches (Griscom and Sprunt 1957).

The yellow-throated warbler is a striking bird with a black-and-white head, a brilliant yellow throat, and a contrasting white belly. It also breeds as far south as central Florida and, like the Parula, can forage creeper-fashion, searching the deeply fissured bark of ancient live oak trunks and larger limbs for insects and spiders (Griscom and Sprunt 1957). Sprunt refers to this warbler as "the animated spirit of the Spanish moss and live oak." It winters from South Carolina to central Florida and in the Bahamas and Antilles. It is one of the most frequently seen songbirds in our swamps, where it nests in late spring.

Two of the most common winter warblers in Florida are the yellow-rumped warbler and the palm warbler. The yellow-rumped, as its name implies, has a distinctive yellow rump patch. In addition, the male in breeding plumage has a yellow crest and yellow patches on the chest just forward of the wings. Most of the winter birds are various shades of brownish-gray, however, with only the bright rump to identify them. The yellow-rumped is also called the myrtle warbler because in winter it feeds primarily on fruit, especially wax myrtle; but it also relishes the small white berries of poison ivy. In addition, it feeds on insects, which it catches by hawking or by hovering and picking them from the bark (Griscom and Sprunt 1957).

The palm warbler, even in breeding plumage, is drab in comparison to the myrtle—mainly brownish on top with an olive-green rump and yellow underparts; a rusty-colored cap is evident in spring. It wags its tail up and down both when standing still and while walking through the grass. The palm warbler feeds primarily on the ground in open areas, but will forage in woodlands when in mixed-species flocks (Griscom and Sprunt 1957). Neither the palm nor the yellow-rumped nests in Florida; but they certainly take advantage of our winter!

Warblers are subject to heavy natural and human-related mortality. In migration, thousands die during their nightly flights by colliding with tall structures like radio antennas, buildings, lighthouses, towers, and monuments. Lights on these structures attract and disorient them. Other warblers are overtaken by storms and die at sea, or just make it to shore only to fall exhausted. Kathy and I spent several Easter vacations on a small cay off Belize, Central America, where spring migrants would find temporary refuge following storms. On a nearby mangrove cay, boa constrictors found the tired birds easy prey. Loss and fragmentation of habitat, both on their northern nesting grounds and in their southern wintering areas, is now reaching crisis proportions for some species (Robbins et al. 1989; Greenwood 1990). Recent data obtained from throughout the East suggests that numbers of warblers and other neotropical migrants are declining (Hagan and Johnson 1992). The specialized habits of many warblers make them sensitive barometers of environmental degradation in both their wintering and breeding areas.

Woodpeckers

Woodpeckers are often seen and heard in our swamps. Eight species occur in Florida, not including the extirpated ivory-bill. The year-round availability of wood-boring insect prey and the wintertime abundance of fruit may explain the variety of woodpeckers in Florida.

Two large woodpeckers were once common in our swamps—the ivory-billed and the pileated. The loud tapping of the largest species, the crow-sized ivory-billed woodpecker, is gone from our swamps forever. It once lived in extensive mature bottomland forests and other swamps from east Texas to North Carolina. Cutting these mature trees destroyed both its food source and its nesting sites. Its food consisted mainly of beetle grubs, which it dug from the sapwood of recently dead hardwoods (Tanner 1942); but it also dug deeper for insect larvae and even fed on fruit (Agey and Heinzmann 1971). Audubon ([1840–44] 1967) mentioned that the ivory-bill would eat persimmons and sugarberries by "hanging by its claws like a titmouse."

Ivory-bills were shot by Indian and white hunters for their meat and colorful feathers. Audubon ([1840–44] 1967) described how the skins were used as ornaments: "Its rich scalp attached to the upper mandible forms an ornament for the war-dress of most of our Indians, or for the shot-pouch of our squatters and hunters, by all of whom the bird is shot merely for that purpose. I have seen entire belts of Indian chiefs closely ornamented with the tufts and bills of this species, and have observed that a great value is frequently put upon them."

In 1939, there were an estimated twenty-two ivory-bills remaining in the United States; all but six were in Florida. The last confirmed sighting of the ivory-bill from Florida was in 1967, when at least one bird was seen in Green Swamp (Agey and Heinzmann 1971). The birds had apparently recently nested in an area of the swamp that was later cleared. Feathers from the nest cavity were identified as being from an ivory-bill by Alexander Wetmore, an ornithologist at the Smithsonian. It was believed that one bird was still present in the area in 1969. There is still hope that a few ivory-billed woodpeckers remain undiscovered in some inaccessible southeastern swamps, but it is highly unlikely.

The distinctive hornlike "toot" of the ivory-bill was unmistakable. Audubon ([1840–44] 1967) poetically described the bird in his classic *Birds of America*:

> Its notes are clear, loud, and yet rather plaintive. They are heard at some considerable distance, perhaps half a mile, and resemble the false high note of a clarinet . . . pait, pait, pait. . . . The transit from one tree to another, even should the distance be as much as a hundred yards, is performed by a single sweep, and the bird appears as if merely swinging itself from the top of one tree to that of the other, forming an elegantly curved line. At this moment all the beauty of the plumage is exhibited, and strikest the beholder with pleasure. . . . I have always imagined, that in the plumage of the beautiful ivory-billed woodpecker, there is something very closely allied to the style of colouring of the great Vandyke. The

broad extent of its dark glossy body and tail, the large and well-defined white markings of its wings, neck, and bill, relieved by the rich carmine of the pendant crest of the male, and the brilliant yellow of its eye, have never failed to remind me of some of the noblest productions of that inimitable artist's pencil. . . . Whenever I have observed one of these birds flying from one tree to another, I have mentally exclaimed, "There goes another Vandyke!"

Perhaps, if bottomland forests in the Southeast are once again allowed to mature, the ivory-bill could be reintroduced from Cuba, where a small population persists (Greenway 1958; Dennis 1988).

Our largest woodpecker is now the pileated, a striking bird with a scarlet-crested head, white neck stripes, and a mostly black body. Its loud and regular tapping, done to proclaim its territory and to excavate wood-boring beetle grubs and carpenter ants from deep within dead wood, carries for long distances, as does its loud "kuk-kuk-kuk" call. Besides insects, the pileated eats fruits, including those of greenbrier, swamp tupelo, wild grape, poison ivy, and Magnolia. Also, both the pileated and red-bellied woodpeckers occasionally prey on nestlings.

The smaller (robin-sized) and more abundant red-bellied woodpecker has a light red cap and a black-and-white–barred back. The indistinct pink belly patch gives this bird its poorly chosen name. Like the pileated, the red-bellied is highly vocal. Alexander Sprunt (1954) described the call as a "rather harsh, rolling chur and penetrating chack." Unlike the pileated, the red-bellied rarely drills into wood. Instead, it probes bark for insects, and searches for fruits and nuts both in trees and on the ground. It will sometimes dig for beetle larvae in live trees. Both the red-bellied and the pileated are cavity nesters; the opening made by the pileated is rectangular, while that of the red-bellied is round.

Carolina Parakeet

"The richness of their plumage, their beautiful mode of flight, and even their scream, afford welcome intimation that our darkest forests and most sequestered swamps are not destitute of charms" (Audubon [1840–44] 1967). With bright, forest-green body, wings, and tail, and a yellow head radiant with an orange face, Carolina parakeets, careening through cypress swamps like animated projectiles, screeching loudly, must have been a memorable sight and sound.

Before the turn of the century, Carolina parakeets were abundant in Florida (Sprunt 1954). In 1881, naturalist Ernst Maynard (in Sprunt 1954) described what led to their extinction: "Their enemies are legion; bird catchers trap them by hundreds for the northern market, sportsmen shoot them for food, planters kill them because they eat their fruit, and tourists slaughter them simply because they present a favorable mark." Earlier, Audubon had described the same carnage and also boasted that he could get "a basketful of birds at a few shots." The birds were viewed as pests since they ruined unripened cultivated fruits to eat the seeds, and destroyed grain crops (Audubon [1840–44] 1967). Although intelligent, Carolina parakeets apparently were unafraid of man. When part of a flock was killed, the remaining birds would still return to the spot, thus exposing themselves to continued slaughter.

Carolina parakeets, like other parrots, were extremely dexterous birds that could open nuts other birds avoided. Besides cypress seeds, they ate seeds of elms, oaks, maples (also the flowers), and pines, in addition to consuming a variety of fruits, and possibly also insects.

The parakeets were nomadic birds, traveling widely to exploit seasonal foods. Audubon ([1840–44] 1967) mentioned that small flocks roosted in tree cavities. Writing in his typical picturesque style, he described their roosting behavior: "Below the entrance [to the cavity] the birds all clung to the bark, and crawl into the hole to pass the night. When such a hole does not prove sufficient to hold the whole flock, those around the entrance hook themselves on by their claws, and the tip of the upper mandible, and look as if hanging by the bill."

Carolina parakeets were last reported from Florida between 1900 and 1920. In February 1920, Henry Redding saw perhaps the last flock at Fort Drum, near Fort Pierce (Dennis 1988).

Barred Owl

The call of the barred owl is as much a symbol of southeastern swamps as the call of the common loon is the emblem of the lakes of Canada and New England. I am always moved when I hear the long "whoo-ah" or the nine-syllable "who-cooks-for-you, who-cooks-for-you-all?" of a barred owl reverberating through a swamp, asking where its mate is or advertising its presence to neighbors.

The barred owl is a medium-sized raptor with brown barring on its buff-colored breast. It is the most common owl of its size (sixteen to twenty inches tall) in the United States, being smaller than the great horned owl but larger than the eastern screech-owl. Our barred owl belongs to the southeastern subspecies called the Florida barred owl (although its subspecific name, *georgica,* suggests it's actually the "Georgia barred owl"). It is the only large owl in the Southeast with a streaked breast and a round face lacking "ears."

The barred owl is widely distributed throughout the East and across southern Canada to the Rocky Mountains. It is closely related to the rare spotted owl, which is an inhabitant of the old-growth Douglas fir forests of the West.

Although the barred owl is ubiquitous in eastern swamps, little is known about its ecology. Most numerous in wetlands, it also lives in pine and upland hardwood forests as well as in forest-margin habitats where there are large, mature trees with suitable nesting cavities. Outside of Florida, barred owls occupy home ranges of about one square mile, but the size of the range is dependent on the availability of prey. Ranges may expand in winter when food is scarce (Johnsgard 1988). The birds maintain this territory and probably become intimately familiar with it, thus knowing where and when prey are most abundant. The average population density is only about one pair per seven square miles. But one night at Blue Spring State Park along the St. Johns River, we heard no fewer than five birds calling. Clearly, the density can be higher at times and is probably at least partially dependent upon the abundance of prey. Barred owls are opportunistic predators, feeding on insects, crayfish, fish, amphibians, reptiles, and birds; however, small rodents, especially voles, are apparently their preferred prey (Johnsgard 1988).

Like most owls, barred owls are nocturnal hunters and have a red eye shine typical of nocturnal birds. Owl feathers are modified so their flight is nearly silent. Audubon ([1840–44] 1967) wrote of the barred owl's flight: "So very lightly do they fly, that I have frequently discovered one passing over me, and only a few yards distant, by first seeing its shadow on the ground, during clear moon-light nights, when not the faintest rustling of its wings could be heard."

Barred owls may form permanent pair bonds, and they may live for more than ten years. Although pairs occupy the same large territory, they may not always be together outside the breeding season. In Fakahatchee Strand, however, I saw a pair mutually preening in July. This was well after the early spring nesting season, suggesting that pair bonds can be maintained by direct contact beyond the breeding season.

Courtship begins in winter. Kathy and I distinctly remember an early winter night in the East Dismal Swamp in North Carolina. It was our first introduction to swamp camping and we were apprehensive about what the night would bring. We pitched our tent beneath a large laurel oak at the edge of a swamp. At about 2 A.M., we were suddenly awakened by indescribable loud noises, just a few feet above our tent, which kept us awake for some time. Peeking outside into the pitch dark, we saw only vague silhouettes. Not until we heard their "normal" calls did we realize that the large flapping shapes were a pair of barred owls, courting.

Besides vocalizations, the courtship display by the male consists of swaying the body from side to side and then raising first each wing in turn, and then both wings. Also, both birds may fluff their feathers repeatedly.

Audubon ([1840–44] 1967) recounted his nocturnal encounters with barred owls in this humorous vein:

How often, when snugly settled under the bough of my temporary encampment, and preparing to roast a venison steak or the body of a squirrel, have I been saluted with the exulting burst of this nightly disturber of the peace, that, had it not been for him, would have prevailed around me, as well as in my lonely retreat! How often have I seen this nocturnal marauder alight within a few yards of me, exposed his whole body to the glare of my fire, and eye me in such a curious manner that, had it been reasonable to do so, I would gladly have invited him to walk in and join me in my repast, that I might have enjoyed the pleasure of forming a better acquaintance with him. The liveliness of his motions, joined to the oddness, have often made me think that his society would be at least as agreeable as that of many of the buffoons we meet with in the world.

The sounds that barred owls make are amazingly varied and have been described as: "cackling," "laughing," and "whooping," as well as the normal "who-cooks-for-you?" territorial call. Calls are given both night and day. Upon hearing the monosyllabic hoot of a daytime owl, a little girl at Highlands Hammock State Park excitedly exclaimed, "There's a whooo!"

In Florida, barred owls begin nesting in late winter or spring; eggs have been found from January to March. Up to three eggs are laid in a tree cavity, a squirrel's nest, or on a stick platform. Incubation takes

Figure 43. The American swallow-tailed kite (*Elanoides forficatus forficatus*), with its splendid fork-shaped tail, is our most striking wetland raptor. Because of habitat loss, it is becoming imperiled. Photo courtesy of Robert Bennetts.

about a month. The young are able to leave the nest after five weeks, but do not fledge until about six weeks. They receive food from the parents for up to four months.

In Audubon's day, barred owls were hunted for food. He noted that the birds were sold in the New Orleans market and that the Creoles made a gumbo of them (Audubon [1840–44] 1967). Barred owls are common in Florida, but if plantation forests continue to spread, the lack of old trees with nest cavities may reduce their numbers.

American Swallow-tailed Kite

Few birds are as distinctive as the swallow-tailed kite. This medium-sized raptor has a long, deeply forked tail, and from below it is mostly white except for its wings and tail, which are deeply edged in black (fig. 43). The beak and feet are surprisingly petite for a raptor, reflecting the small size of its prey and its aerial feeding mode: with the grace of a swallow, this kite swoops down to pluck anoles and small snakes from trees or to hawk insects in midair.

From March to September, the swallow-tailed kite is found mostly in Florida, where more than half of the known U.S. population of about three thousand birds live (Millsap 1987; Meyer and Collopy in press). It winters in South America. Its northern range extends from

South Carolina around the gulf to Louisiana; formerly it also extended up the Mississippi valley as far north as Minnesota (Bent [1937] 1961).

When in its breeding range, the swallow-tailed kite is primarily a resident of wetlands, where it forages and nests. The ornithologist A. C. Bent described his first encounter with this bird near Cape Sable in the Everglades (Bent [1937] 1961): "We saw seven of these lovely birds sailing about over the prairie, soaring in circles high overhead, or scaling along close to the ground, like glorified swallows. . . . It was a joy to watch their graceful movements and a pity to disturb them, but my companion, the late Louis A. Fuertes, and I both wanted specimens. . . . We shot no more; they were too beautiful; and we were rapt in admiration of their graceful lines, the purity of their contrasting colors, and the beautiful grapelike bloom on their backs and wings. . . . I shall never forget the loving reverence with which the noted bird artist admired his specimen, as he began at once to sketch its charms."

Swallow-tailed kites forage on the wing, making use of wind and thermals to stay aloft. They sometimes gather where dragonflies are plentiful. One June, in the northern section of the Big Cypress within the Seminole Indian Reservation, I watched a group of kites hawking dragonflies. Their seemingly effortless aerobatic movements were reminiscent of the flight of frigatebirds, which also have a deeply forked tail. Audubon ([1840–44] 1967) vividly described their feeding method: "They dive in rapid succession amongst the branches, glancing along the trunks, and seizing in their course the insects and small lizards of which they are in quest. Their motions are astonishingly rapid, and the deep curves which they describe, their sudden doublings and crossings, and the extreme ease with which they seem to cleave the air, excite the admiration of him who views them. . . . They soar to an immense height, pursuing the large insects called Musquito Hawks [dragonflies], and performing the most singular evolutions that can be conceived, using their tail with an elegance of motion peculiar to themselves."

The kites' prey consists primarily of large flying and crawling insects like grasshoppers, cicadas, and dragonflies, as well as frogs, anoles, and snakes; they also eat young songbirds and even bats (Bent [1937] 1961; Snyder 1974; Meyer and Collopy in press). Adults mainly consume insects, but nestlings are fed vertebrates. Prey are eaten on the wing, a practice unlike that of most raptors, which usually fly to a perch to dismember prey.

Nesting takes place in cypress and hardwood swamps throughout Florida in late February or early March, soon after the birds arrive from South America (Snyder 1974; Meyer and Collopy in press). Again unlike most raptors, swallow-tailed kites both nest and roost in colonies—usually in tall open cypress and pine trees (Snyder 1974; Millsap 1987; Meyer and Collopy in press). Their nests consist of long sticks interwoven with Spanish moss and threadlike *Usnea* and *Ramalina* lichens (Meyer and Collopy in press). Very protective of their nests, adults will mob potential predators such a crows. The young are fed until the migration period, which begins in late August or early September.

In south Florida's agricultural areas, kites use the exotic Australian pines for nesting (Meyer and Collopy in press). In such locations, the nests are easily destroyed by winds. Brian Millsap, a state nongame biologist, recently described a previously unknown communal roost of swallow-tailed kites near Fisheating Creek, on the west side of Lake Okeechobee, where more than five hundred birds were seen between July and September (Millsap 1987).

Their habit of returning to the same nesting and roosting sites makes these kites especially vulnerable to timber cutting and wetland loss; also, migration mortality may be significant, adding further uncertainty about the future of this imperiled species (Meyer and Collopy in press).

Red-shouldered Hawk

The red-shouldered hawk is the most common raptor in Florida's forested wetlands, and could be described as the "swamp hawk." Its high-pitched "keee-ah, keee-ah, keee-ah" is frequently heard in swamps of all kinds, especially during the early spring breeding season.

The red-shoulder is somewhat larger than a crow (about eighteen inches tall), and has rufous-colored shoulders and a light rusty chest (fig. 44). Young birds' shoulder patches and chest are paler, but the breast is more visibly streaked. The adult's tail is dark with multiple thin white bands. In juveniles, the tail is banded black and gray. In peninsular Florida, a lighter-colored subspecies (*Buteo lineatus alleni*) is recognized.

When hunting, red-shouldered hawks are silent and not easily discovered. They generally perch low in the canopy, often only twenty to thirty feet up on a horizontal limb, and search the ground below for

Figure 44. Red-shouldered hawks (*Buteo lineatus*) are often seen in swamps where they perch low in the canopy and watch for frogs, snakes, and other prey.

small prey. They only rarely soar like other buteos. Red-shoulders are highly opportunistic predators, feeding on earthworms, insects, crayfish, spiders, snails, amphibians, turtles, snakes, lizards, birds, and mammals (Bent [1937] 1961; Ogden 1974).

Red-shoulders can kill prey nearly their own size. They have been known to attack fully grown eastern gray squirrels, small opossums, and tricolored herons, which weigh about as much as the hawk (Edscorn 1974). Kathy and I have seen red-shouldered hawks on occasion dive into the underbrush and retrieve three- to four-foot-long snakes, generally rat snakes. Also, at Highlands Hammock, I watched a red-shouldered hawk only a few yards away, feeding on a juvenile armadillo that it had just killed. The armadillo was too large to be carried off, so the hawk ate it on the ground.

Red-shouldered hawks breed in Florida in the late winter and early spring. The dramatic aerial displays, involving several pairs, include steep dives, "sky dancing" and "high-circling," and a great deal of calling (Palmer 1988). The large and bulky nest, built in tall cypress or pine trees at the edge of a swamp, is often two to three feet in diameter; it consists of sticks and other vegetation, including Spanish moss. Pairs mate for life. A succession of birds may use the same nest year after year, or a pair may build a new nest each year. Red-shoulders' nests may also be used by barred owls or other hawks, and vice versa. Occasionally, barred owls and red-shouldered hawks nest in the same tree. Even more bizarre are reports of both species simultaneously laying eggs in the same nest (Sprunt 1954)! Other reports, however, suggest that barred owls and red-shoulders are intolerant of one another when nesting (Ogden 1974).

Although red-shouldered hawk populations in Florida declined drastically between the 1940s and 1960s, they have since remained rather stable (Kiltie 1987). In contrast, red-tailed hawk populations increased between 1940 and 1980. One explanation for this difference was that deforestation provided more open habitat for red-tails, but reduced the forest habitat necessary for red-shoulders (Kiltie 1987).

Mammals

Mammals, like birds, are diverse in size and ecological function. Although our mammal fauna is not particularly rich, Florida is fortunate in that it is still home to several large carnivores, such as the river otter, panther, and black bear, which have been extirpated elsewhere in the East. About fifty species of land mammals live in Florida (Stevenson 1976; Layne 1988). South Florida alone has thirty-two native species and about fifty subspecies (Layne 1984, 1988). The large number of mammalian subspecies living here is apparently due to the many relict populations that have been isolated in Florida for thousands of years. Unfortunately, most people are only aware of our mammal fauna from the specimens that are killed on our roads. Highways, in fact, may be the main source of mortality for many of our wildlife species (Harris and Gallagher 1989).

Swamps offer food and protection to a host of mammals. In south Florida, where wetlands predominate, nearly 70 percent of the mammals occur in wetlands (Layne 1988). Other than the ubiquitous raccoon, marsh rabbit, opossum, white-tailed deer, eastern gray squirrel, and the introduced nine-banded armadillo, however, most of the mammal fauna remains unseen amid dense cover. Among the animals easily overlooked are small and secretive shrews like the short-tailed shrew and the least shrew and rodents like the cotton mouse, rice rat, and hispid cotton rat. Bats such as the evening bat can be more common in swamps than in other habitats, thanks to the abundance of moths, beetles, and other nocturnal flying insects, plus tree cavities for roosting (Robson 1990). Several large carnivores also frequent swamps; these include the Florida black bear, the bobcat, the Florida panther, the river otter, and the mink. Although many mammals use wetlands, only six species (rice rat, round-tailed muskrat, beaver, marsh rabbit, mink, and river otter) are primarily wetland species (Layne 1988).

Extensive loss or degradation of other habitats makes swamps increasingly crucial as sources of food and cover for our mammals. During the dry season, ponds in cypress domes may provide much-needed water for mammals. Because of increased habitat fragmentation, riverine wetlands (riverside habitats) have become crucial travel routes for mammals and other animals (Harris and Gallagher 1989; Harris and Scheck 1991). Florida panthers can use linear woodlands, such as strands, as corridors through their vast territories (Maehr et al. 1991). Florida is fortunate to have many riverine wetlands linking habitats across the state. But improper placement of roads and power lines, as well as agricultural and urban development, could reduce the habitat value of these important landscape features.

Mammals that live primarily in wetlands show specialized adaptations (Layne 1988). For example, they often have a waterproof coat and webbed feet; and some species have long hind legs to help them jump through marshy terrain. Also, their reproductive cycles may be correlated to rainfall.

The beaver, our largest rodent, is well adapted to an aquatic life. Awkward on land, it is an adept swimmer and can stay submerged for up to fifteen minutes. Although once occurring as far south as central Florida, beavers were extirpated from much of their former range in the East by unregulated trapping. They are now plentiful in parts of the Panhandle, where they are considered a nuisance because their dams cause localized flooding of roads, as well as the death of flood-intolerant trees (James Layne, Archbold Biological Station, pers. comm., 1991). Nonetheless, beavers can be beneficial because their dams provide aquatic habitat and enlarge riparian wetlands. Left alone, beaver ponds eventually fill with sediment and become rich bottomland hardwood forests.

Another wetland rodent, the round-tailed muskrat (listed by the state as a species of special concern) is an inhabitant of marshes, cypress domes, and other wetlands (Layne 1984; Humphrey 1992). This muskrat is so dependent on water that it must burrow into moist peat during the dry season; many die during droughts. It builds hemispherical houses up to two feet in diameter and constructs feeding platforms from vegetation in ponds. Its tunnel-like runways radiate through adjacent marshes, where it feeds on emergent vegetation.

One of the most common wetland mammals is the marsh rabbit, which is widely distributed in swampy habitats from Florida to Virginia along the southeastern coastal plain. It is short-eared, and dark brown in color. Our other common rabbit, the eastern cottontail, prefers drier places and is more often found in residential areas (Layne 1984). On some evenings a dark brown marsh rabbit sits outside my office window, nibbling the grass. Its short ears make it appear quite unrabbitlike.

Raccoon

By far our most abundant midsized mammalian carnivore is the raccoon. This masked bandit of garbage cans and campsites is becoming so numerous in residential areas that large numbers are killed on roads. Raccoons are expanding their range into areas they have never inhabited before; presently they occur from Canada to Panama. Sanderson (1983) reported that raccoons now live in areas of Canada where the native Indians previously had no local name for them.

Raccoons are very much at home in wetlands. Their long-toed tracks are ubiquitous around cypress ponds and other wetlands where they search for aquatic prey. Their acute sense of touch enables them to catch amphibians, fish, mussels, and crayfish, simply by feel. Raccoons always seem to wash their food before eating it. In fact, their species name, the Latin word *lotor,* means "the washer." But, as Sanderson (1983) points out, raccoons don't necessarily wash their food to clean it. This stereotyped behavior, seen primarily in captive animals, apparently stems from the normal searching behavior of wild animals who capture much of their food in water. Part of the success of this species comes from its ability to exploit whatever food is available (a trait also demonstrated by the Florida black bear). Thus, raccoon foods range from aquatic animals to fruits and seeds, along with whatever we inadvertently provide.

The abundance of raccoons in Florida and elsewhere is cause for concern. Along the Wekiva River north of Orlando, raccoons have become accustomed to eating food placed daily on the riverbank. Kathy and I have seen more than a hundred raccoons attracted to this spot. Rabies, distemper, and other diseases are readily spread under such conditions. Raccoons can carry canine distemper, a fatal disease that can be transmitted to gray foxes. Raccoons are also the major carriers of rabies in the state (Donald Forester, Univ. of Florida, School of Veterinary Medicine, pers. comm., 1991). They may be cute, but raccoons are also significant predators of birds' eggs and nestlings, and may be contributing to the decline of both songbirds (Robbins et al. 1989) and wading birds (Ruckdeschel and Shoop 1989). At one time, big alligators may have regulated raccoon populations in wetlands, but now there are too few large gators to have much impact. The superabundance of raccoons is an indicator that natural population control is defunct.

River Otter

Another familiar wetland carnivore is the river otter. Its fluid grace in water as it dives after fish and other aquatic prey has probably captured the attention of all of us. Otters, unlike most of our other carnivores, are social even outside the breeding season, although adults may also be solitary. The family is usually composed of a female and her young. Other unrelated adult otters will temporarily join a family, however, and several families may merge (Melquist and Hornocker 1983). Group bonding occurs through mutual grooming and play (Beckel 1990).

Otters eat a variety of aquatic animals including amphibians and crustaceans, but fish less than eight inches in length were found in one study to be the principal prey (Beckel 1990). Surprisingly, solitary otters capture more prey than otters in a group (Beckel 1990), but otters within a group might be able to exploit a greater variety of prey by learning from one another how to capture particular prey. Also, being in a group may confer some protection from alligators.

Although river otters adapt well to disturbed habitats, their overall abundance in Florida may be declining because of wetland losses (Layne 1984). Water pollution could also adversely affect otter numbers. For example, the abnormally high mercury levels found in largemouth bass from areas in south Florida (Roelke 1990; Roelke et al. 1991; Simons 1991) could accumulate in otters, with potentially dangerous effects. Additional unnecessary mortality comes from state-sanctioned fur trapping. In a number of other states, the otter is protected; and in some states efforts are even underway to reintroduce it where it has been extirpated. In Florida, the river otter has been ranked tenth out of thirty species needing management (Millsap et al. 1990). Florida should closely monitor otter populations as indicators of wetland ecosystem integrity.

Bobcat

Florida has two species of native cats, the bobcat and the Florida panther. The bobcat is the more common. Adult bobcats are about three feet long (including the short tail) and two feet high at the shoulder, and they weigh about twenty pounds. They are widely distributed in the United States and are found throughout Florida in wooded habitats including swamps and hammocks. In one study in northeast Florida, bottomland hardwoods were their preferred habitat (Progulske 1982).

Like the otter, the bobcat is still legally trapped in large numbers in Florida for its fur (Maehr and Brady 1986). Although naive animals are easily trapped, bobcats that have been caught and manage to escape are understandably reluctant to be trapped again. In one study, a female bobcat that was trapped and then released marked the trap with fecal or urine scrapes (Wassmer, Guenther, and Layne 1988). Apparently as a consequence, her kittens avoided the trap.

In Florida, the density of bobcats is about one per square mile in appropriate habitats (Conner 1982; Layne 1984; Wassmer, Guenther, and Layne 1988). The size of their home range was estimated to be ten to fifteen square miles for males and about half that for females (Progulske 1982; Wassmer, Guenther, and Layne 1988). Often the range of a male overlaps that of a female, but the ranges of adjacent males rarely overlap. Wassmer and coworkers (1988) suggested that overlapping ranges of male and female bobcats indicate that social interactions occurring outside of the breeding season may maintain pair bonding. Territory boundaries coincided with natural and humanmade habitat edges, including roads, fire trails, power-line rights-of-way, and pastures. This suggests that, as contiguous forests diminish in size and are increasingly crisscrossed by roads and other barriers, they become less suitable for bobcats. Yet bobcats make extensive use of inactive roads and fire trails, and these habitat edges may actually increase their access to such prey as rabbits (Wassmer, Guenther, and Layne 1988).

Bobcats mark their boundaries by scraping the ground and then urinating or defecating in the depression, in much the same way domestic cats do. These scrapes alert bobcats to the boundaries of their own territories as well as those of their neighbors and may also provide information on the age, sex, and reproductive status of neighbors.

In one study, bobcats in Florida were found to breed from August to March (Wassmer, Guenther, and Layne 1988). It was also noted that females less than one year old can give birth, but they have smaller litters than do older cats, which can have up to five kittens (two to three is the norm). Generally only one litter is produced per year, but some females produce two.

Bobcats are superb hunters, agile enough to capture small birds but with the strength to take much larger game, including feral hogs and deer. Small mammals like rabbits and cotton rats dominate their diet in Florida, with birds composing only 10 percent of total prey (Maehr and Brady 1986; Wassmer, Guenther, and Layne 1988). Perhaps not surprisingly, bobcats rarely attack adult armadillos. The ability of the bobcat to feed on rabbits and other small mammals—which are relatively abundant in both human-altered and natural habitats—has no doubt enabled bobcats to prosper in increasingly altered habitats.

Natural mortality rates of bobcats in Florida can be high. In one study in central Florida by Wassmer and coworkers (1988), mortality ranged from 16 percent per year for adults to 24 percent per year for juveniles. Half of the cats died from viral infections (mainly feline panleucopenia). Mange, a parasite, was also prevalent, causing animals to weaken or die. Human-induced deaths, such as road kills and those attributable to gunshots, were less significant than infections and parasites. Mortality would have been even greater had the population been exploited by fur trapping (during the study, there was no trapping). Human-induced mortality not only decreases the abundance of bobcats but also disrupts social organization, perhaps putting additional stress on the cats (Wassmer, Guenther, and Layne 1988). Large predators like bobcats are still considered by some people to be competitors for deer and other game, or are killed for their fur. Should we continue to exploit ecologically important predators and allow the management of individual game species to take precedence over the proper functioning of ecosystems?

Florida Panther

The hammocks, swamps, pine flatwoods, and other wild habitats of southwest Florida are the last refuge of our largest native cat, the endangered Florida panther, a subspecies of *Felis concolor*. Also known as puma, mountain lion, and cougar, *F. concolor* formerly ranged from Canada to Argentina and was once the most widespread terrestrial mammal in the New World with the exception of humans. Now the Florida panther is the sole remaining *F. concolor* subspecies in the eastern United States and Canada.

Prior to this century, Florida panthers were abundant and widely dispersed, ranging from east Texas to Florida and as far north as Tennessee. Today, fewer than about fifty animals are left, living primarily in hammocks, flatwoods, and swamps in Collier, Hendry, Lee, and Highlands Counties in southwest Florida (Belden 1989; Maehr 1990, 1992; Maehr, Land, and Roof 1991) (fig. 45). The catastrophic decline in panther populations is tragic, considering that they were once so common as to be considered pests.

How did Florida panther populations become so dangerously low? As in many similar situations involving large predators, misconceptions rather than scientific fact dictated the animal's fate. Considering the panther's present legal protection, as well as its revered status among the public and wildlife biologists trying to rescue it from extinction, it is stunning to reflect that just a few decades ago the Florida panther was more valuable dead than alive. Persecuted because they were considered a threat to humans and a killer of livestock, panthers were already uncommon by the early part of this century. Deer were their natural prey; but in the 1930s, deer populations were thinned because they were suspected of transmitting tick fever, a disease

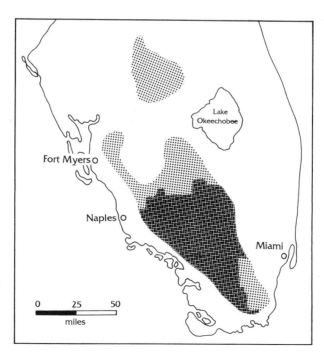

Figure 45. Present distribution of the Florida panther. Light hatching represents total panther range. Dark hatching represents range in public ownership. Redrawn from Maehr, Land, and Roof 1991.

affecting cattle. With fewer deer, some panthers were probably forced to attack cattle, which resulted in ranchers in turn escalating their assault on panthers.

From 1950 to 1958, the Florida panther was partially protected by the state, which allowed panthers to be hunted legally only during the deer season. Animals suspected of killing livestock, however, could be shot at any time, by permit (Belden 1989). Many others were probably illegally killed by poachers. In 1958, the Florida panther was given further protection by the state, but it was too late, as populations had already plummeted. Finally, in 1967 the Florida panther was officially listed as endangered by the U.S. Fish and Wildlife Service, and it was federally protected under the Endangered Species Act when it was enacted in 1973.

Intensive scientific research over the past decade has provided much information about this cat's biology. Mature panthers are quite variable in weight, ranging from about sixty-five to 160 pounds, with males being larger (Belden 1989). Florida panthers are tawny in color, and many have a right-angled crook at the tip of the tail, a cowlick, and other minor anomalies resulting from inbreeding—a consequence of small population size.

Panthers are primarily nocturnal, spending the day in dense cover, and hence are extremely difficult to observe (Maehr et al. 1991). Consequently, biologists have had to infer much about their behavior by tracking radio-collared cats. To collar one, the selected panther is first pursued by trained hounds. Once treed, the panther is immobilized by a dart gun. A veterinary team (present at all captures) ensures that the cat is safely handled and determines the state of its health (Roelke 1990). Each cat is measured, immunized for rabies, distemper, and other diseases and then fitted with a radio collar. Between 1981 and 1993, fifty-two Florida panthers were fitted with transmitters (David Maehr, Florida Game and Fresh Water Fish Commission, pers. comm., 1993).

Telemetry has provided crucial data on panther movements that could not be obtained by other methods (fig. 46). Searching for tracks, scrapes, scat, kills, or beds is labor-intensive and provides less information about movements than telemetry. Stress put on the cats by the chase, capture, and anesthesia, however, must be significant, and it no doubt has led to some mortality. Nevertheless, capturing the cats is the only way to obtain data on their health, and it also allows researchers to immunize the cats against diseases.

Figure 46. The Florida panther (*Felis concolor coryi*) is one of Florida's most endangered species. Radio tracking of collared panthers provides essential information on their biology. Photo courtesy of David Maehr, Florida Game and Fresh Water Fish Commission.

Radio-tracking has shown that panthers hunt mainly at night, with peaks in activity at dawn and dusk (Maehr 1990; Maehr et al. 1991). Foraging panthers can cover distances of more than ten miles per night, but the average is two to five miles for adults. During the day, panthers rest in thick vegetation, especially saw palmetto. Females with kittens spend most of the day at a maternal den consisting of a bed of vegetation or soil. Tracking has also shown that panthers use a variety of habitats, depending on availability; hardwood hammocks and pine flatwoods are preferred (Maehr, Land, and Roof 1991).

Before this century, white-tailed deer were the primary prey of panthers. Although deer still are important prey, feral hogs and armadillos became significant as these exotics proliferated; now they make up half of the panther's diet (Maehr et al. 1989a; Maehr et al. 1990). Other significant prey are raccoons and rabbits. Even though panthers share range lands with cattle, researchers found that livestock are rarely eaten (Maehr et al. 1990). If an animal is too large to be consumed in one meal, panthers cover the carcass with debris and return later to resume feeding.

The home range of individual panthers is vast, covering about two hundred square miles for adult males and about seventy square miles for females (Belden 1989; Maehr 1990; Maehr, Land, and Roof 1991).

These are more than ten times the size of the ranges of the smaller bobcat.

The size of a panther's home range depends on several factors. Adult males occupy territories adjacent to those of other males; but, although their ranges may overlap somewhat, the cats tend to avoid one another and generally are separated by a distance of at least half a mile (Maehr 1990; Maehr, Land, and Roof 1991). The size of each territory may also depend on prey densities and on the presence of females. State biologist David Maehr (1990), who has studied the panther extensively, found that a male panther whose territory did not overlap with that of a female would either enlarge its range or shift territorial boundaries in an attempt to find a female, even moving to an area of lower prey density. Thus, social interactions have a significant effect on the ranges of males.

The home range of a female panther depends on whether or not she has kittens, how old they are, and on prey densities (Maehr et al. 1989a). Immediately following the birth of her kittens, a female panther has a small range because the kittens must be nursed frequently. Later her range increases, depending on prey abundance, especially deer. If females must travel widely to secure prey, the young will receive less food, and the female will lose weight from the added activity. This may reduce reproduction and increase mortality (Roelke 1990).

Ranges of both males and females shift when other panthers of the same sex leave or occupy adjacent territories. Young males disperse to unoccupied territories. Because suitable panther habitat is severely limited, young males have difficulty finding unoccupied territory (Maehr 1990; Maehr, Land, and Roof 1991). During this dispersal phase, young male panthers are sometimes killed by adult males. In fact, it is believed that this type of panther mortality may soon surpass the major documented killer, vehicle collisions (Jordan 1991). Dispersing females, on the other hand, apparently have less difficulty securing a territory; in fact, one young female raised her first litter within her mother's home range. Maehr (1990) further determined that although resident males may not kill each other in encounters, all adult males are heavily scarred. In contrast, females are apparently nonaggressive toward one another, or to adult or juvenile males.

Other than females with kittens, adult panthers are mostly solitary except during the brief period each year when females are in estrus (heat) (Maehr 1990). As is the case with bobcats, adult male panthers probably ascertain the reproductive condition of females through direct contact or from scent cues present in urine scrapes (Roof and Maehr 1988).

Female Florida panthers can give birth when they are as young as nineteen months, but males are not sexually active until three years of age (Maehr, Roof, and Land 1989; Maehr 1990). Births occur throughout the year. Up to four kittens are in a litter, but mortality is high and few kittens survive to adulthood. The number of surviving young probably depends on the availability of large prey, especially feral hogs and deer (Roelke 1990). Panthers may live more than fifteen years, but ten years is normal (Belden 1989).

As part of the panther recovery program, state and federal agencies seek to increase panther populations to five hundred animals—about ten times the present estimate and a number that would allow the maintenance of genetic diversity. As with any animal population, genetic variability is essential for long-term health, enabling the species to adapt to a changing environment.

With the present small population size, it is no wonder that Florida panthers have the lowest genetic diversity of any of the cougar subspecies (Roelke 1990). Furthermore, this diversity is decreasing with time, and without population increases diversity will soon be so low that extinction will become inevitable. Inbreeding has already led to several debilitating abnormalities, including congenital heart defects and a condition in males called cryptorchidism, whereby only one testis is functional (Roelke 1990). Interestingly, several male panthers from the Everglades National Park did not have this problem, and studies of their DNA revealed that these cats were intercross offspring—progeny of Florida panthers that had mated with "cougars" (of another subspecies) released into the park in the 1950s and 1960s (Roelke 1990).

The discovery of healthy panther-cougar crosses in the Everglades suggests that further introductions of cats from other cougar subspecies could reduce the congenital problems caused by inbreeding. Although hybrids were not previously protected by the Endangered Species Act, the Fish and Wildlife Service stated in 1991 that protection of hybrids will be considered on a case-by-case basis. The Service has now listed all subspecies of *F. concolor* in Florida as threatened, except for *F. concolor coryi*—the Florida panther, which is still considered endangered. Thus both cougars and panthers—and their hybrid offspring—are legally protected.

The health of Florida panthers is also compromised by a new factor. In the Everglades, two female panthers found dead in 1989 and 1991 contained potentially lethal concentrations of mercury. Mercury, like DDT, is known to move up the food web and accumulate in top predators. High levels of mercury have been found in alligators, bass, and raccoons from the Everglades area (Department of Environmental Regulation 1990; Roelke 1990; Roelke et al. 1991; Simons 1991).

The origin of the mercury is undetermined. Some mercury may have accumulated in the peat over aeons. And increased amounts are now being released into the atmosphere by solid-waste incinerators. As long as mercury is buried deep within the peat, it is relatively benign. When it reaches the surface, it can move into the food chain—in this case from fish to raccoons and finally to panthers.

Other sources of mortality are more directly related to humans. Between 1979 and 1991, thirty-two panther deaths were documented (Roelke 1990; Maehr, Land, and Roelke 1992). Of these, natural or unidentified causes accounted for thirteen deaths; the rest were all human-related, primarily collisions with vehicles. Barely excluded from the mortality lists are additional panthers that were hit by autos but received medical attention and survived.

Statistics show that nearly twice as many male panthers were hit by vehicles as females. Maehr (1990) discovered that males, because of their larger territories, were much more likely to cross roads than females. In Collier and Hendry Counties, only one male panther had a territory devoid of a paved road (Maehr 1990), while most adult females had ranges without roads.

Panther roadkills have been concentrated along two highways, Interstate 75 and State Road 29—both adjacent to Fakahatchee Strand (Maehr 1990). Most of the deaths occurred where the roads bisected swamps. Wildlife underpasses and associated fences along I-75 have already proven effective and should be used in all areas where panthers cross highways.

Panthers face seemingly insurmountable difficulties—inbreeding, mercury poisoning, poaching, vehicle collisions, habitat loss, and disease and parasites. The future of the panther is totally dependent on whether its number can quickly be increased.

A hybrid Florida panther could perhaps survive in the wild indefinitely if its habitat needs were met. Much potential habitat is already in public ownership, but panthers do not recognize property lines and will roam into adjacent private lands. Compounding that is the fact that much of the public land in Florida is extensively used by people, and potential conflicts could occur. The success of any recovery program will require tolerance by ranchers, farmers, hunters, loggers, and others who live, work, and hunt near the panthers.

To increase panther numbers to robust levels will be difficult and expensive. But the unacceptable alternative is a continued decline in the health of the wild population, and long-term custody of captive cats with no hope of their being released. The choice is ours.

I wish I could describe a close encounter with a Florida panther or black bear in the wilds of Fakahatchee or elsewhere, but I have never had such an experience. Exchanging eye contact with a wild animal, especially a large predator, is an experience that is perhaps primal and dramatically illustrates that we are still part of nature. Setting aside land for large carnivores or simply as wilderness may seem wasteful to some but to me it is essential. As E. O. Wilson, the Pulitzer prize–winning author and originator of the theory on biophilia explains in his book of the same name, we cannot escape our connection to the natural world, nor should we. Our lives are enriched by panthers just as they are by books and art. The natural world is part of the human experience.

Florida Black Bear

The black bear is Florida's largest land mammal, reaching weights of six hundred pounds. Once common throughout the Southeast, the Florida black bear is now restricted to a few swamps, hammocks, and other dense woodlands in Florida and southeast Georgia where it finds food and adequate cover (Maehr 1984a; Brady and Maehr 1985; Maehr and Wooding 1992).

Listed by the state as threatened, the black bear is sensitive to habitat loss. Millsap and others rated the Florida black bear seventh out of thirty species needing management attention (Millsap et al. 1990). In the past ten years, nearly seven hundred bears have been killed by hunters and collisions with vehicles; and others are killed by poaching. Hunting of black bears occurred in Apalachicola and Osceola National Forests and on private land in Baker and Columbia counties until it was banned in 1993. There are healthy bear populations in parts of the Southeast, but black bears are becoming increasingly rare and now occupy only 10 percent of their former range (Pelton 1986).

As in the case of the panther, the black bear's numbers are difficult to assess because of the cover in which they live, and because bears

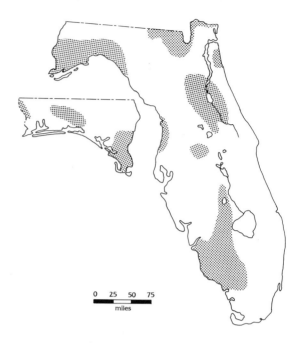

Figure 47. Present distribution of the
Florida black bear in Florida. Redrawn
from Maehr and Wooding 1992.

0   25   50   75
miles

avoid humans. Within Florida and in adjacent areas of Georgia there
may be one thousand bears, largely confined to forested areas of
Apalachicola, Ocala, and Osceola National Forests, Big Cypress National Preserve, and Okefenokee Swamp (Maehr 1984a; Brady and
Maehr 1985) (fig. 47). This number could be much smaller, or even
larger, and further study of black bear populations in Florida is war-
ranted.

There is concern that because the Florida black bear is mostly
confined to "habitat islands," there may be limited gene flow among
the small, isolated populations. If so, this puts the bears at risk of inbreeding, which has already stricken panthers. Black bears are more
adaptable than panthers, however, and they occupy smaller ranges
(averaging thirty square miles versus the panther's one hundred to
two hundred square miles). There is also evidence that black bears
will use vegetated corridors such as river swamps to move between
regions. This was demonstrated by one two-year-old male Florida
black bear that was tracked by biologists as it moved seventy-five
miles from Collier to Highlands County during a one-month period
(Maehr et al. 1988).

Although classified as carnivores, Florida black bears are mostly
vegetarians, subsisting primarily on fruit, berries, and nuts (Maehr
1984b; Maehr and Brady 1985; Maehr and DeFrazio 1985). The variety
of hard and soft mast eaten by Florida black bears includes nearly ev-

ery fruiting plant in their environment, including palms (cabbage palm, saw palmetto, needle palm), arum berries, greenbrier, pond apple, wild coffee, beautyberry, and peppertree, to name just a few (Maehr and DeFrazio 1985). Surprisingly, insects are also important in bears' diets: they eat wasps, bees, ants, beetles, walking sticks, and others. Among vertebrate prey, armadillo, birds, deer, and feral hogs are taken occasionally. This wide array of foods enables bears to occupy relatively small territories. Since the diet of black bears changes seasonally, such forestry practices as burning may locally affect bear populations by altering the availability of certain foods.

Because bears eat many kinds of fruit, their extensive roaming causes wide dispersal of seeds. Although beneficial to native plants, such dispersal contributes to the spread of exotic species. For example, David Maehr (1984b) found that peppertree seeds, of which about one-fourth germinate, may be present at densities of up to one thousand sprouts per bear scat. In addition, if bears and other animals feed on peppertree fruit, they are ignoring wild plants that may be dependent on these animals for seed dispersal. The problems we have created by altering habitats and introducing exotic species often have many unforeseen ramifications; and to rectify these problems is in many cases now impossible.

Feral Hog

Although pigs were once native to Florida, they became extinct long before man arrived. Feral hogs were first introduced by the Spanish as early as 1539, when de Soto explored Florida (Tabor 1989). The ancestors of most feral hogs were domestic pigs that escaped; there may also be crosses between introduced European wild hogs and domestic pigs. These wild animals have little in common with their barnyard relatives. They are thin and muscular with massive shoulders and have long snouts, straight tails, and a coat of thick hair. Boars have long, curled, tusklike canine teeth that are used for fighting during the breeding season.

Feral hogs live in palmetto thickets, hydric hammocks, and in swamps, where they feed on mast, grass, roots, bulbs, and snakes and on any other small animals they can catch. When searching for roots and bulbs, hogs disturb areas of forest. In doing so, they uproot and kill rare ferns, wildflowers, and tree seedlings. When I first saw the damage caused by their rooting, I was amazed. It is not uncommon in many of our state parks to see hundreds of square feet of soil completely tilled, looking exactly as if someone had gone over it with a rototiller.

During a trip to Highlands Hammock State Park in July 1994, I was struck by the destruction that feral hogs created. Nearly everywhere I saw areas recently swept clean of herbaceous vegetation by the rooting activity of hogs. The following day I saw two young pigs as they rooted in the soil not far from one of the paths. When I approached they sauntered off, barely noticing my presence.

Feral hogs can give birth twice a year to as many as ten piglets; thus, their populations can soar, with dire consequences. In addition, hogs compete with native animals like deer and turkeys for acorns and other mast, and they have been implicated in the spread of such noxious weeds as Hydrilla (James Layne, Archbold Biological Station, pers. comm., 1990). Although hunting reduces their numbers in some areas, and others are killed by panthers, black bears, bobcats, and even gators, the feral hogs in our parks and other areas where hunting is banned, and where there are few predators, are a serious concern.

Armadillos, another introduced species in Florida, also dig into the ground. They make small cone-shaped pits only a few inches deep in order to find mole crickets and other insects and worms; they do relatively little damage in comparison to hogs.

 Epilogue

" *The salvation of the Florida scene*
will come about only if the public savors
its beauty, understands its limitations,
and speaks up for its preservation."

Marjorie Harris Carr (1990)

Floridians are lucky that their state has ample wetlands dappled by colorful wildflowers and enriched by fascinating animals. They should be proud that Florida has more lands in public ownership— eleven thousand square miles—than any other eastern state. Florida also has some of the toughest wetland-protection laws in the nation.

But wetlands in Florida are an environmental testing ground. Our list of imperiled species grows steadily and is one of the largest in the country. Alligator reproduction has been disrupted by DDT spilled into Lake Apopka. The Florida panther cannot survive without human intervention. Manatee deaths occur almost weekly. South Florida's wading bird populations have plummeted, and mercury levels threaten other wetland animals. The Kissimmee River and Lake Okeechobee ecosystems have been disrupted by dredging and diking and by pollution. The Everglades are choking from excessive nutrients from agricultural runoff. The Florida Bay and Florida Reef Tract systems are under extreme stress. We have altered an incredibly rich and complex natural system we know little about and that in these fiscally stressed times we can barely afford to fix. Anyway, the cost of repairing environmental damage once it occurs is greater than the cost of protecting fragile areas in the first place.

What can we do to protect our wetlands? Each of us can make a difference. The most important tool we have for protecting Florida wetlands—and the environment in general—is education. Our environmental problems are chiefly caused by lack of environmental understanding. Much of the damage originated before we had adequate information on the consequences of our actions. This is no longer the case. We now have considerable empirical data on the results of human environmental alteration. We also know that technical solutions to environmental problems are nearly always flawed.

But this knowledge is not being used effectively. The people who most frequently alter the parts of Florida that should be protected—engineers, architects, industrial chemists, heavy equipment operators, farmers, loggers, real estate developers, and the like—usually have little understanding of applied ecology. We wouldn't let untrained people provide our health care. Why do we allow them to affect the health of our environment? Every person who has the power to impact the environment should have an understanding of basic ecological principles and the long-term implications of his or her actions.

We need to take steps to ensure that our children are better educated in environmental science than we are. Check with your local school board to find out what instruction your children are receiving concerning the environment. Get to know your child's science teachers and let them know that you think environmental sensitivity is a vital part of science education. Help teachers find instructional materials on wetlands and other environments. Help them arrange field trips to wetlands and encourage them to invite informed speakers into the classroom. And educate yourself and your family. Take your kids to local parks so they can see the beauty of nature themselves. Read books and magazine articles on environmental problems. Drop by your local library and see what instructional materials it has—including videos. Let your librarian know about your interest in the environment and ask him or her to obtain more material on the subject. Governmental resource agencies, such as your water management district office, can provide information on wetlands, and their staffs might be able to help you develop a reading list.

There's so much environmental information out there that ignorance about the effects of our actions is no longer acceptable.

The second tool we have is advocacy. Many of our environmental problems have arisen because the public hasn't exerted enough pressure to halt the destruction. Proponents of development projects generally have something tangible to gain, while opponents often are only indirectly affected. Also, environmental damage many go unnoticed for years; by the time people *do* notice they can rarely trace the cause of the damage back a single action. This is often true in wetlands, where problems accumulate over years until they finally result in an ecological crisis like the one now evident in the Everglades.

The environmental and monetary costs of past abuses to Florida's wetlands and other ecosystems mean that we can no longer afford to be apathetic. People really do make a difference, especially concerning projects involving public funds, like the Cross-Florida Barge Canal proposal.

You can involve yourself in local issues. If every community protected its local environment, many of the problems facing the state as a whole could be avoided. We could make a lasting difference in our own lives if each of us worked with our neighbors to consider the environmental effects of our actions. We need to make the achievement of a healthy and functioning environment a community-based goal that is just as crucial as good schools, roads, hospitals, and other public necessities.

Join or form a community-based group advocating environmental protection. Almost everyone appreciates abundant open space and natural habitats with diverse fauna and flora. But undeveloped lands will not remain undeveloped without protection. As part of its growth strategy, your county should identify its wetlands and other environmentally sensitive lands. Involve your organization in the monitoring of such areas and help your county government identify its wetlands and other fragile ecosystems. Find out what plans your local government has for developing these ecosystems and work with your representatives to minimize the impact of these projects on the environment.

You may be surprised to find out that experts and advocates live in your own community—right down the street, maybe! Get to know staff people in local, state, and federal agencies that make the regulatory decisions. Ask to be included on their mailing lists so you'll receive notices about permits being considered in your area. Network with other people in organizations to share information and to learn how to improve the effectiveness of your own group. Learn about land trusts and how conservation easements can protect key habitats and provide tax benefits for landowners.

Together, education and advocacy can make a difference. If you don't get involved, someone who may not share your concerns will make the decisions. It's no accident that Florida still has many wonderful natural areas, including swamps; the reason we are so fortunate is because people like you took notice and fought to protect a natural legacy for future generations to enjoy.

References

Agey, H. N., and G. M. Heinzmann. 1971. The ivory-billed woodpecker found in central Florida. *Florida Naturalist* 44(3):46–47.

Arbogast, R. T. 1966. Migration of *Agraulis vanillae* (Lepidoptera: Nymphalidae) in Florida. *Florida Entomologist* 9:45–46.

Ashton, R. E., and P. S. Ashton. 1988. *Handbook of reptiles and amphibians of Florida*. Miami: Windward Publishing Co.

Audubon, J. J. [1840–44] 1967. *The birds of America*. 7 vols. New York: Dover Publications.

Auffenberg, K., and L. A. Stange. 1986. *Snail-eating snails of Florida*. Entomological Circular no. 285. Gainesville: Florida Department of Agriculture and Consumer Services.

Austin, D. F., J. L. Jones, and B. C. Bennett. 1990. Vascular plants of Fakahatchee Strand State Preserve. *Florida Scientist* 53(2):89–117.

Austin, E. S., ed. 1967. *Frank M. Chapman in Florida: His journal and letters.* Gainesville: University of Florida Press.

Barbour, T. 1944. *That vanishing Eden: A naturalist's Florida.* Boston: Little, Brown.

Barron, G. 1992. Jckyll-Hyde mushrooms. *Natural History* (March): 46–52.

Bartram, W. [1791] 1955. *The Travels of William Bartram.* Ed. M. Van Doren. Reprint, New York: Dover Publications.

Beckel, A. L. 1990. Foraging success rates of North American river otters, *Lutra canadensis*, hunting alone and hunting in pairs. *Canadian Field Naturalist* 104:586–88.

Belden, R. C. 1989. *The Florida panther.* Audubon Wildlife Report, 1988–89. New York: National Audubon Society.

Bent, A. C. [1937] 1961. *Life histories of North American birds of prey.* Vol. 1. Reprint, New York: Dover Publications.

Benzing, D. H. 1980. *The biology of the bromeliads.* Eureka: Mad River Press.

————. 1990. *Vascular epiphytes.* Cambridge: Cambridge University Press.

Berry, E. W. 1916. The physical conditions and age indicated by the flora of the Alum Bluff Formation. *U.S. Geological Survey Professional Papers* 98:41–53.

Bierzychudek, P. 1982. The demography of jack-in-the-pulpit, a forest perennial that changes sex. *Ecological Monographs* 52(4):335–51.

Bildstein, K. L., W. Post, J. Johnson, and P. Fredrick. 1990. Freshwater wetlands, rainfall, and the breeding ecology of white ibises in coastal South Carolina. *Wilson Bulletin* 102:84–98.

Blake, N. M. 1980. *Land into water—water into land.* Gainesville: University Presses of Florida.

Blest, A. D. 1957. The function of eyespot patterns in the Lepidoptera. *Behaviour* 11:209–56.

Brady, J. R., and D. S. Maehr. 1985. Distribution of black bears in Florida. *Florida Field Naturalist* 13(1):1–7.

Breen, R. S. 1963. *Mosses of Florida: An illustrated manual.* Gainesville: University of Florida Press.

Breil, D. A. 1970. Liverworts of the mid-Gulf Coastal Plain. *Bryologist* 73(3):409–91.

Brown, C. A. 1984. Morphology and biology of cypress trees. In *Cypress swamps,* ed. K. C. Ewel and H. T. Odum, 16–24. Gainesville: University Presses of Florida.

Brown, C. L., and L. K. Kirkman. 1990. *Trees of Georgia and adjacent states.* Portland: Timber Press.

Brown, D. 1988. *Aroids.* Portland: Timber Press.

Brown, K. E. 1973. Biological life history and geographical distribution of the cabbage palm, *Sabal palmetto.* Ph.D. diss., North Carolina State University.

Brown, L. N. 1972. The silkmoths of Florida. *Florida Naturalist* 45(2):40–43.

Brown, S. L. 1984. The role of wetlands in the Green Swamp. In *Cypress swamps,* ed. K. C. Ewel and H. T. Odum, 405–15. Gainesville: University Presses of Florida.

Burdick, D. M., D. Cushman, R. Hamilton, and J. G. Gosselink. 1989. Faunal changes and bottomland hardwood forest loss in the Tensas Watershed, Louisiana. *Conservation Biology* 3(3):282–92.

Butler, J. 1974. Pineapples of the tree tops. *Florida Naturalist* 47(4):13–17.

Carr, A. F. 1940. *A contribution to the herpetology of Florida.* Gainesville: University of Florida Publications in the Biological Sciences Series 2, no 1.

————. 1973. *The Everglades.* New York: Time-Life Books.

Carr, M. H. 1990. Foreword to *Ecosystems of Florida,* ed. R. L. Myers and J. J. Ewel, xi-xiii. Gainesville: University Presses of Florida.

Carter, E. F., and J. L. Pearce. 1990. *A canoeing and kayaking guide to the streams of Florida.* 2 vols. Birmingham: Menasha Ridge Press.

Carter, L. J. 1974. *The Florida experience: Land and water policy in a growth state.* Baltimore: Johns Hopkins University Press.

Cerulean, S. I., and A. J. Morrow. 1993. *Florida wildlife viewing guide.* Helena: Falcon Press.

Chiu, S., and K. Chou. 1962. Observations on the biology of the carnivorous snail *Euglandina rosea* Ferussac. *Bulletin of the Institute of Zoology, Academia Sinica* 1:17–24.

Clarke, S. C. 1874. Among the alligators. *Lippincott's* 13 (February): 223.

Clewell, A. F. 1977. Geobotany of the Apalachicola River region. *Florida Marine Research Publication* 26:6–14.

———. 1985. *Guide to the vascular plants of the Florida Panhandle.* Gainesville: University Presses of Florida.

Cohn, J. P. 1994. Salamanders slip-sliding away or too surreptitious to count? *Bioscience* 44(4):219–23.

Comstock, J. H. 1948. *The spider book.* Ithaca: Comstock Publishing Co.

Conant, R., and J. T. Collins. 1991. *A field guide to reptiles and amphibians of eastern and central North America.* Peterson Field Guide Series no. 12. Boston: Houghton Mifflin.

Conner, D. M. 1982. Determination of bobcat (*Lynx rufus*) and raccoon (*Procyon lotor*) population abundance by radioisotope marking. Master's thesis, University of Florida.

Correll, D. S. 1950. *Native orchids of North America north of Mexico.* Waltham, Mass.: Chronica Botanica Co.

Covell, C. V., Jr. 1984. *A field guide to the moths of eastern North America.* Peterson Field Guide Series no. 30. Boston: Houghton Mifflin.

Cox, J. 1988. The influence of forest size on the transient and resident bird species occupying maritime hammocks of northeastern Florida. *Florida Field Naturalist* 16(2):25–34.

Craig, C. L., and G. D. Bernard. 1990. Insect attraction to ultraviolet-reflecting spider webs and web decorations. *Ecology* 71(2):616–23.

Craighead, F. C. 1963. *Orchids and other airplants of the Everglades National Park.* Coral Gables: University of Miami Press.

———. 1984. Hammocks of South Florida. In *Environments of south Florida, past and present II,* ed. P. J. Gleason, 191–97. Miami: Miami Geological Society.

Crowder, J. P. 1974. *Some perspectives on the status of aquatic wading birds in South Florida.* Project, Ecological Report no. DI-SFEP-74-29.

Davis, H. 1984. Mosquito populations and arbovirus activity in cypress domes. In *Cypress swamps,* ed. K. C. Ewel and H. T. Odum, 210–15. Gainesville: University Presses of Florida.

Deckert, R. F. 1915. Further notes on the Salientia of Jacksonville, Florida. *Copeia* 18:3–5.

Deisler, J. E. 1982. Species of special concern. Florida tree snail. In *Rare and endangered biota of Florida.* Vol. 6, *Invertebrates,* ed. R. Franz, 15–18. Gainesville: University Presses of Florida.

Delany, M. F. 1990. Late summer diet of juvenile alligators. *Journal of Herpetology* 24(4):418–21.

Delany, M. F., and C. L. Abercrombie. 1986. American alligator food habits in northcentral Florida. *Journal of Wildlife Management* 50(2):348–53.

Delany, M. F., A. R. Woodward, and I. H. Kochel. 1988. Nuisance alligator food habits in Florida. *Florida Field Naturalist* 16:90–96.

Dennis, J. V. 1988. *The great cypress swamps.* Baton Rouge: Louisiana State University Press.

Department of Environmental Regulation. 1990. *Mercury, largemouth bass, and water quality: A preliminary report.* Tallahassee.

Douglas, M. M. 1986. *The lives of butterflies.* Ann Arbor: University of Michigan Press.

Douglas, M. S. 1947. *The Everglades: River of grass.* New York: Rinehart.

Doust, J. L., and P. B. Cavers. 1982. Sex and gender dynamics in the jack-in-the-pulpit, *Arisaema triphyllum* (Araceae). *Ecology* 63(3):797–808.

Dressler, R. L., D. W. Hall, K. D. Perkins, and N. H. Williams. 1987. *Identification manual for wetland plant species of Florida.* Gainesville: Institute of Food and Agricultural Sciences, University of Florida.

Duever, M. J. 1984. Environmental factors controlling plant communities of the Big Cypress Swamp. In *Environments of south Florida, past and present II,* ed. P. J. Gleason, 127–36. Miami: Miami Geological Society.

Duever, M. J., and L. A. Riopelle. 1984. Tree ring analysis in the Okefenokee Swamp. In *The Okefenokee Swamp: Its natural history, geology, and geochemistry,* ed. A. D. Cohen, D. J. Casagrande, M. J. Andrejko, and G. R. Best, 112–31. Los Alamos: Wetlands Surveys.

Duever, M. J., J. E. Carlson, and L. A. Riopelle. 1984. Corkscrew Swamp a virgin cypress strand. In *Cypress swamps,* ed. K. C. Ewel and H. T. Odum, 334–48. Gainesville: University Presses of Florida.

Duever, M. J., J. E. Carlson, J. F. Meeder, L. C. Duever, L. H. Gunderson, L. A. Riopelle, T. R. Alexander, R. L. Myers, and D. P. Spangler. 1986. *The Big Cypress National Preserve.* Research Report no. 8. New York: National Audubon Society.

Duever, M. J., J. F. Meeder, and L. C. Duever. 1984. Ecosystems of Big Cypress Swamp. In *Cypress swamps,* ed. K. C. Ewel and H. T. Odum, 249–303. Gainesville: University Presses of Florida.

Dundee, H. A., and D. A. Rossman. 1989. *The amphibians and reptiles of Louisiana.* Baton Rouge: Louisiana State University Press.

Dunkle, S. W. 1990. *Damselflies of Florida, Bermuda and the Bahamas.* Gainesville: Scientific Publishers.

Earley, L. S. 1990. Clues from the Methuselahs. *Audubon* (July): 68–77.

Edman, J. D. 1974. Host-feeding patterns of Florida mosquitos: IV. *Deinocerites. Journal of Medical Entomology* 11(1):105–7.

Edman, J. D., and J. S. Haeger. 1977. Host-feeding patterns of Florida Mosquitos: V. *Wyeomyia. Journal of Medical Entomology* 14(4):477–79.

Edscorn, J. B. 1974. Remarkable weights carried by red-shouldered hawks. *Florida Field Naturalist* 2:12–13.

Edwards, G. B. 1988. *A spiny orb weaver, Gasteracantha cancriformis, in Florida (Araneae: Araneidae).* Entomological Circular no. 308. Gainesville: Florida Department of Agriculture and Consumer Services.

Eisner, T., and S. Nowicki. 1983. Spider web protection through visual advertisement: role of the stabilimentum. *Science* 219:185–87.

Ernst, C. H., and R. W. Barbour. 1972. *Turtles of the United States.* Lexington: University Press of Kentucky.

Ewel, J. J. 1986. Invisibility: Lessons from South Florida. In *Ecology of biological invasions of North America and Hawaii.* Ecology Studies vol. 58, ed. H. A. Mooney and J. A. Drake, 214–30. New York: Springer-Verlag.

Ewel, J. J., D. S. Ojima, D. A. Karl, and W. F. DeBusk. 1982. *Schinus in successional ecosystems of Everglades National Park.* Report T-676. Homestead, Fla.: National Park Service.

Ewel, K. C. 1990. Swamps. In *Ecosystems of Florida,* ed. R. L. Myers and J. J. Ewel, 281–323. Gainesville: University Presses of Florida.

Fairchild, G. B., and H. V. Weems, Jr. 1973. *Diachlorus ferrugatus (Fabricius), a fierce biting fly (Diptera: Tabanidae).* Entomological Circular no. 139. Gainesville: Florida Department of Agriculture and Consumer Services.

Farrar, D. R. 1978. Problems in the identity and origin of the Appalachian *Vittaria* gametophyte, a sporophyteless fern of the eastern United States. *American Journal of Botany* 65:1–12.

Ferguson, D. C. 1971. *The moths of North America. Fascicle 20.2A. Bombycoidea, Saturniidae.* London: Curwen Press.

Finn, M. A. 1965. For Fakahatchee Strand . . . the time is now. *Florida Naturalist* 38(3):85–87.

Fish, D. 1976. Insect-plant relationships of the insectivorous pitcher plant *Sarracenia minor. Florida Entomologist* 59:199–203.

Foelix, R. F. 1982. *Biology of spiders.* Cambridge, Mass.: Harvard University Press.

Fogarty, M. J. 1978. American alligator. In *Rare and endangered biota of Florida,* ed. R. W. McDiarmid, 65–67. Gainesville: University Presses of Florida.

———. 1984. The ecology of the Everglades alligator. In *Environments of south Florida, past and present II,* ed. P. J. Gleason, 211–18. Miami: Miami Geological Society.

Folkerts, G. W. 1982. The Gulf Coast pitcher plant bogs. *American Scientist* 70(3):260–67.

Foote, L. E., and S. B. Jones, Jr. 1989. *Native shrubs and woody vines of the Southeast.* Portland: Timber Press.

Frank, J. H. 1983. Bromeliad phytotelmata and their biota, especially mosquitoes. In *Phytotelmata: Terrestrial plants as hosts for aquatic insect communities,* ed. J. H. Frank and L. P. Lounibos, 101–25. New York: Plexus Publishing.

Frank, J. H., and G. A. Curtis. 1981. Bionomics of the bromeliad-inhabiting mosquito *Wyeomyia vanduzeii* and its nursery plant *Tillandsia utriculata. Florida Entomologist* 64(4):491–506.

Frank, J. H., and G. F. O'Meara. 1984. The bromeliad *Catopsis berteroniana* traps terrestrial arthropods but harbors *Wyeomyia* larvae (Diptera: Culicidae). *Florida Entomologist* 67(3):418–24.

Franz, R., and S. E. Franz. 1990. A review of the Florida crayfish fauna, with comments on the nomenclature, distribution, and conservation. *Florida Scientist* 4:286–96.

Frayer, W. E., and J. M. Hefner. 1991. *Florida wetlands: Status and trends, 1970's to 1980's.* Atlanta: U.S. Fish and Wildlife Service.

Garth, R. E. 1964. The ecology of the Spanish moss (*Tillandsia usnoides*): Its growth and distribution. *Ecology* 45(3):470–80.

Gerberg, E. J., and R. H. Arnett. 1989. *Florida butterflies*. Baltimore: Natural Science Publications.

Gertsch, W. J. 1979. *American spiders*. New York: Van Nostrand.

Gibbons, J. W. 1990. Turtle studies at SERL. In *Life history and ecology of the slider turtle,* ed. J. W. Gibbons, 19–44. Washington, D.C.: Smithsonian Institution Press.

Gilbert, L. E. 1972. Pollen feeding and reproductive biology of *Heliconius* butterflies. *Proceedings of the National Academy of Science* 69:1403–7.

Gillespie, A. K., and J. Mechling. 1987. *American wildlife in symbol and story*. Knoxville: University of Tennessee Press.

Gleason, P. J. 1984. Introduction: Saving the wild places—a necessity for growth. In *Environments of south Florida, past and present II,* ed. P. J. Gleason, viii–xxiv. Miami: Miami Geological Society.

Godfrey, R. K. 1988. *Trees, shrubs, and woody vines of northern Florida and adjacent Georgia and Alabama*. Athens: University of Georgia Press.

Godfrey, R. K., and J. W. Wooten. 1979. *Aquatic and wetland plants of the southeastern United States: Monocotyledons*. Athens: University of Georgia Press.

Goodwin, T. M., and W. R. Marion. 1977. Occurrence of Florida red-bellied turtle eggs in north-central Florida alligator nests. *Florida Scientist* 40:237–38.

———. 1979. Seasonal activity ranges and habitat preferences of adult alligators in a north-central Florida lake. *Journal of Herpetology* 13(2):157–64.

Gorman, J. 1992. Wet-lands? Wet-lands? Whatever happened to swamps? *Audubon* (May-June): 82–83.

Gould, S. J. 1992. Magnolias from Moscow. *Natural History* (September): 10–17.

Green, C. H. 1939. *Trees of the South*. Chapel Hill: University of North Carolina Press.

Greenberg, N. 1977. A neuroethological study of display behavior in the lizard *Anolis carolinensis* (Reptilia, Lacertilia, Iguanidae). *American Zoologist* 17:191–201.

Greenway, J. C. 1958. *Extinct and vanishing birds of the world*. Special Publication no. 13. New York: American Committee for International Wildlife Protection.

Greenwood, J. J. D. 1990. What the little birds tell us. *Nature* 343:22–23.

Griscom, L., and A. Sprunt, Jr. 1957. *The warblers of America*. New York: Devan-Adair.

Grow, G. O. 1993. *Florida parks: A guide to camping in nature*. Tallahassee: Longleaf Publications.

Gunderson, L. H. 1984. Regeneration of cypress in logged and burned strands at Corkscrew Swamp Sanctuary, Florida. In *Cypress swamps,* ed. K. C. Ewel and H. T. Odum, 349–57. Gainesville: University Presses of Florida.

Hagan, J. M., and D. W. Johnson, eds. 1992. *Ecology and conservation of neotropical migrant landbirds*. Washington, D.C.: Smithsonian Institution Press.

Hamilton, D. B. 1984. Plant succession and the influence of disturbance in the Okefenokee Swamp. In *The Okefenokee Swamp: Its natural history, geology, and geochemistry,* ed. A. D. Cohen, D. J. Casagrande, M. J. Andrejko, and G. R. Best, 86–111. Los Alamos, N.M.: Wetlands Surveys.

Harris, L. D., and P. B. Gallagher. 1989. New initiatives for wildlife conservation: The need for movement corridors. In *In defense of wildlife: Preserving communities and corridors,* ed. G. Mackintosh, 11–34. Washington, D.C: Defenders of Wildlife.

Harris, L. D., and J. G. Gosselink. 1990. Cumulative impacts of bottomland hardwood forest conversion on hydrology, water quality, and terrestrial wildlife. In *Ecological processes and cumulative impacts: Illustrated by bottomland hardwood wetland ecosystems,* ed. J. G. Gosselink, L. C. Lee, and T. A. Muir, 259–322. Chelsea: Lewis Publishers.

Harris, L. D., and R. Mulholland. 1983. Southeastern bottomland systems as wildlife habitat. In *Appraisal of Florida's wetland hardwood resource,* ed. D. M. Flinchum, G. B. Doolittle, and K. R. Munson, 63–73. Gainesville: School of Forest Resources and Conservation, University of Florida.

Harris, L. D., and J. Scheck. 1991. From implications to applications: The dispersal corridor principle applied to the conservation of biological diversity. In *Nature conservation 2: The role of corridors,* ed. D. A. Saunders and R. J. Hobbs, 189–220. London: Surrey Beatty.

Hefner, J. M. 1986. Wetlands of Florida, 1950's to 1970's. In *Managing cumulative effects in Florida wetlands,* ed. E. D. Estevez, J. Miller, J. Morris, and R. Hamman, 23–31. Environmental Studies Program Publication no. 38. St. Petersburg: New College of the University of South Florida.

Holland, W. J. [1903] 1968. *The moth book. A guide to the moths of North America.* Reprint, New York: Dover Publications.

Howard, J. 1988. Swampwalking. *Walking* (June-July): 96.

Huck, R. B. 1987. Plant communities along an edaphic continuum in a central Florida watershed. *Florida Scientist* 50(2):111–28.

Humphrey, S. R., ed. 1992. *Rare and endangered biota of Florida.* Vol. 1, *Mammals.* Gainesville: University Press of Florida.

Ingram, W. M. 1949. Natural history observations on *Philomycus carolinianus* (Bosc). *Nautilus* 62(3):86–90.

Jennings, W. L. 1958. The ecological distribution of bats in Florida. Ph.D. diss., University of Florida.

Johnsgard, P. A. 1988. *North American owls: Biology and natural history.* Washington, D.C.: Smithsonian Institution Press.

Johnson, C. 1962. Breeding behavior and oviposition in *Calopteryx maculatum* (Beauvais) (Odonata: Calopterygidae). *American Midland Naturalist* 68(1):242–47.

Jones, F. M. 1930. The sleeping heliconias of Florida. *Natural History* 30:635–44.

Jordan, D. 1991. *Draft supplemental environmental assessment: A proposal to establish a captive breeding population of Florida panthers.* Washington, D.C.: U.S. Fish and Wildlife Service.

Kale, H. W. II, and D. S. Maehr. 1990. *Florida's birds: A handbook and reference.* Sarasota, Fla.: Pineapple Press.

Kautz, R. S., D. T. Gilbert, and G. M. Mauldin. 1993. Vegetative cover in Florida based on 1985–1989 Landsat thematic mapper imagery. *Florida Scientist* 3:135–54.

KBN Engineering and Applied Sciences, Applied Technology and Management, G. Burgess, and E and S Environmental Chemistry. 1990. *Steinhatchee River management plan.* Prepared for Suwannee River Water Management District. Live Oak.

Kiester, A. R. 1971. Species density of North American amphibians and reptiles. *Systematic Zoology* 20:127–37.

Kiltie, R. A. 1987. Winter abundances of red-tailed and red-shouldered hawks in Florida: An analysis of Christmas bird count data, 1946–1983. *Florida Field Naturalist* 15:45–51.

Kushlan, J. A. 1990. Freshwater marshes. In *Ecosystems of Florida,* ed. R. L. Myers and J. J. Ewel, 324–63. Gainesville: University Presses of Florida.

Kushlan, J. A., and M. S. Kushlan. 1975. Food of the white ibis in southern Florida. *Florida Field Naturalist* 3:31–38.

Kushlan, J. A., J. C. Ogden, and A. L. Higer. 1975. *Relation of water level and fish availability to wood stork reproduction in the southern Everglades.* U.S. Geological Survey Open-File Report, 75–434.

Laird, M. 1988. *The natural history of larval mosquito habits.* London: Academic Press.

Lakela, O., and R. W. Long. 1976. *Ferns of Florida.* Miami: Banyan Books.

Layne, J. N. 1984. The land mammals of South Florida. In *Environments of south Florida, past and present II,* ed. P. J. Gleason, 269–95. Miami: Miami Geological Society.

———. 1988. Overview of mammals of south Florida. In *Wildlife in the Everglades and Latin American wetlands,* ed. G. H. Dalrymple, W. F. Loftus, and F. S. Bernardino, Jr., 6–7. Miami: Florida International University.

Leitman, H. M., J. E. Sohm, and M. A. Franklin. 1983. *Wetland hydrology and tree distribution of the Apalachicola River flood plain, Florida.* U.S. Geological Survey Water-Supply Paper 2196-A.

Leitman, H. M., M. R. Darst, and J. L. Nordhaus. 1991. *Fishes in the forested flood plain of the Ochlockonee River, Florida, during flood and drought conditions.* U.S. Geological Survey Water-Resources Investigation Report 90-4202.

Lounibos, L. P., and L. B. Dewald. 1989. Oviposition site selection by *Mansonia* mosquitos on water-lettuce. *Ecological Entomology* 14:413–22.

Luer, C. A. 1972. *The native orchids of Florida.* New York: New York Botanical Garden.

———. 1975. *The native orchids of the United States and Canada.* New York: New York Botanical Garden.

Maehr, D. S. 1984a. Distribution of black bears in eastern North America. *Proceedings of the Seventh Eastern Workshop on Black Bear Research and Management* 7:74–76.

———. 1984b. The black bear as a seed disperser in Florida. *Florida Field Naturalist* 12:40–42.

———. 1990. *Florida panther movements, social organization, and habitat utilization.* Final Performance Report no. 7502. Tallahassee: Bureau of Wildlife Research, Florida Game and Fresh Water Fish Commission.

————. 1992. Florida panther. In *Rare and endangered biota of Florida.* Vol. 1, *Mammals,* ed. S. R. Humphrey, 176–89. Gainesville: University Press of Florida.

Maehr, D. S., and J. R. Brady. 1985. Fall food habits of black bears in Baker and Columbia Counties, Florida. *Proceedings of the Annual Conference of Southeastern Fish and Wildlife Agencies* 36:565–70.

————. 1986. Food habits of bobcats in Florida. *Journal of Mammalogy* 67(1):133–38.

Maehr, D. S., and J. T. DeFrazio, Jr. 1985. Foods of black bears in Florida. *Florida Field Naturalist* 13:8–12.

Maehr, D. S., and J. B. Wooding. 1992. Florida black bear. In *Rare and endangered biota of Florida.* Vol. 1, *Mammals,* ed. S. R. Humphrey, 265–75. Gainesville: University Press of Florida.

Maehr, D. S., M. C. Conner, and J. Stenberg. 1982. Bird diversity and abundance in three plant communities in Putnam County, Florida. *Florida Field Naturalist* 10(4):69–73.

Maehr, D. S., E. D. Land, and M. E. Roelke. 1992. Mortality patterns of panthers in southwest Florida. *Proceedings of the Annual Conference of Southeastern Fish and Wildlife Agencies* 45:201–7.

Maehr, D. S., E. D. Land, and J. C. Roof. 1991. Florida panthers. *National Geographic Research and Exploration* 7(4):414–31.

Maehr, D. S., J. C. Roof, and E. D. Land. 1989. First reproduction of a panther (*Felis concolor coryi*) in southwest Florida, U.S.A. *Mammalia* 53:129–31.

Maehr, D. S., R. C. Belden, E. D. Land, and L. Wilkins. 1990. Food habits of panthers in southwest Florida. *Journal of Wildlife Management* 54(3):420–23.

Maehr, D. S., E. D. Land, J. C. Roof, and J. W. McGowan. 1989a. Early maternal behavior in the Florida panther. *American Midland Naturalist* 122:34–43.

————. 1991. Day beds, natal dens, and activity of Florida panthers. *Proceedings of the Annual Conference of Southeastern Fish and Wildlife Agencies* 45:310–18.

Maehr, D. S., J. N. Layne, E. D. Land, J. W. McGowan, and J. Roof. 1988. Long distance movements of a Florida black bear. *Florida Field Naturalist* 16(1):1–6.

Maehr, D. S., J. C. Roof, E. D. Land, J. W. McGowan, R. C. Belden, and W. B. Frankenberger. 1989b. Fates of wild hogs released into occupied Florida panther home ranges. *Florida Field Naturalist* 17(2):42–43.

Mallet, J. 1986. Gregarious roosting and home range in *Heliconius* butterflies. *National Geographic Research* 2:198–215.

McPherson, B. F. 1984. The Big Cypress swamp. In *Environments of south Florida, past and present II,* ed. P. J. Gleason, 69–77. Miami: Miami Geological Society.

Means, D. B. 1976. Endangered species: Pine barrens treefrog. *Florida Naturalist* 49(5):15–20.

————. 1977. Aspects of the significance to terrestrial vertebrates of the Apalachicola River drainage basin, Florida. *Florida Marine Research Publication* 26:37–68.

————. 1990. Florida wetlands. *Florida Wildlife* (September-October): 32–37.

————. 1992. Pinebarrens treefrog. In *Rare and endangered biota of Florida.* Vol. 3, *Amphibians and reptiles,* ed. P. Moler, 20–25. Gainesville: University Press of Florida.

Melquist, W. E., and M. G. Hornocker. 1983. Ecology of river otters in west central Idaho. *Wildlife Monographs* 83:1–60.

Metzler, S., and V. Metzler. 1992. Texas mushrooms: A field guide. Austin: University of Texas Press.

Meyer, K. D., and M. W. Collopy. In press. Threatened: American swallow-tailed kite *Elanoides forficatus* (Linnaeus), family Accipitridae, order Falconiformes. In *Rare and endangered biota of Florida,* Vol. 5, *Birds,* ed. H. W. Kale II. Gainesville: University Press of Florida.

Millsap, B. A. 1987. Summer concentration of American swallow-tailed kites at Lake Okeechobee, Florida, with comments on post-breeding movements. *Florida Field Naturalist* 15(4):85–112.

Millsap, B. A., J. A. Gore, D. E. Runde, and S. I. Cerulean. 1990. Setting priorities for the conservation of fish and wildlife species in Florida. *Wildlife Monographs* 111:1–57.

Mitsch, W. J., and J. G. Gosselink. 1986. *Wetlands.* New York: Van Nostrand Reinhold.

Monk, C. D. 1966. An ecological study of hardwood swamps in north-central Florida. *Ecology* 47:649–54.

————. 1968. Successional and environmental relationships of the forest vegetation of north central Florida. *American Midland Naturalist* 79(2):441–57.

Moore, B. J. 1968. The macrolichen flora of Florida. *Bryologist* 71:161–266.

Myers, R. L. 1984. Ecological compression of *Taxodium distichum* var. *nutans* by *Melaleuca quinquenervia* in southern Florida. In *Cypress swamps,* ed. K. C. Ewel and H. T. Odum, 358–64. Gainesville: University Presses of Florida.

Nayar, J. K. 1982. Bionomics and physiology of *Culex nigripalpus* (Diptera: Culicidae) of Florida: An important vector of diseases. Florida Agricultural Experiment Stations. Institute of Food and Agricultural Sciences, University of Florida Bulletin no. 827.

Ogden, J. C. 1974. Aspects of red-shouldered hawk nesting in southern Florida. *Florida Field Naturalist* 2(1):25–27.

Palmer, R. S. 1988. Red-shouldered hawk, *Asturina lineata.* In *Handbook of North American Birds,* vol. 4, ed. R. S. Palmer, 413–29. New Haven: Yale University Press.

Pelton, M. R. 1986. Habitat needs of black bear in the East. In *Wilderness and natural areas in the eastern United States: A management challenge,* ed. D. Kulhavy, 49–53. Nacogdoches, Tex.: Stephen Foster State University.

Perrin, L. S. 1986. Wetland status and restoration agenda from the channelized Kissimmee River. In *Managing cumulative effects in Florida wetlands,* ed. E. D. Estevez, J. Miller, J. Morris, and R. Hamman, 83–91. Environmental Studies Program Publication no. 37. St. Petersburg: New College of the University of South Florida.

Platt, W. J., and M. W. Schwartz. 1990. Temperate hardwood forests. In *Ecosystems of Florida,* ed. R. L. Myers and J. J. Ewel, 194–229. Gainesville: University Presses of Florida.

Presley, D. E. 1984. Life and lore of the swampers. In *The Okefenokee Swamp: Its natural history, geology, and geochemistry,* ed. A. D. Cohen, D. J. Casagrande, M. J. Andrejko, and G. R. Best, 18–37. Los Alamos, N.M.: Wetlands Surveys.

Pride, R. W., F. W. Meyer, R. N. Cheery. 1961. *Interim report on the hydrologic features of the Green Swamp area of central Florida.* Information Circular no. 26. Tallahassee: Florida Geological Survey.

Pritchard, P. C. H. 1978. Florida palms. *Florida Naturalist* 51(1):12–24.

Progulske, D. R., Jr. 1982. Spatial distribution of bobcats and gray foxes in eastern Florida. Master's thesis, University of Florida.

Ritland, D. B. 1991. Variation in palatability of queen butterflies (*Danaus gilippus*) and implications regarding mimicry. *Ecology* 75(3):732–46.

Robbins, C. S., D. K. Dawson, and B. A. Dowell. 1990. Habitat area requirements of breeding forest birds of the middle Atlantic states. *Wildlife Monographs* 103:1–34.

Robbins, C. S., J. R. Sauer, R. S. Greenberg, and S. Droege. 1989. Population declines in North American birds that migrate to the neotropics. *Proceedings of the National Academy of Science* 86:7658–62.

Robinson, S. K., and R. T. Holmes. 1982. Foraging behavior of forest birds: The relationship among search tactics, diet, and habitat structure. *Ecology* 63(6):1918–31.

Robson, M. 1990. *Status survey of the Florida mastiff bat (Eumops glaucinus floridanus).* Final Performance Report. West Palm Beach: Florida Game and Fresh Water Fish Commission, Nongame Wildlife Section.

Roelke, M. E. 1990. *Florida panther biomedical investigation.* Final Performance Report no. 7506. Tallahassee: Florida Game and Fresh Water Fish Commission, Bureau of Wildlife Research.

Roelke, M. E., D. P. Schultz, C. F. Facemire, S. F. Sundolf, and H. E. Royals. 1991. *Mercury contamination in Florida panthers.* A Report of the Florida Panther Technical Subcommittee to the Florida Panther Interagency Committee, Gainesville.

Roof, J. C., and D. S. Maehr. 1988. Sign surveys for Florida panthers on peripheral areas of their known range. *Florida Field Naturalist* 16(4):81–85.

Rosen, M., and R. E. Lemon. 1974. The vocal behavior of spring peepers, *Hyla crucifer. Copeia* 1974(4):940–49.

Ruckdeschel, C. A., and C. R. Shoop. 1989. Aspects of wood stork nesting ecology on Cumberland Island, Georgia. *Oriole* 52:21–27.

Sanderson, G. C. 1983. *Procyon lotor* (Mapache, Raccoon). In *Costa Rican Natural History,* ed. D. H. Janzen, 485–88. Chicago: University of Chicago Press.

Sargent, C. S. 1947. *The silva of North America.* Vol. 9. New York: Peter Smith Publishers.

Sargent, T. D. 1976. *Legion of night: The underwing moths.* Amherst: University of Massachusetts Press.

Savage, H. 1982. *The mysterious Carolina bays.* Columbia: University of South Carolina Press.

Schlesinger, W. H. 1978. Community structure, dynamics and nutrient cycling in the Okefenokee cypress swamp-forest. *Ecological Monographs* 48:43–65.

Schneider, R. L., and R. R. Sharitz. 1988. Hydrochory and regeneration in a bald cypress-water tupelo swamp forest. *Ecology* 69(4):1055–63.

Schnell, D. E. 1976. *Carnivorous plants of the United States and Canada.* Winston Salem, N.C.: John F. Blair.

Schwartz, D. M. 1989. It takes more than repellent to make flying pests bug off. *Smithsonian* (July):76–87.

Scott, J. A. 1986. *The butterflies of North America: A natural history and field guide.* Stanford: Stanford University Press.

Scriber, J. M. 1986. Origins of the regional feeding abilities in the tiger swallowtail butterfly: Ecological monophagy and the *Papilio glaucus australis* subspecies in Florida. *Oecologia* (Berlin) 71:94–103.

Sehlinger, B., and D. Otey. 1980. *Southern Georgia canoeing.* Birmingham, Ala.: Menasha Ridge Press.

Sharitz, R. R., and J. W. Gibbons. 1982. *The ecology of southeastern shrub bogs (pocosins) and Carolina bays: A community profile.* FWS/OBS-81/37. Washington, D.C.: U.S. Fish and Wildlife Service.

Shoop, C. R., and C. A. Ruckdeschel. 1990. Alligators as predators on terrestrial mammals. *American Midland Naturalist* 124:407–12.

Sigmund, W. R. 1983. Female preference for *Anolis carolinensis* males as a function of dewlap color and background coloration. *Journal of Herpetology* 17(2):137–43.

Simons, J. N. 1991. Mercury in the Everglades. What is the role of agriculture? *Florida Naturalist* 164(1):7–9.

Simons, R. W., S. W. Vince, and S. R. Humphrey. 1989. *Hydric hammocks: A guide to management.* U.S. Fish and Wildlife Service Biological Report no. 85 (7.26 Supplement).

Skeate, S. T. 1987. Interactions between birds and fruits in a northern Florida hammock community. *Ecology* 68(2):297–309.

Slack, A. 1979. *Carnivorous plants.* Cambridge, Mass.: MIT Press.

Small, J. K. 1932. *Ferns of Florida.* Lancaster, Penn.: Science Press.

Snyder, N. F. R. 1974. Breeding biology of swallow-tailed kites in Florida. *Living Bird* 13:73–97.

Southwest Florida Water Management District. 1985. *The Green Swamp project: Environmental report.* Brooksville.

Sprunt, A., Jr. 1954. *Florida bird life.* New York: Coward-McCann.

Stalter, R., S. Dial, and A. Laessle. 1981. Some ecological observations of the arborescent vegetation in Highlands Hammock State Park, Florida. *Castanea* 46:30–35.

Stange, L. A. 1978. *The slugs of Florida (Gastropoda: Pulmonata).* Entomological Circular no. 197. Gainesville: Florida Department of Agriculture and Consumer Services.

Stevenson, H. M. 1976. *Vertebrates of Florida.* Gainesville: University Presses of Florida.

Stubbs, T. 1974. A moccasin may be more than a shoe. *Florida Naturalist* 47(1):17–20.

Swayze, L. J., and B. F. McPherson. 1977. *The effects of the Faka Union Canal Sys-*

tem on the water levels in the Fakahatchee Strand, Collier County, Florida. U.S. Geological Survey Water-Resources Investigations 77–61.

Tabor, J. 1989. The wild boar is a formidable foe and an admirable pest. *Smithsonian* (September): 115–25.

Tanner, J. T. 1942. *The ivory-billed woodpecker.* Research Report no. 1. New York: National Audubon Society.

Taylor, D. S. 1990. Adaptive specializations of the cyprinodont fish *Rivulus marmoratus. Florida Scientist* 53(3):239–48.

Thomas, B. 1976. *The swamp.* New York: Norton.

Van Meter, V. B. 1987. *Florida's alligators and crocodiles.* Miami: Florida Power and Light Co.

Vernon, R. O. 1947. Cypress domes. *Science* 105:97–99.

Vince, S. W., S. R. Humphrey, and R. W. Simons. 1989. *The ecology of hydric hammocks: A community profile.* U.S. Fish and Wildlife Service Biological Report no. 85 (7.26).

Voss, G. L. 1976. Observation on the ecology of the Florida tree snail, *Liguus fasciatus* (Müller). *Nautilus* 90(2):65–69.

Waage, J. K. 1973. Reproductive behavior and its relation to territoriality in *Calopteryx maculata* (Beauvois) (Odonata: Calopterygidae). *Behaviour* 47:240–55.

Wallace, D. R. 1989. *Bulow hammock: Mind in the forest.* San Francisco: Sierra Club Books.

Ward, D. B., ed. 1979. *Rare and endangered biota of Florida.* Vol. 5, *Plants.* Gainesville: University Presses of Florida.

Ward, D. B., and D. Fish. 1979. Threatened: Powdery Catopsis. In *Rare and endangered biota of Florida,* Vol. 5, *Plants,* ed. D. B. Ward, 74–75. Gainesville: University Presses of Florida.

Wassmer, D. A., D. D. Guenther, and J. N. Layne. 1988. Ecology of the bobcat in south-central Florida. Bulletin of the Florida State Museum. *Biological Sciences* 33(4):159–228.

Webb, S. D. 1974. *Pleistocene mammals of Florida.* Gainesville: University Presses of Florida.

———. 1990. Historical biogeography. In *Ecosystems of Florida,* ed. R. L. Myers and J. J. Ewel, 70–100. Gainesville: University Presses of Florida.

Weems, H. V., Jr., and G. B. Edwards, Jr. 1978. *The golden silk spider, Nephila clavipes (Linnaeus) (Araneae: Araneidae).* Entomological Circular no. 193. Gainesville: Florida Department of Agriculture and Consumer Services.

Wharton, C. H. 1977. *The natural environments of Georgia.* Atlanta: Georgia Department of Natural Resources.

Wharton, C. H., W. M. Kitchens, E. C. Pendleton, and T. W. Sipe. 1982. *The ecology of bottomland hardwood swamps of the southeast: A community profile.* FWS/OBS-81/37. Washington, D.C.: U.S. Fish and Wildlife Service.

Wharton, C. H., V. W. Lambour, J. Newsom, P. V. Winger, L. L. Gaddy, and R. Mancke. 1981. The fauna of bottomland hardwoods in southeastern United States. In *Wetlands of bottomland hardwood forests,* ed. J. R. Clark and J. Benforado, 87–160. New York: Elsevier Scientific Publishing Co.

Wharton, C. H., H. T. Odum, K. Ewel, M. Duever, A. Lugo, R. Boyt, J. Bartholomew, E. DeBellevue, S. Brown, M. Brown, and L. Duever. 1976. *Forested wetlands of Florida: Their management and use.* Final report to Florida Division of State Planning. Gainesville: Center for Wetlands, University of Florida.

Wood, W. W. 1989. *Jacksonville's architectural heritage: Landmarks for the future.* Gainesville: University Presses of Florida.

Wright, A. H., and A. A. Wright. 1949. *Handbook of frogs and toads of the United States and Canada.* Ithaca: Comstock Publishing Co.

Young, A. 1991. *Sarapiqui chronicle.* Washington, D.C.: Smithsonian Institution Press.

Zona, S. 1990. A monograph of *Sabal* (Arecaceae: Coryphoidae). *Aliso* 12(4):583–666.

 Index